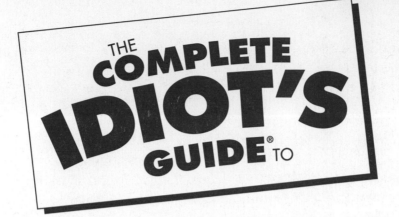

Target Marketing

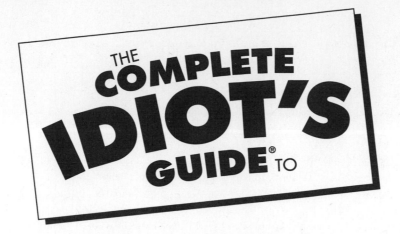

THE COMPLETE IDIOT'S GUIDE® TO

Target Marketing

by Susan Friedmann

ALPHA

A member of Penguin Group (USA) Inc.

This book and everything I do is dedicated to the one I love ... Alec (my rock)!

ALPHA BOOKS

Published by the Penguin Group

Penguin Group (USA) Inc., 375 Hudson Street, New York, New York 10014, USA

Penguin Group (Canada), 90 Eglinton Avenue East, Suite 700, Toronto, Ontario M4P 2Y3, Canada (a division of Pearson Penguin Canada Inc.)

Penguin Books Ltd., 80 Strand, London WC2R 0RL, England

Penguin Ireland, 25 St. Stephen's Green, Dublin 2, Ireland (a division of Penguin Books Ltd.)

Penguin Group (Australia), 250 Camberwell Road, Camberwell, Victoria 3124, Australia (a division of Pearson Australia Group Pty. Ltd.)

Penguin Books India Pvt. Ltd., 11 Community Centre, Panchsheel Park, New Delhi—110 017, India

Penguin Group (NZ), 67 Apollo Drive, Rosedale, North Shore, Auckland 1311, New Zealand (a division of Pearson New Zealand Ltd.)

Penguin Books (South Africa) (Pty.) Ltd., 24 Sturdee Avenue, Rosebank, Johannesburg 2196, South Africa

Penguin Books Ltd., Registered Offices: 80 Strand, London WC2R 0RL, England

Copyright © 2009 by Susan Friedmann

International Standard Book Number: 978-1-59257-903-7
Library of Congress Catalog Card Number: 2009920703

11   10   09   8   7   6   5   4   3   2   1

Interpretation of the printing code: The rightmost number of the first series of numbers is the year of the book's printing; the rightmost number of the second series of numbers is the number of the book's printing. For example, a printing code of 09-1 shows that the first printing occurred in 2009.

Printed in the United States of America

Note: This publication contains the opinions and ideas of its author. It is intended to provide helpful and informative material on the subject matter covered. It is sold with the understanding that the author and publisher are not engaged in rendering professional services in the book. If the reader requires personal assistance or advice, a competent professional should be consulted.

The author and publisher specifically disclaim any responsibility for any liability, loss, or risk, personal or otherwise, which is incurred as a consequence, directly or indirectly, of the use and application of any of the contents of this book.

Most Alpha books are available at special quantity discounts for bulk purchases for sales promotions, premiums, fundraising, or educational use. Special books, or book excerpts, can also be created to fit specific needs.

For details, write: Special Markets, Alpha Books, 375 Hudson Street, New York, NY 10014.

Publisher: *Marie Butler-Knight*
Editorial Director: *Mike Sanders*
Senior Managing Editor: *Billy Fields*
Senior Acquisitions Editor: *Paul Dinas*
Development Editor: *Jennifer Moore*
Senior Production Editor: *Megan Douglass*
Copy Editor: *Jan Zoya*

Cartoonist: *Steve Barr*
Cover Designer: *Kurt Owens*
Book Designer: *Trina Wurst*
Indexer: *Tonya Heard*
Layout: *Ayanna Lacey*
Proofreader: *Laura Caddell*

Contents at a Glance

Appendixes

Contents

Appendixes

Introduction

It's not easy being small—and there's no place that's more true than in the business world. In a climate where megaretailers and chain service providers have seemingly bottomless pockets to blanket the world with their advertising, how can the small business owner possibly compete?

The trick is to work smarter, not harder. That's the key concept in target marketing: by identifying and connecting directly with your customer base, you will not only out-maneuver the large, behemoth corporations, but you will outperform them!

Everything you'll find in these pages has been road-tested by business owners just like you. Over the course of writing this book, we've interviewed literally hundreds of people, from the real estate agent who sells multimillion dollar homes from the deck of his boat to the owner of a small chain of specialty stores. They've shared what works—because they know how hard it is to reach their customer without breaking the bank!

This is real-world knowledge, and it's delivered in real-world language. You don't need an advanced academic degree to be a great small business owner, and you certainly don't need one to be an effective target marketer. You just need to understand your customer and pinpoint the best possible way to connect with them.

The Complete Idiot's Guide to Target Marketing will give you that knowledge. We've cut out absolutely everything that wasn't essential: every single word in this book was selected so you can begin making your business better right now!

How to Use This Book

This book is divided into four parts. Target marketing is a process, with the success of each step resting directly on the step before it. As you work through the book, you'll learn everything you need to forge a long-lasting, profitable relationship with your customers.

In **Part 1, "Beginning the Journey,"** you'll discover the most critical aspects of target marketing: what it is, why you should do it, and when, where, and who benefit from target marketing the most.

Part 2, "Components of Target Marketing," introduces the conceptual framework that makes target marketing work. In this part, you'll learn what you need to know about your target market, and exactly how you're going to get that information without spending a million bucks on market research.

In **Part 3, "The Whole Nine Yards,"** you'll find the techniques and strategies that enable you to connect with your customers. This is where you learn how to establish a relationship and convince your customers that you are the very best source for whatever they're in the market for: products, services, or expertise.

Finally, in **Part 4, "Actions Speak Louder Than Words,"** the concept of customer retention comes into play. Eighty percent of most businesses' profits come from 20 percent of their customer base. It's essential to identify and retain that 20 percent—and in this part, you'll learn exactly how to do that.

Signs You'll See Along the Way

Throughout these pages, you'll see four distinct sidebars. These sidebars are designed to help make the material easier to understand, remember, and most important, use! Here's what they are:

On Target
Real-world examples of how other business owners succeed.

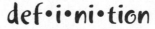

def•i•ni•tion

Explains new or unfamiliar terms.

Insight

Interesting information and helpful advice.

Danger Zone

Look out! Common pitfalls and mistakes.

Acknowledgments

Target marketing is fundamentally about working smarter, not harder, and identifying and connecting the right people to make things happen. In other words, it's a collaborative effort. Without the many individuals who unselfishly shared their insights, intelligence, energy, and generosity, a work of this magnitude would never happen.

So many wonderful individuals supported me throughout this exciting project, and to say that I'm deeply grateful hardly seems enough. It's every author's fear when writing an acknowledgment page that someone gets left out. I am no different from my peers, so if you happen to fall into that category, know that I truly appreciate your help, however small.

First, I would like to thank Paul Dinas at Alpha Books and his dedicated team for their insight and willingness to partner with me on this exciting project. Your interest and total support helped make this book a true expression of my belief in the incredible power of target marketing.

The primary sources for this book were hundreds of small business owners who represent a variety of professions—chiropractors, massage therapists, accountants, doctors, lawyers, retailers, consultants, online marketers, and more. These incredibly giving individuals shared life experiences that help give this book its strong backbone. I am deeply appreciative of their willingness to share the good, the bad, and the ugly so that others can learn.

Specifically, my thanks go out to the following top-notch target marketers, in no specific order of importance: Donna Smallin-Kuper, Dave Ratner, Dr. Pat Raymond, Brian Dominic, Roland Lacey, Shawn Clements and Lorna Hinson, John Scalzi, J. Craig Williams, Cynthia MacGregor, Steve Ouellette, Tracey Coenen, Melody Morris, Lenka Reznicek. Thank you so much for unselfishly sharing your nuggets of wisdom. In addition, I have to thank the following gurus for their inspiration and influence: Rick Segel, CSP; Bob Bly; Jeffrey Gitomer, CPAE; and Seth Godin.

Some of my best ideas come from my clients. It's difficult to single you all out, but I thank you from the bottom of my heart for allowing me the privilege of working with you.

As the old saying goes, "Save the best for last," so here is the crème de la crème!

Words fail me when it comes to thanking my devoted and extremely talented research assistant, Cynthia Potts. She worked tirelessly, all hours of the day and night, despite her young family, to make sure I included the best possible up-to-date information available. If I had the power to canonize you, "Saint Cindy," I most certainly would. But, in the meantime, just know how much I truly appreciate all your hard work and dedication to this project. (Know that it was okay for you to be bossy!) I couldn't have done it without you! I'm also eternally grateful to my devoted assistant, Kathy Scriver, who has the unrelenting job of keeping me organized. Thank you for all that you do for me!

Throughout this project I also had an extra special group of cheerleaders, who continuously support me, come rain or shine. I'm referring, of course, to my nearest and dearest—my beloved family, Alec, my life partner, Dov and Yael, my incredibly talented children from whom I constantly learn. Thank you, thank you, and thank you again for believing in me and for always being my rock. Everyone should be so fortunate to have such a wonderful team on their side. My endless love and thanks to you all!

Trademarks

All terms mentioned in this book that are known to be or are suspected of being trademarks or service marks have been appropriately capitalized. Alpha Books and Penguin Group (USA) Inc. cannot attest to the accuracy of this information. Use of a term in this book should not be regarded as affecting the validity of any trademark or service mark.

Part 1

Beginning the Journey

Chances are you've got a good business. In fact, you might even have a great business, a fantastic business—but if no one knows about you, you're not going to be in business for long.

Attracting the attention of customers is more difficult than ever: the marketplace is growing more crowded by the day, and anything your customers want can be found online.

You know this. You also know that if you want your business to survive, you've got to be the business that stands head and shoulders in the crowd.

In this part, you'll discover one route to attracting customer attention in the face of overwhelming, constant competition: target marketing.

NO, NO, FENWICK! THAT'S *NOT* WHAT WE MEANT WHEN WE TOLD YOU TO TARGET SPECIFIC CUSTOMERS AND BRING THEM BACK IN!

BARR

Chapter 1

Zeroing In: What Is Target Marketing?

In This Chapter

- ◆ Target marketing defined
- ◆ The forces that make target marketing an appealing option
- ◆ The three Rs of target marketing
- ◆ The role of advertising in target marketing

Every business needs one thing to succeed: *customers*. Someone has to buy the products you sell or the services you offer. That's simple enough.

But who are your customers? How do you persuade people to take time out of their busy day to come check out your business? Customers aren't blank slates. They come to you with a history: stores where they like to shop, businesses they patronize, service providers they've worked with for years.

Attracting customers is difficult. The marketplace is crowded, and your competition seems to have bottomless pockets to spend on marketing and advertising. However, strategic thinking and understanding how your customers want to be treated can give you a competitive advantage. That's the heart of target marketing: working smarter, not harder.

def•i•ni•tion

No matter what you call your **customers**—clients, clientele, patrons, guests, members—it doesn't matter. The term refers to the person who buys your products and/or services.

Comparing Regular and Target Marketing

The first question everyone asks about target marketing is "How is that different than regular marketing?" So let's clarify how the two marketing styles differ.

Regular marketing is the art and science of presenting your products and services to every possible customer. Literally, you're trying to sell to everyone: regardless of gender, location, or income level. It's the commercial attempt to be all things to all people.

Insight

Target marketing applies to companies of every shape and size. Nike, one of the largest shoe companies in the world, does an excellent job target marketing to athletes in 16 different disciplines, including basketball, baseball, football, running, dancing, and more!

This approach can work, and work really, really well. Wal-Mart, for example, uses a mass-market approach, and they claim to be extremely successful.

Target marketing uses some of the same tools and techniques as regular marketing, but rather than trying to reach everyone and anyone, it concentrates on marketing to specific market segments. There is a conscious and continuous effort to identify the most profitable portion of the marketplace and adopt the strategies that will resonate the most effectively with that target audience. This model is more efficient and profitable.

Kissing Cousins: Target and Niche Marketing

The phrases "target marketing" and "niche marketing" get tossed around quite a bit and are often used interchangeably—yet the two are not quite the same thing.

Both target marketing and niche marketing involve looking at the entire potential audience for their products and services, and then breaking that huge group into smaller pieces. Understanding the people who make up each group enables you, as the business owner, to create highly specific marketing campaigns that will resonate with customers and inspire them to buy—usually at much higher rates than more generalized, mass-marketing campaigns.

One of the primary differences between target marketing and niche marketing is the size of the market segment you approach. If the entire marketplace is a pie, target marketers cut that pie into eight pieces. A niche marketer, on the other hand, cuts that pie into 16 pieces. Or 32. Or, in some exceptional cases, 64.

You can cut that pie until you have no more than the merest sliver of filling and crust remaining, and still have a lucrative niche. Niche marketing is targeted marketing reduced to its purest essence: connecting the business owner directly with those customers—and only those customers—who are interested in exactly what the business owner offers.

Niche marketing is a great strategy, but it's not for everyone.

Target marketing offers business owners the ability to be efficient and connect with a clearly defined audience, without confronting the sometimes self-limiting nature of niche marketing.

To illustrate the difference, let's go back to our Nike shoe example. Nike targets several different groups when marketing athletic shoes: basketball players, runners, dancers, walkers—even yoga aficionados!

> ### On Target
>
> Stacey Kanneberg identified a lucrative niche market—parents of young children who want to be sure their children are prepared for school—and capitalized on it by starting a publishing company that produces titles such as *Let's Get Ready for Kindergarten!* and *Let's Get Ready for First Grade!*

Yet there are athletic shoes that Nike doesn't sell. People with diabetes and other health concerns often require specific types of athletic shoes—shoes like those from Drew Shoes. Drew Shoes serves a niche marketplace: medical shoes that are sporty and attractive.

Could Nike make these shoes? Probably, as they are "the experts." However, they've decided that the medical shoe market is not for them right now. They've stayed out of it. What that means is that they've provided an opportunity for a smaller manufacturer like Drew Shoes to thrive.

Why Do This?

Not sure whether target marketing is right for you? Perhaps the following benefits will convince you.

Follow the Money

Let's be completely honest, most of us started businesses to make money. Part of the appeal of target marketing, and why it is increasingly being adopted as the "go-to" strategy for the small business owner, is that target marketing produces great results for minimal cash outlay.

That's the small "e" economic reason to consider target marketing. There are other, larger, big "E" Economic reasons to adopt a target marketing strategy, that all have to do with the way we, as customers all around the world, do business now.

Reason #1: Globalization

Disney was right. It is a small world, after all!

Globalization is a really complex phenomenon. There are many competing viewpoints about whether the lowering of trade barriers, taxes, and tariffs is a good thing or not—but for our purposes, we need to sidestep the merits of globalization and look at its effects on you, the small business owner.

What does globalization mean to you? It means that there are many more products and services in the marketplace than ever before. Many of these are made in places that aren't as restrictive regarding minimum wage or environmental regulations. This means they cost less to make—and hence can compete aggressively with products and services that are produced in countries that do have such regulations in place.

Effectively, this means that as a small business owner, you can't position yourself solely based on price. While you may once have been able to have "The Best Prices in Town," chances are that you'll never have "The Best Prices in the World."

Reason #2: Internet Commerce

A generation ago, only the supremely technologically advanced knew about the Internet. Today, grandmothers are logging on to check out their grandchildren's bands on MySpace … when they're not busy shopping online.

Over 90 percent of customers begin any major purchase of products or services by researching online. This has led to an increasingly informed and demanding consumer base: they know what they want, they know it's available, and they have a pretty good idea what they should expect to pay.

Target marketing works with the Internet-savvy generation because you're provid-ing them with exactly what they want: specific information about the products and services they're already researching. They're by and large already well informed: your approach will either validate what they think—leading them to do business with you— or open them to new possibilities that are better than the ones they've already discovered. Again, you come out the winner.

Of course, this means your products and services have to be at least as good as those your target customer finds online. That's critical—but all things being equal, most people prefer to do business with local companies and vendors. Target marketing lets your customers know you're a viable alternative to the worldwide web.

Follow the Crowd

Target marketing works. Why? Because people have become accustomed to getting what they want whenever they want it. As a nation, we demand individualized attention. There are two reasons this has happened.

Reason #1: Omnipresent Media

Customers are being marketed to almost every minute of the day—simply because they're engaged with the media from the moment they wake up until they close their eyes at night.

Television used to be the primary form of media most people related to, having long ago supplanted print for all but a select minority. Now, however, television's power has been eclipsed by the Internet.

The beauty of the net is that everything is available. But, at the same time, that is a strange and terrible beauty, for now customers want equal and immediate access to what they see online—and they want it delivered by local business owners. This obviously adds enormous pressure to your offering.

Reason #2: The Customization Culture

The mass market has lost much of its appeal. While once a nervous society, rattled by the fallout of a World War, found comfort in suburbia's regular features and cookie-cutter architecture, today the "one-size-fits-all" model fails to suit anyone.

The trend in every consumer industry is toward the individualized, the one of a kind, the custom made. Obviously, the more individualized and unique an item appears, the higher the price tag. Most customers balance the need to have the item or service that is exactly what they want with the need to purchase that item or service at a reasonable price.

There's a clear and direct relationship between price and customization. However, advances in technology have significantly reduced the cost of manufacturing, marketing, and distributing many things, leading the customer base to become accustomed to a higher level of customization than was ever previously available.

Today's customers have an expectation of being able to get pretty close to exactly what they want without spending big bucks. This makes target marketing essential.

The Three Rs of Target Marketing

What makes target marketing work? We're going to spend chapters discussing exactly that, but to get you started, here's a look at the three Rs of target marketing.

The Power of Relevancy

To make target marketing work for your business, you have to face a really unpleasant fact: people don't, by and large, care about you or your business. People care about themselves. They are only interested in things that are relevant—things that will impact their personal or professional lives.

That's the concept most marketers totally fail to grasp. They spend unbelievable amounts of time, energy, and money spreading the word about their business, never once thinking about the people they're marketing to.

Yet every customer comes to us with one, and only one, question:

What's in it for me?

Customers want any of an infinite number of things. They want to improve themselves. They want to save money, save time, make money, avoid effort, and be more comfortable. It's not difficult to identify products and services that enable people to have a clean home, escape physical or emotional pain, enjoy praise, or ensure popularity. The list is literally endless.

Danger Zone

Relevancy is descriptive, not prescriptive! That means you have to react to what customers want—not what you think they should have or should want!

You have to know what your customers want from you. More important, you have to know why they want it. It is that understanding that enables you to craft relevant marketing messages.

When a message is relevant, customers buy. You'll know you're relevant when your customers say, "This is exactly what I was looking for!" or, "You are exactly the right person to fix this problem!"

The reason relevancy is so important comes down to numbers. Customers are deluged with thousands of marketing messages daily. They can't possibly interact with, much less respond to, all of them. They have to pick and choose, and they only choose to respond to those offers that have meaning to them—in other words, the messages that are relevant.

The Power of Rare

Target marketing means abandoning the safety of the crowds, that is, all those companies that use the same old mass-marketing strategies. Daring to be unique and newsworthy is the name of the game.

If you're going to target market, you're presenting yourself as an alternative to the mass market: the one ideal solution to a problem, the one store that carries the perfect product.

> ### On Target
>
> Donut shops are a dime a dozen. No one pays much attention because they're all the same. However, Voodoo Donuts, located in Portland, Oregon, chose to be different. With freaky flavors and an offbeat atmosphere—they even perform weddings!—Voodoo Donuts has become a cult destination location with a very loyal target audience.

Being rare—unique, different, one of a kind—is a choice. You, as a business owner, have to decide if you're going to stand out from the crowd. Having decided that, you need a way to differentiate yourself: that point of *differentiation* is what is going to attract your target market. By the way, this strategy takes guts.

def•i•ni•tion

Differentiation involves identifying, leveraging, and promoting those characteristics of your business that are distinctly different from those of your competition.

The Power of Repetition

Picture an empty glass, situated directly under a dripping faucet. As each small drop plops down, the glass slowly fills. It takes a significant number of drops to fill the cup, but the glass will fill. In fact, eventually the glass fills to the brim, and each subsequent drop will send water spilling over the sides, cascading in all directions.

Target marketing is just like that! You have to constantly repeat your message, putting it out there and out there and out there, until you reach a critical mass where seemingly everyone is aware of, and engaged with, your business in some form or other.

It's important that your marketing message be consistent with your branding. Just as each one of those drops falling into the glass is similar to the drop that fell before it, your marketing messages need to share a resemblance as well.

This doesn't mean you need to run 8,000,000 identical marketing campaigns. However, you do need to have a recognizable "presence" in all of your marketing efforts. Be consistent in how you communicate who you are and what you do. This includes a consistent use of visual cues such as color, font choice, and graphics, as well as more subtle factors such as language choice and design.

The power of branding is consistency.

Insight _____

It is far better to have one strong marketing message that is repeated consistently than numerous weaker messages that diverge from your branding.

Obviously, marketing messages have to change over time. You need to be responsive to what's happening in your customer's world.

Yet while being responsive, you want to keep your branding recognizable and consistent. For a great example of this, look at the financial services world. Upheaval in the marketplace has left more than a few individual investors feeling skittish—but brokerages still have to do business.

Ameritrade, which once positioned itself as a tool for investors who wanted to be free from the restrictions other investment companies required, changed position by touting itself as an educational resource that advocates for investors and provides critical support when needed. All the while, Ameritrade's branding remained recognizable and consistent. They have even kept the same spokesman—*Law and Order*'s Sam Waterson.

Reach Your Customers Where They Are

Reach your customers where they are. It sounds like commonsense, and it is. However, it's commonsense that few business owners take full advantage of.

Dedicate your marketing efforts to presenting your products and services in an environment where your target audience is currently located. This is far easier than trying to persuade customers to come to where you think they should be!

By marketing to your customers where they are, you realize a great deal of efficiency. You save time—you're not crafting campaigns no one will see. You'll save money by not paying for advertising in publications your target audience doesn't read, not participating in events they don't attend, and not committing to causes they don't care about. Most of all, you'll eliminate frustration: you won't have to worry about why a particular campaign isn't working—because you'll be able to focus on targeted campaigns that do work.

You can stand on the street corner all day long, shouting about how wonderful your business is—but if your customers aren't there to hear you shouting, you're not going to capture their business!

For example, Tom's of Maine, a specialty toothpaste company, advertises on the Comic Book Resource Forums—a web community devoted to people who read and create comic books. If someone's looking for an alternative toothpaste, chances are they won't seek out a comic book website for recommendations. If that were Tom's of Maine's only advertising venue, they'd lose out on a substantial chunk of their target audience.

By the same token, you wouldn't put signage in an airport to market to your customers if your customers don't fly. There's no sense sponsoring the community skating rink if your target audience has no awareness or interest in peewee hockey or junior ice skating.

Be where your audience is. Pass on everything else.

On Target

Community colleges are constantly recruiting students. Understanding their target audience of nontraditional students has led savvy community college recruiters to some nontraditional locations, such as county fairs and local sporting events—where they realize great results!

How Target Marketing Differs from Advertising

Many, many people confuse marketing and advertising. The two are not the same. Advertising is merely one tool that marketers use. It's an important tool—you'll find an entire chapter devoted to advertising techniques in Chapter 16—but it's not the only tool.

Small business owners don't have a ton of money. It's important to realize the maximum value of every dollar that you spend. You want your investments to work for you.

Insight

Marketing always has a price. Sometimes you have to pay with money, while other marketing requires an investment of time. Target marketing focuses on the time-side of the equation.

Advertising can eat up a tremendous amount of money in a very short time. Target marketing, on the other hand, focuses on making strategic choices with your limited financial resources. Many of the tools you'll find discussed in this book are low cost.

For example, target marketing includes using public relations tools such as press releases to get exposure in local media, at very little cost to the business owner. Cultivating a working relationship with the media can take years, but the dividends editorial coverage pays to your business can be tremendous.

Web-based target marketing strategies are particularly important alternatives to advertising. From participating in social networking sites to posting regular blog entries, there are a ton of things the small business owner can do online to increase visibility and drive sales.

Target Marketing Can Enhance Advertising

An old business joke says: Half of all my advertising works, but I don't know which half!

This joke is borne out of the mass-marketing model: when you're advertising trying to reach everybody and anybody, there's a better than fair chance that your message is going to fall on deaf ears.

Target marketing helps ensure you're not wasting your advertising dollars. By identifying who your customers are, what media they enjoy, and what types of messages they respond to, you stand a much better chance of crafting effective ads that really generate business.

The Least You Need to Know

◆ Instead of being all things to all people, target marketing zeros in on the most profitable portion of specific market segments.

◆ Target marketing is a more efficient and profitable marketing model because our culture has become accustomed to getting what they want, when they want it.

◆ For target marketing to really work, your strategies need to be relevant, rare (different), and repeated continuously.

◆ To save time, money, and frustration, dedicate your marketing efforts to offering your products and services in an environment where your target audience is currently located.

Chapter 2

Why Should You Target Market?

In This Chapter

- ◆ The benefits of target marketing
- ◆ Common marketing mistakes to avoid
- ◆ The four fundamental reasons to target market

If you've made it this far into the book, you now know what target marketing is. You might even have some idea about how target marketing works. The main question facing you now is simple: why should you consider target marketing for your business?

In a way, you're just like your customers. They consider your products and services and say, "What's in this for me?" Similarly, you are probably wondering what's so fantastic about target marketing that you should take time out of your already-busy schedule for it.

Or maybe you're more interested in the bottom line. What will target marketing do to your balance sheet? Is this endeavor going to promise you a lot, cost a ton of money, and deliver very little? Or are you missing out on lucrative opportunities by not pursuing target marketing?

In this section, we'll address those very questions!

The Benefits of Target Marketing

Target marketing has many benefits, the most important of which is that it enables you to take charge of your business's success.

By exploring the thought process and underlying target marketing techniques, you can guide your business in exactly the direction you want it to go. The time you spend understanding your customers' wants and needs helps clarify your business vision and refine your decision-making process, which gives you the freedom to enjoy what you do each and every day.

That's only the tip of the iceberg. There are four major benefits derived from target marketing, as you'll see below.

Benefit #1: Build Your Business Quicker

As a business owner, time is not your friend. Did you know that the vast majority of small businesses fail within the first two years? This means there's tremendous pressure to succeed, and succeed early.

The beauty of target marketing is that it helps build your business quickly, far quicker than trying to bend mass-marketing tools to fit your specific needs. Rather, you shape your marketing strategy based on your target audience.

Danger Zone

A surprisingly common mistake for small business start-ups is to avoid marketing activities mainly because they don't know what to do or how to do them.

One of the most common hurdles small business owners face is attracting awareness in the marketplace—letting people know you exist! Making the public aware that you offer products or services to help them isn't as simple as it sounds.

More often than not, small business owners open their doors and think that customers will magically appear. When customers fail to materialize, they close the doors, convinced that no market exists for their offerings.

Target marketing helps small business owners sidestep this problem by introducing their business to their market segment. Strategic media appearances, an effective web presence, and carefully targeted advertising all serve as that vital first step, raising your business's profile and encouraging people to become customers.

It may seem counterintuitive, but target marketing helps you grow your business simply by the sheer number of things you don't have to do.

In business, every minute counts, which means not wasting time on marketing activities that don't generate positive results. Every marketing campaign needs to give you a positive return on investment: you want to get more out of your efforts than you put into them!

To help you do that you should avoid these following common mistakes.

> **On Target**
>
> Brian Dominic, of YourLakefrontSpecialist.com, had to build his real estate business in a hurry. Strategic use of target marketing techniques enabled him to catapult to the top in a very competitive market—in under two years!

> **Insight**
>
> Increasingly, savvy small business owners use target marketing techniques to generate buzz about their business—before ever opening their doors! Talk about the ultimate presell: you have customers before you have a storefront—physical or virtual!

Common Mistake #1: Marketing to the Wrong Customers

Traditional marketing works by crafting a marketing message to appeal to as many potential customers as possible, and then distributing that message all over the place to attract potential customers.

For example, let's look at Geico Car Insurance. Geico has achieved a dominant position in the car insurance industry largely by supersaturating the marketplace with their message. Their adorable lizard mascot—and its equally omnipresent counterpart, the Geico Cavemen—show up everywhere: on television commercials, on bus signage, in the children's toy aisle. Chances are that whatever the media, on or offline, you've encountered these Geico characters.

Market saturation with fun distinguishable and memorable characters accounts for why this strategy works for Geico. Even if 90 percent of their marketing fails, they'll still be more than profitable.

The same can't be said for most small business owners. For starters, you're unlikely to have the marketing budget to attempt this type of campaign. Plus, a failure rate of 90 percent is simply not acceptable. By using target marketing techniques, you zero in on those customers who are most likely to be interested in your products and services. You then force that failure rate down from 90 percent to a far more acceptable number—simply by choosing to not market to people who have no interest in your offerings!

Common Mistake #2: Marketing in the Wrong Venues

Any good target marketing strategy focuses on identifying the most effective ways to reach customers. For example, if you have a target market who would be absolutely lost without their BlackBerries and who check their messages 50 times a day, it's smart to explore mobile platform marketing. However, if your target audience thinks that a Blackberry belongs in a pie, you don't want to waste time, energy, and resources exploring that avenue!

The time you save sidestepping ineffective, inappropriate marketing campaigns frees you to channel that energy into more lucrative opportunities. The research you do as a target marketer enables you to identify your most likely prospects, and pinpoint, from that pool, those customers most likely to buy a lot from you—often!

Insight

Nothing moves faster than the speed of light—except for a news story. Target marketing is the art and science of making your business newsworthy. A strategic plan to showcase your products and services in the media or prominently online is one of the fastest ways to grow your business.

Some companies stumble into the limelight, serendipitously showing up on the *Today* show, seemingly by accident. They're the exception, rather than the rule! Savvy business owners make strategic use of target marketing techniques to garner a prominent position for their company, directly in the media spotlight. Customers respond to what they see on the small screen, leading to increased sales and business growth.

Benefit #2: Increase Customer Loyalty

You can hear a Harley from a mile away: the constant low-rumble of a high-power motor, the distinctive roar of tires against the pavement. They don't sound like any other motorcycle out there.

That's music to the legions of Harley enthusiasts out there: they know what they like about their bikes and they don't want anything to change. They're so loyal to Harley Davidson that they'll spend thousands of dollars over the course of their bike's life keeping it in top-notch condition. That's love—and who doesn't want love?

After decades of hard-core marketing and almost constant media exposure, today's customers are incredibly brand conscious. They're also capable of being fervently loyal to their favorite brands—if their brands give them a reason to be loyal.

That's good news, because according to many experts, customer loyalty is the critical, must-have component of a successful business. To thrive in a competitive marketplace, a business must have a core group of loyal customers who keep coming back again and again for more.

Insight

Harley Davidson tried to trademark the very distinctive and unique sound their bike motor makes. However, after a six-year battle to do so, they withdrew their trademark application.

On Target

Black Phoenix Alchemy Labs produces high-end specialty perfumed oils—definitely not your everyday body spray! Their customers meet up online and in person to discuss and swap scents; it's a cult phenomenon that landed the company in *The Village Voice!*

What Makes Customers Loyal?

Chances are you're not the CEO of Harley Davidson, nor one of the people behind Black Phoenix Alchemy Labs. With both of those options off the table, you might be wondering, what can you do to make customers loyal to your company?

Many reasons exist why customers choose to be loyal to a business. They may like the person who operates the business and value working with him. They may enjoy the level of service they receive. Perhaps it's the expertise and wisdom that simply can't be found anywhere else. Maybe the merchandise is the best ever.

These are some of the top reasons customers cite when they're explaining their loyalty to a particular business. Other reasons might include the fact that customers favor one business because of a convenient location, or low prices, or because all the right people go there.

At the end of the day, it doesn't usually matter to your customers why they're loyal. What's critical is that you know why they're loyal. That's where target marketing comes in.

How Target Marketing Increases Customer Loyalty

Target marketing connects you with your customers at a very fundamental, concrete level. To be a great target marketer, you have to really understand your customers. You must spend time learning about them: who they are, and what makes them tick.

Danger Zone

Never assume that you know why your customers buy from you. They may not be coming for the reasons you think they are! Only research will validate their motivation.

On Target

Tractor Supply Company's slogan, "The stuff you need out here," demonstrates a fundamental understanding of their very loyal customer base. Combined with images of wide-open country, farm yards, and ranches, "out here" appeals to the rural, agricultural customer Tractor Supply wants to reach.

In the process, you will learn what your customers value the most. It's possible to pinpoint, with crystal precision, what exactly brings customers to your business time and time again.

Once you've identified the reason your customers value you, you must let them know you know. Target marketing increases customer loyalty because it clearly articulates the reason your existing customers value your business.

Simply understanding is not enough. Letting the customer know you understand them is the first step. Making that understanding an integral part of your target marketing campaign lets customers know that you "get it," that you're the right business for them.

Communication is key. Using target marketing strategies enables you to remind customers why they enjoy doing business with you. The most powerful selling tool any small business owner has at their disposal is known as the friendly reminder. That little nudge, in whatever format, lets customers know you're still around and are just waiting to make their lives better.

Because many target marketing tools are no- to low-cost, it's easy to deliver those friendly reminders often. You probably know from experience as a customer yourself, you're continually bombarded by marketing messages. Any organization that is not part of the mix might as well be invisible—and invisible companies go out of business!

Better still, using target marketing strategies helps you to deliver your marketing message—the friendly reminder—in the most appropriate, effective venues. With careful planning, you remind customers of your company at the time they're likely to need you, in the locations they're most likely to visit.

On Target

Enfamil, a major manufacturer of baby formula, reaches out to new mothers right from day one. Their gift diaper bags, loaded with coupons and promotional materials, are handed out in countless maternity wards nationwide.

Creating Community

One extremely profitable target marketing technique for small business owners is the ability to create a community around your products and services. Sometimes known as "fandoms," these groups are fervent admirers of what you do—so much so that they want to congregate with other people who enjoy your products.

Communities often spring up around three types of products and services:

1. Those that have a collectible element, such as American Girls Dolls.

2. Those that have an interactive element, such as Hasbro's Littlest Pet Shop.

3. Those that enable users to create something, such as Ravelry, devoted to the fiber arts.

Insight _____

Often, a customer's loyalty to the community becomes more important than their initial attachment to the brand behind it!

Benefit #3: Do More with Less

How big is your marketing budget? If you've got a heap of money just sitting there waiting to be ploughed into marketing and promotion, you'll want to skip this benefit.

However, if you're like most business owners, you worry about inventory and payroll and overhead and professional association memberships, and the countless other expenses that have to be met. The benefit of target marketing to money-conscious business owners is that it helps you to effectively promote without spending a fortune.

Insight _____

According to the experts, a marketing budget is usually between 5 and 10 percent of sales.

How Much It Costs to Play the Game

As you read through this book, you'll discover that many target marketing tools are very low cost. A select few are even free!

However, as with most things, there is a trade-off. The low-cost target marketing resources often require a substantial time commitment. Generally, most small business owners have more time than money—and many of the available target marketing tasks can be done after hours if you choose to do them yourself. If you update your website at 6 A.M. rather than in the middle of the working day, no one's the wiser—and you still reap all the benefits!

Appearances Can Be Deceiving

Strategic use of target marketing tools and techniques can result in your company having a much larger and more impressive appearance than you might otherwise imagine.

This is essential. Customers place a tremendous amount of value on appearances. To attract any but the most desperate or price-conscious crowd, you need an image that meets at least a minimum standard of professionalism.

Think about it. If you're going to the bank to open a line of credit for your business, do you want to do business with a man sitting at a card table with a laptop in a rented cubicle, or do you expect to go to a proper bank, with tellers at the counter, bank officers in offices with doors, and perhaps some marble columns gracing the facade?

> **On Target**
>
> Gateway Computers started on a farm in Iowa. Smart target marketing, including the famous spotted cow boxes, helped the company grow rapidly. It wasn't until they'd been in business four years and had established branding that they actually opened a store!

Chances are you won't be too confident doing business with the first guy—even if his terms are much more favorable than the more traditionally appointed bank.

Target marketing strategies help you to create that impressive image without devoting considerable resources. No, there's no quick and easy route to getting a building with a marble facade! However, many of the cues customers use to determine the size and stability of an organization are readily accessible to target marketers.

Eliminate Waste

Target marketing is an attractive option for many small business owners because it makes prudent use of resources and eliminates and avoids potentially wasteful marketing campaigns.

Because target marketing is based on research, you know what type of customer is likely to respond to your message. More than that, you know what type of message they're most likely to respond to—and which ones will turn them right off! In addition, you know when and where the best opportunities lie to interact with your customers.

Armed with all this information, it's easy to identify and eliminate any marketing and promotional opportunities that simply won't work for you. Generally, small businesses don't make one huge marketing mistake. Instead, their budgets are attacked by dozens of small unproductive campaigns. An ad in the wrong paper here, a series of commercials on a radio station no one listens to there, and before you know it, there's no money left to market your business!

Target marketing also enables you to leverage your campaigns to realize the maximum value from them. For example, if the local newspaper interviews you, then the resulting article can be archived on your website, used in a media kit when you're soliciting future coverage, and perhaps used as a calling card to secure community-level speaking engagements. One small pebble won't change the course of a stream, it's true, but throw enough pebbles in the water, and pretty soon you've got a dam!

Benefit #4: Increase Sales

The final benefit of target marketing makes any business owner's heart sing. Plain and simple, when you target market, you sell more. Sell more products, sell more services, book more appointments!

The reason target marketing generates more sales than any other type of marketing lies in the simple act of presenting a specific marketing message to a group of individuals highly likely to be receptive to it. They've already demonstrated that they'll purchase similar products and services. They have emotional needs your offerings meet, or a belief system that renders your products irresistible.

Target marketing is about making connections. Every product and service has a target market, a corps of customers who long for what that product offers. However, there's a good chance that the majority of these customers don't know you exist. Target marketing makes the introduction for you. Once they know you're there, they'll buy from you.

A Friend of a Friend

Target marketing is particularly powerful and effective right now due to the rising influence of social networking and other online media. Our customers are online, and they're making friends in cyberspace.

Insight

Introducing yourself is just as critical if you're opening a small business in a small town: just because you hang out a new sign on Main Street doesn't mean everyone knows what you're all about.

For many years, word-of-mouth marketing was the gold standard. We've all been told that referrals from colleagues, relatives, friends, and peers was one of the most powerful influences any customer was exposed to.

This still holds true. What has changed, with the advent of social media, is the number and types of friendships our customers develop. The average MySpace user has well over 100 online friends. These friends are influential. If they're raving to their friends about your products and services, chances are their friends will at least check out your business.

Have Your Customers Buy More, More Often

One of the really powerful components of target marketing is that it helps you to connect with your customer at a deeper level. We've discussed why this works from an efficiency standpoint—you won't waste time or money on marketing that doesn't appeal or won't be seen by your potential customers. We've talked about how strong relationships are critical to customer loyalty.

Now let's take a moment to discuss the money-making aspect of target marketing. Today more than ever, customers want to feel connected to the companies they do business with. They want relationships with the people they buy clothes from, with the woman who prepares the tax return, and the man who adjusts their back. They want to know more than the storefront: they want to know the people who work there.

When customers feels like they know a business and have a relationship with it, they'll give that company their business each and every time over a business they know nothing about!

In fact, target marketing can be used to make customers feel like they're invested in the success of a particular business. Inviting customers to give you "how to improve service" suggestions offers you opportunities you may never have thought of. When customers are invested in your success, they buy more.

Finally, target marketing makes you more money, because your satisfied customers will refer their friends, family, and colleagues to you. This is especially true for service providers, where referrals are the order of the day. Really savvy target marketers can even develop other businesses sending clients their way.

Insight

The Internet has made it possible to have a relationship with someone you've never met. Many loyal customers don't know anything more about an organization than what they read on a blog—but that's often enough to build a relationship. They feel a relationship!

On Target

Old Navy, a clothing retailer, invited customers to help them select a new mascot and found themselves deluged with responses.

The Least You Need to Know

- ◆ The most important benefit of target marketing is that it enables you to take charge of your business's success.

- ◆ Target marketing helps build your business quickly because you shape your marketing strategy based on your target audience.

- ◆ To be a great target marketer, you have to really understand who your customers are and what makes them tick.

- ◆ Target marketing generates more sales than any other type of marketing because it presents a precise marketing message aimed at a specific group of individuals.

The Three Ws of Target Marketing

In This Chapter

- ◆ What types of small businesses benefit most from target marketing
- ◆ The many venues where target marketing takes place
- ◆ How to adjust your target marketing strategy for the maturity level of your business
- ◆ The importance of realistic expectations

Target marketing looks appealing on the surface. After all, you can increase sales, enhance profitability, grow your business, and enjoy greater visibility—all without working any harder than you are right now!

That being said, you might be wondering if target marketing is right for you. More important, there are the logistics to consider. Even if target marketing works half as well as people claim, the questions are these: Will it work for you? What's involved? What are the costs?

Those are great questions, and as a small business owner, they're exactly the type of questions you need to be asking! In this section, we're going to answer them for you. Read on to discover who should target market, and when and where this marketing should take place.

Who Should Target Market?

At this point in the book, you may be thinking, "This sounds great, but is it really for me? Do I have the right kind of company to use target marketing? Will this strategy build my business?"

This section is designed to answer that question. As you'll see, target marketing is a tool that can be adopted by almost any organization. Read on to find out how your business fits in the picture.

It's the Brand, Baby

Only one type of business should consider target marketing. That's the one where branding matters!

Your organization's brand is your company's personality—it conveys who you are, what you do, and how you do it to the public. Or, as Amazon.com founder Jeff Bezos said, "Your brand is what other people say about your company when you're not in the room."

Customers live in a world of too many choices. There's an almost-infinite supply of services and merchandise to choose from. Without an objective way to make apples-to-apples comparisons between offerings, how is the customer supposed to make an informed purchasing decision?

Increasingly, the public relies on branding to help them make their purchasing decisions. A brand conveys your reputation. Consider Rolex: even if you've never touched a Rolex watch or even seen one, you know Rolex watches mean quality. The same goes for a Rolls-Royce. You may have never been closer to a Rolls than a model in the toy aisle, yet the mental connection is clear: a Rolls-Royce is the crème de la crème—the very best of the very best.

To bring our examples a little more down to Earth, consider the fact that the poultry company Perdue

> **Insight**
>
> Service providers need branding just as much as retailers and manufacturers. Think about it: what tax preparer gets more business—H&R Block or Joe Jones, tax preparer?

brands chicken parts. What could be more interchangeable than chicken? A chicken breast is a chicken breast is a chicken breast—but Perdue sells an awful lot of chicken breasts, at higher prices than nonbranded chicken breasts, due to their reputation for quality.

If your customers make decisions based on branding, you need to target market!

Size

Target marketing works for organizations of every size.

Coca-Cola is one of the largest companies in the world, a veritable behemoth. You could land virtually anywhere on this planet and find a Coke product for sale—but Coca-Cola target markets. They offer over 450 brands, many of which are highly targeted to a specific geographic region and demographic group.

Coke's Chaudfontaine, for example, is an unflavored water available only in Belgium, France, Luxembourg, and the Netherlands.

Why does a huge organization like Coca-Cola market to a comparatively small portion of the world's beverage market? If you think about it, water drinkers in four small European countries can, by definition, only be a proverbial drop in Coca-Cola's bucket.

Coke does it because marketing to this group makes money for Coke. It's profitable, pure and simple.

Adding one product to an extensive product selection is one end of the spectrum. On the other end of the size scale, small organizations and individual business owners can also target market effectively!

Torquere Press, a small publishing house focusing on same-sex romance novels, started life as an Internet conversation among friends. They're only a fraction of the size of larger romance publishers, such as the more familiar Harlequin. Yet with strategic use of web-based target marketing, augmented with in-person networking, Torquere Press has formed a thriving business, even at a time when publishing reports to be in a decline.

In other words, companies from the one-person operation to the global giants can benefit from target marketing tools and techniques. No matter how large your

Insight _____

As a rule of thumb, the smaller a company is, the more essential target marketing becomes!

organization, everyone can benefit from strategic use of marketing resources! Saving money and realizing a good return on investment is what it's all about.

Function

We've looked at the size of your organization, and what impact that has on your target marketing decisions. But a company is more than its size. You also want to consider what type of company you are!

If you step back and look at the business world in the broadest perspective possible, you'll discover that there are really only three types of companies.

Some companies make things; they're manufacturers. Others do things for people; these are service providers. Still others sell products to customers; they're retailers.

Obviously, there are companies that fall into more than one of these categories. However, for our purposes, and to make your life easier, you're going to want to concentrate on the function that makes up the majority of your business.

Let's look at each option in turn.

Manufacturing

Target marketing is absolutely essential for manufacturers. When you're creating a product, you need to know that there's a large-enough pool of people who want to buy what you're making. This holds true especially if you want to cover the costs of researching, developing, and producing your wares!

To see this concept in action, you need to go no farther than the nearest parking lot. Check out all of the vehicles there. Let's say there's a sporty little convertible, parked next to a full-sized pickup truck. Next to the truck, there's a tricked-out Mercedes, shiny and loaded up with enough chrome that you can see it from space. Beside it, a minivan, and beyond that, a pair of motorcycles—one sleek and aggressively athletic, ready to tear down a speedway, and the other, a fully-dressed Harley with tassels hanging from the handlebars.

Who drives each of these vehicles? Is the soccer Mom walking out from the parking lot, a toddler holding each hand, going to climb onto the racing bike? Is the tough bearded dude in leather, sporting more ink than today's *Wall Street Journal*, going to get into the Mercedes?

Maybe. As you'll see, appearance isn't the only factor in determining a target market.

But just for a moment, let's go with the trends. Chances are Mom is headed for the minivan, and the biker for the bike. Each vehicle has its target market. So, before a frame goes through the first station on the assembly line, the manufacturer knows who is going to want to drive that vehicle.

Service

Organizations that provide services to customers form a vast and diverse group. Accountants and hairdressers, piano teachers and surgeons, life coaches and chiropractors … all have the same basic business model. They succeed by providing a service requiring some measure of skill to those individuals who do not have that skill for themselves.

Target marketing is essential for this group, because not all service providers work the same way, or offer the same type of service. One piano teacher might prefer to work with small children, introducing them to the joys of music and reveling as tots bang ham-handed on the keyboard. Another may prefer to work only with those students clearly bound for Julliard and, from there, the professional stage.

Clearly, the two piano teachers are unlikely to be happy with each other's customer lists!

Service providers are not interchangeable, but often, the public has a hard time determining which service provider is right for them. Strategic use of target marketing conveys that essential information to the public, so they can make more informed decisions.

Additionally, target marketing shines a spotlight on the specialist. An attorney who markets himself as "The Divorce Doctor" will attract a clientele interested in ending marriages. He won't waste time and resources reaching out to those who aren't married, who are married and plan to stay that way, or who need a lawyer to help them figure out the best way to sell a piece of property, settle a billing dispute, or defend them in a defamation suit!

Retail

A retailer acts as a middleman, selling the products manufactured by another organization to the public. This sounds simple enough—and it would be, if there weren't more retailers than ever before!

Competition in the retail world is incredibly intense. It is a difficult environment, particularly for the small, independent retailer. Megaretailers and deep discounters can undercut on price and generally offer a wider selection. Then, the Internet trumps the independent store-owner on selection, price, and convenience.

To succeed, an independent retailer has to do something to stand out from the crowd. This can vary from the type of merchandise, the level of service, the personality of the store, to any of a dozen other things. However, simply doing something different isn't enough. You have to let your customers know what sets you apart.

Enter target marketing. A low-cost, highly effective style of marketing, retailers use it to continually remind customers why they're different, and persuade them to forgo the omnipresent megaretailers and the convenience of the web to come in and shop.

Independents vs. Franchisees

Franchisees are a particular type of small business owner. Purchasing a particular franchise allows you the right or license to market specific products or services in a specific territory. Having committed to a franchise agreement that dictates much of how you do business, you may think that target marketing is no longer an option.

However, that's not necessarily true. Even a franchise business can develop a target market, and, working within the requirements of the franchise agreement, market themselves to a specific group of customers. This strategy is likely to result in greater sales, which makes you and your franchise-holder very happy!

On Target

The UPS Store in Lake Placid, New York, looks much the same as any other UPS Store across the nation. However, they've developed a specialty in shipping large Adirondack furniture—and market themselves very successfully to the numerous tourists in the region with oversized souvenirs!

Where Do You Target Market?

Asking "Where do you target market?" may seem like a strange question. After all, marketing isn't generally tied to a tangible location—a billboard strategically positioned along a high-traffic road being the rare exception.

However, crucial to the concept of target marketing is the premise that you're putting your message directly in front of an audience likely to respond to it. This means you must consider location. After all, putting a message in the right place means that you need to know where that right place is!

For now, we're going to concentrate on three primary locations: online, in person, and in the media.

Working the Web

To understand the Internet, you must realize that the web is the ultimate mass market. It has, quite literally, positioned itself to be all things to all people.

No matter what your personal viewpoint—from arch-conservative to cutting-edge—there's a community of like-minded individuals online. Blogs, discussion forums, news sites, social networks, and wikis abound, each and every one catering to a specific target market.

The problem is that there's no clear road map to the wilds of the Internet. You can't simply say, "I want to identify all of the websites that my customers enjoy," and then find that information in one tidy package. The web is a dynamic, constantly shifting environment. A site that's red hot one day may fade into obscurity the next. Also, realize that popularity is not an indication of quality.

That being said, every small business owner today needs to have an effective online presence. That's the very first step to take as a target marketer. The deeper understanding you have of your target audience, the more efficient you will be connecting with them.

Identifying where your target market congregates online is the first step to connecting with your customers. Be open to exploring new corners of the web. This is second nature to some of you reading this book, but to an older entrepreneur who wasn't raised with a keyboard in hand, don't despair! The learning curve flattens with practice!

Insight

Target marketing on the Internet is truly a circular process: researching your customers leads to interacting with your customers, which leads to more research!

Face Time

People like to do business with people they know and trust. As a small business owner, you know the value of relationships. Your connections with others help determine the success of your business.

Connecting with your customers in person can certainly take place within your business—however, that's only the tip of the iceberg.

In-person target marketing opportunities abound! In a cultural environment that places a heightened value on information and expertise, presenting seminars, classes, and workshops is a valuable in-person target marketing tool.

Networking is another form of in-person target marketing. Connecting with professional colleagues and peers is a critical target marketing strategy, particularly for those small business owners who thrive on referrals. Service professionals, such as accountants, attorneys, and financial advisors, when confronted with a case outside their purview, often steer business to those peers with whom they have the strongest relationship.

def•i•ni•tion

> **Networking events** are special opportunities to meet colleagues, peers, vendors, and other professionals. These events often occur at trade shows, annual conventions, and industry-sponsored gatherings.

Another type of networking happens when you engage directly with your community. Participating in local-level events such as wellness fairs, community celebrations, county fairs, and so on, may not seem to have any business value—yet these *networking events* enable the customer to see your business in another setting and, often, to begin building that essential relationship.

In the Media

Like the web, the media doesn't have a tangible physical location—the iconic *New York Times* building notwithstanding!

Instead, locating your target marketing efforts within the media hinges on appearing in the right venues. That is, you need those media outlets most valued by your target market.

That's why a financial advisor would love to be quoted in *The Wall Street Journal*, while the same appearance might not have quite the same appeal to a florist. Put that florist and her work on the cover of a bridal magazine, however, and there's no doubt, you've got one happy small business owner!

Insight

> Never lose sight of the fact that much media consumption takes place online. Of the countless people who read *The New York Times* every day, only a small percentage ever actually turn a page to do so!

Unfortunately, there is no one definitive guide that lets you know what media your target market most enjoys. Once again, this is something you'll have to research. Understanding where your customers get their information offers you great insight into their decision-making process and buying motivations. For example, a viewer of FOX News is often a very different type of customer than an MSNBC fan.

Target marketing in the media has great appeal to the small business owner for a number of reasons. It's a great credibility enhancer, it raises the visibility of your business, and best of all, it's free. The same considerations that make target marketing in the media so appealing lead to it's major challenge. There's a limited number of opportunities to appear in the press, and an endless number of small business owners who want to be there. This is why strategic thinking and smart target marketing are essential!

When Do You Target Market?

Timing plays a role in target marketing. We're not referring to the time of day—although that consideration can play a role in specific scenarios!

Instead, we're focusing on when, in the course of your business's life, it's appropriate to embrace target marketing.

Every business has a natural lifespan. It begins with an idea, nothing more than a spark of passion in someone's mind.

From there, begins a fledgling firm in the universe. A growth stage follows, during which many businesses expand and gain momentum. Finally, a company matures as an established player at whatever its size. In maturity, the organization focuses more on maintaining the status quo and remaining competitive than on future growth.

Every stage in this process offers a unique opportunity to embrace target marketing.

Three Phases in a Company's Life

Stage One: Young, Emerging Companies. Can you start selling your products before you build your store? In some cases, the answer is absolutely! Target marketing opportunities begin when your business is still in the planning stage and develop throughout the period when you're becoming established.

During this phase, you should begin to identify and learn everything possible about your target audience. This may be a community you're already well connected to, or you may need to start forging new relationships.

The launch of a new business is a natural point to begin engaging with the media. This is your chance to introduce yourself to your customers, and let them know what you're all about. At the same time, aggressive use of the web helps you rapidly build a customer base, establish a reputation, and garner brand recognition.

Young, emerging organizations tend to be more flexible and responsive to their target audience. They're not "locked into" concepts, mindsets, or strategies that don't work!

Stage Two: Steadily Growing Companies. When your organization is in a growth phase, you have two tasks ahead of you. You need to identify who your customers think you are and pinpoint the direction you want to continue growing.

The two tasks dovetail nicely together. Understanding who your customers think you are plays a critical role in determining how you want your business to grow.

If, for example, your target market's vision of who you are meshes with your own vision, you simply need to refine and reinforce what you're already doing! However, if the two visions differ, some adjustments are clearly in order.

Additionally, target marketing during this phase helps you identify potential customer groups and reach out to them in the most effective way possible. During a growth phase, it's essential to control costs. Conducting targeted marketing campaigns helps you to achieve growth without spending money or time foolishly.

Insight

Growth is a time of experimentation; this is the phase where many business owners test various target marketing campaigns to see what works and what doesn't.

Stage Three: Established Companies. When an organization is in stage three, it means it has grown as large as the owners want it to. This size may be limited to the type of business you're in. For example, a sports medicine trainer who only works with professional bowlers has a self-limiting pool of customers to offer services to! On the other hand, the business owner might have purposely limited the size of his business so that it is just big enough to serve professional bowlers.

Either way, reaching this point does not eliminate your need for target marketing. Customer loyalty is about as strong as a wet tissue: the slightest bit of distraction from a competitor who promises to do a better job for less money with more benefits will likely lure customers away.

Customer retention as a target marketing strategy becomes essential when you're an established organization. Identifying and retaining your very best customers is one route to success. At the same time, you want to continually reach out to new customers who will appreciate the products and services you offer. Some will replace customers you do lose, through natural attrition, while others contribute to the necessary required level of growth every business needs.

Straight Talk and Realistic Expectations

Any time you make a change in your business—from changing the sign on your front door to adopting a new marketing strategy—you want to ensure you're making an informed, appropriate decision.

Let's take a moment to consider the effectiveness of target marketing and the costs inherent in adopting this promotional strategy. That way, as you read through the tips and techniques that follow, you'll be fully prepared to decide if this approach is right for your business.

Can You Believe the Hype?

Target marketing is one tool a business owner can use to promote her business, attract customer attention, build brand loyalty, and drive sales.

Sounds great, doesn't it? Bear in mind, however, that for target marketing to really work, you need a good business to promote.

What happens after you attract the customers' attention? Do you have the skills to provide the services they're looking for? Do you stock the merchandise they want? Can you *wow* them like no one's ever *wow*ed them before?

In short, can you deliver on your promise? Target marketing is making a promise to your customers: you're saying, "We're the right business for *you!*"

No amount of target marketing in the world can make up for it if you can't deliver on that promise.

If you're looking for a magic bullet that will transform a substandard business into a fantastic one, you haven't found it in target marketing.

What Can Target Marketing Really Do?

Target marketing can, however, transform a good business into a great one. By pinpointing likely customers and clearly identifying what appeals to those customers and what motivates them to buy, a strategic small business owner can grow her business and enjoy greater profitability with target marketing.

Perhaps the most powerful aspect of target marketing is increasing the visibility and brand awareness of your business. Customers can't do business with you unless they know you exist—and increasingly, they won't do business with you until they know who you are!

Target marketing enables you to address both issues. It's a powerful way to introduce yourself to the public and to convince them that you're the company to do business with.

How Much Time Does It Take?

There's no such thing as a free lunch. That's certainly not news to the small business owner. One of the first things an entrepreneur learns is that everything has a price.

This holds true for target marketing, as well. There are two ways to pay for your target marketing efforts.

Target marketing is an investment in time and money. As the small business owner, you must decide if you want to invest the time equity or the financial resources into funding your target marketing campaign.

In the beginning, most small business owners have more time than money. That's great news, for many effective target marketing strategies—writing articles, blogging, teaching classes and seminars—require a good amount of time, but not much in the way of financial resources.

Other strategies—creating television commercials, video blogging, and podcasting—require more funding.

With that in mind, let's look at just how much time we're talking about.

Running a small business takes a tremendous amount of time. There's no doubt about that. Experts recommend budgeting between 5 and 10 percent of one's budget to marketing and promotion; this recommendation applies to both time and money.

Danger Zone

Conventional wisdom states that you have to devote the most time and energy to marketing your business in the first days, and that requirement will taper off after the business is established. However, this is not true: marketing and promoting your business is an essential, ongoing requirement.

This means that if you're working a 60-hour week (not uncommon for most small business owners) you're looking at devoting between three to six hours to marketing on a weekly basis.

In the grand scheme of things, that's not a lot of time. Assuming a four-week month, you're spending the equivalent of one day a month promoting your business.

The appeal of target marketing is that you're making the most effective use of that time. You're devoting that day to getting your message in front of customers who are likely to be interested in what you're offering.

Time is a finite resource, so you don't want to waste it marketing to people who will never, ever buy your products and services.

A Few Cautions

Running a small business is challenging, period. Marketing and promoting that business is part of that challenge. However, you want to make sure that you keep your target marketing campaign in perspective.

This is not an all-or-nothing scenario. Don't read this book thinking you have to try every technique detailed here, or adopt every strategy. Everything is not going to work for everyone; the efficiency of a technique depends entirely on your target market!

For example, Hunt Country Vineyards, a wine-maker from western New York, introduces new customers to their product with frequent tastings—including one in the parking lot in front of the store. This makes it possible for new customers to try their product without stepping foot in the store. This engaging, accessible approach works for their brand. However, it wouldn't be appropriate for a vineyard trying to promote an exclusive, high snob-appeal product. Hosting a glitzy event might be a more fitting way for them to lure potential buyers into their store.

Focus on knowing your customer. Identify what techniques will resonate with them. Keep your own personal comfort level in mind. You do best with those techniques that feel natural and authentic to you. However, sometimes it is worth stepping outside your comfort zone to explore new venues. Be realistic! If the thought of writing a blog post makes you break out in a nervous sweat, stomach churning with fear, pick something else. Alternatively, explore finding an employee or contractor to do the work for you!

The Least You Need to Know

- Only consider using target marketing if promoting your brand matters!

- Companies of every size, from the one-person operation to the global giants, benefit from target marketing tools and techniques.

- There are only three types of companies: manufacturers, service providers, and retailers.

- Target marketing is an investment in time and money. It is a powerful tool that helps you to promote your business, attract customer attention, build brand loyalty, and drive sales.

Part 2

Components of Target Marketing

Do you believe in soul mates? Do you know that somewhere out there, there's the perfect person for you, the person who was created to fall in love with you?

Businesses have soul mates, too. They turn up as customers, the customers who will shop at your store before they go anywhere else, who will seek out your services exclusively, rather than consider trusting another professional. These customers not only visit your business often but direct their family and friends to do the same.

What does your business's soul mate look like? Who are your perfect customers? Where do they live, what do they do, and when do they need your products and services?

The more you know about your customers, the easier it becomes to attract them to your business. In this part, we're going to cover how you go about recognizing your business's soul mate.

Chapter 4

Begin at the Beginning

In This Chapter

- ◆ The two critical components of target marketing
- ◆ Your target marketing objectives
- ◆ The tools you necd to use

Target marketing is the art and science of reaching your ideal customers in the most efficient, effective manner possible.

This sounds great, but how do you actually do that? What is targct marketing made of? What do you need to have in order to call yourself a target marketer?

In this chapter, we're going to take a look at the parts of target marketing. Each one of these components is important, but it's not until they're used together that you truly realize the value and potential of target marketing.

Much like how lettuce, carrots, tomatoes, and cucumbers are all healthy vegetables to eat on their own, it's only when they meet together in the salad bowl that they turn into a really enjoyable meal. The same is true for target marketing!

The Components of Target Marketing

You need two things to be a great target marketer. First and foremost, a small business owner needs to have a complete, thorough, and total understanding of his target audience. From this understanding, you develop insight into the best way to reach your customer base. That's the second element: the ability to reach your customers where they are.

Let's look at each component in turn. You want to really take the time to read through and fully understand this chapter: everything you read from this point forward hinges on these two very important concepts!

Understanding Your Target Audience

Understanding, Eleanor Roosevelt said, is a two-way street. While the former First Lady may not be famed for her target marketing prowess, she certainly hit the nail on the head with that statement!

Before we get into what you need to know about your target audience, let's take a moment to take a closer look at who your *target audience* is.

def•i•ni•tion

A **target audience** consists of the people who share some or all of the characteristics of your ideal customer—the customer who cannot resist your products and services!

Throughout this book, we're going to use the terms target market and target audience interchangeably; the two are synonymous.

The Target Marketing Cycle

First, a small business owner has to identify the customers she wants to appeal to. Then she has to learn about them, and craft marketing messages in such a fashion that customers can't help but respond!

That's stage one in the cycle. Most target marketers find themselves in a continual process, always going through some stage in order to grow. There's always an opportunity to identify new customers, to better serve existing customers, or to recapture customers who have slipped away.

Understanding can always be enhanced. You can always learn more about your customers. And keep in mind that customers change.

Why Might Your Customers Change?

The customers you have today are not the customers you had a year ago. Sure, they may look the same—but a lot happens in the course of 12 months.

For one thing, your customers grow older. For example, if you sell products or services targeted at children or young adults, your customer base is continually aging out, moving on to the next big thing, while smaller versions of themselves toddle into the store for the first time.

It's not only children who get older. Age has a tremendous impact on the types of products and services that we purchase: the jacket that a 25-year-old guy wears out on the weekend is hardly the same garment a grandfather in his 60s puts on!

Age is only one consideration that can change in a year. Financial status can be very volatile—the swings the economy takes means that a customer who was comfortably well off one season might be pinching pennies the next—or vice versa!

Trends, fads, and fashions all change. Sometimes these changes occur over several years, but a fashion can flare up, capture lots of customer attention, and burn out within a matter of weeks.

Trends and fads have a great influence on some target markets. Sell fashion to pre-teen girls, and you'll learn that any given style might have a moment in the sun that lasts from Monday all the way to Thursday! The high-tech sector is particularly susceptible to the power of fads. We discuss the concept of trends and fads in much greater detail in Chapter 8 because of its impact on target marketing.

Insight

Early adopters are the customers who pride themselves on being the first to try a new product or service. They like to discover the best things first, and often don't mind paying high prices for the privilege.

Why It Is So Important to Understand Your Target Audience

Retail expert Rick Segel perhaps says it best, when he says, "The more you know about your customers, the better job you'll do selling to them."

Segel concentrates on the retail world, but it turns out his wisdom works no matter what business you're in.

Insight

Some businesses sell directly to customers. Other businesses engage in what's known as B2B (business to business) marketing: selling their products and services primarily to other businesses.

For example, understanding a customer's driving habits and expectations enables the manufacturer to design the perfect car. Knowing a bride's dreams helps the wedding cake designer present the ultimate in individualized pastry. Understanding the fears, hopes, and aspirations a client has for the future helps the financial planner to recommend great investment strategies, and the attorney to navigate the challenges that client may encounter along the way.

Reaching Your Target Audience

One of the benefits of understanding your target audience means that it becomes easier to determine the best way to reach your customers.

There are literally hundreds of ways that people connect with businesses today. Some log on to Twitter to see what their favorite sports trainer is doing that morning, while others turn to the pages of the newspaper. Increasingly, people go online to research businesses, but a significant part of the marketplace still much prefers to do business face to face.

Danger Zone

Don't rule marketing options in or out because you assume your target market does or doesn't do something. This is too important to trust to a gut reaction. Make sure you actually know what your market is doing!

When you know the types of people who make up your target market, you can better identify the best method to reach them. This is often a process of elimination.

For example, if your target market seldom travels, staying within the confines of your small town, you can safely opt out of buying billboard space on a busy highway across the state. If your customers are online, you need to be online. If they're not reading *The Economist*, you probably don't need to knock yourself out to be interviewed by their writers.

Who Are These People, Anyway?

We're going to spend quite a bit of time going over the demographic and psychographic information you need to know about your target market in Chapter 6. So for right now, let's go through the down-and-dirty guide to identifying your target market.

Identify Your Ideal Customer

As much as you might like it, you're unlikely to meet your ideal customer in person. Chances are this person doesn't exist. Most people come equipped with an annoying amount of free will, which means they act in unpredictable ways and make purchasing decisions that make no sense whatsoever.

That's why your customer who always adores the color purple and cashmere sweaters might never, ever look at the great purple cashmere sweaters you've just brought in. Although previous purchasing behaviors indicate she should adore the sweater, she doesn't. You have no way of knowing that because her hated second-grade teacher wore a purple cashmere sweater every Friday afternoon, buying a similar garment is out of the question.

Creating an ideal customer helps you to make decisions without factoring in that uncontrollable variable. You're constructing an imaginary person who represents most of your customers; they share the same socioeconomic background, the same values, the same approach to life.

Ask yourself: "Who would want the products or services I'm offering?" Answer that question in as much detail as possible. How old are your ideal customers? What gender are they? How much money do they make? How is their health?

Danger Zone

Be realistic when constructing your ideal customer. It's nice to imagine that dozens of bored millionaires are just lounging around, waiting to come to your restaurant, but chances are you might find yourself needing to cater to a more common clientele!

Understanding Your Ideal Customer

Human beings are social animals. It's a rare person indeed who isn't connected to someone else—from a spouse or partner to parents, children, colleagues, and peers.

Connections imply responsibility and obligations. The decisions your ideal customer makes may have everything to do with their position with their employer, in their community, or in their faith.

A knowledge of these connections and obligations helps you better present products and services that appeal to your customer base.

Begin acquiring this knowledge by asking these four important questions:

Insight

The Internet can greatly influence and impact your target market. Check out the role of blogs and social networks as influencers for your segment.

♦ Who influences the person who wants my products and services?

♦ Who makes decisions for the person who wants my products and services?

♦ What are the pressures and challenges that face this person?

♦ What other products or services are vying for this person's attention?

How Much You Need to Know

Researching your target market can, quite seriously, occupy the rest of your life. How deeply can we ever understand another person? There's no defined demarcation point at which we can say confidently that we know everything there is to know about a person.

That's okay. To be an effective target marketer, you don't need to know everything there is to know about your customer.

Balance is key. You want to know enough about your customers to make informed, effective decisions about marketing campaigns without becoming so bogged down in details you lose sight of the big picture.

Using Market Research

One of the best ways to learn about your target market without drowning yourself in extraneous detail is to use *market research*.

There are several types of market research. In the next chapter, we're going to be taking an extensive look at the different types of market research the small business owner can do on his own.

def•i•ni•tion

Market research is the organized consideration of customer behavior, preferences, and purchasing history.

For now, let's look at the categories of market research available to you.

Primary Market Research

Primary market research comes directly from the source. This means you're getting information right from your customers and would-be customers, with no middleman asking questions on your behalf.

Primary research has some benefits: it's immediate and unvarnished. An eyewitness to a car accident is a valuable resource because she was right there and she saw what she saw.

As a small business owner, you're already conducting some level of primary research, even if you're unaware of it. Every time you ask a customer what he thinks of a product, or the best time of day for him to schedule an appointment, or where he found your name, you're conducting primary research.

There are a couple of drawbacks to primary research. First, it's time-consuming. Talking to numerous people and getting information you need to make decisions can take hours out of every day. Then there's the problem of managing all of the data you collect. If you don't have experience in crafting and conducting surveys, for example, you can easily wind up with reams of unusable information that actually makes your decisions harder.

With that in mind, primary market research is a great tool for getting the feel of what your existing customer base thinks and feels. However, it is tricky to know exactly how much weight you should give to individual customer responses to questions that impact your marketing and other business decisions. The information you get is directly linked to the questions you asked.

Secondary Market Research

Secondary market research is the small business owner's secret weapon! When you conduct secondary market research, you're delving into the work done by a third party. Your goal is to look for useable data in order to make informed decisions about your business.

Secondary market research is all over the place, and much of it is either free or low cost. Beginning with the powerhouse of the U.S. Census Bureau, which documents demographic information about everyone in the country, and ranging through the files kept by your local newspapers' advertising department, you can access an almost-infinite amount of information.

The advantage of secondary market research is that much of the work is already done for you. All the interviewing, recording, and organization of data has been taken care of. Additionally, secondary market research tends to encompass a larger sample size than the individual business owner can manage.

Danger Zone

Subtle biases have a tendency to creep into the data: people often answer what they think they *should* say rather than what they *would* say in a given circumstance.

The drawbacks to secondary market research are two-fold. First, the further away you get from the original source of information (i.e., your customer or would-be customer) the less accurate and immediate the information.

Second, becoming comfortable with and understanding secondary market research takes time. Demographic and psychographic information tend to be statistical in nature. However, once you become familiar with the specialized lingo researchers use, the value far outweighs any inconvenience.

Exploratory Market Research

Are you a real innovator? A cutting-edge free thinker who regularly comes up with the ideas that others only dream of imagining?

Then you're going to want to know about exploratory market research. Exploratory market research is the art and science of determining the market for a product or service that previously did not exist, or if it did exist, has never been successfully marketed as a commercial product.

Think about it, 20 years ago, no one had an MP3 player. They simply did not exist. When the iPod was developed, you'd better believe a great deal of research went into the best way to make an MP3 player that would appeal to the widest-possible group of customers.

That's exploratory market research. In a nutshell, exploratory market research is about potential: what would the market be if the market existed?

Insight

A specific subset of exploratory market research focuses on exploring wholly new markets for an existing product or service.

Conclusive Market Research

While exploratory market research focuses on possibility, conclusive market research determines viability. A highly structured research model, conclusive market research determines if a particular product or service is going to be profitable.

Conclusive market research is a sophisticated tool. It's also very labor intensive and expensive; therefore, generally, if an organization pursues market research of this type, they hire professionals.

Yet even conclusive market research cannot provide that which every business owner wants: a guarantee that a given product or service will be a best-seller!

It's important to remember that, at the end of the day, all market research is based on that least quantifiable and most quixotic of creatures: the human being. We can use market research to increase our chances of connecting with customers, but it's never an absolute guarantee!

The Least You Need to Know

♦ To be a great target marketer, you must have a complete and thorough understanding of your target audience and know how to reach them.

♦ Target marketing is an ongoing cycle of identifying new customers, better serving existing customers, and recapturing lost customers.

♦ You can always learn more about your customers, as they are complex characters who change over time.

♦ Even with the most sophisticated market research, there is never any guarantee of business success.

Chapter 5

Market Research, Pure and Simple

In This Chapter

- ◆ Understanding the value of market research
- ◆ Focusing on do-it-yourself market research
- ◆ Finding out how to hire the best help—on a budget!

The more you know about your customers, the better you can reach them. Target marketing hinges on understanding your customers: who they are, what motivates them, and what, at the end of the day, they consider important.

Once you know who your customers are, you still have to discover the best way to reach them. What media is the most effective? What messages will resonate? Will this great promotional campaign you're considering draw in the crowds—or draw down scorn from the very people you're trying to reach?

To discover the information that you need to understand and reach your customers, you have to do some market research. At its broadest, market research is the organized study of customer groups and behaviors.

The DIY Formula: Can You Do Customer Research Yourself?

The organized study of customer groups and behaviors is quite a mouthful and sounds very intimidating.

Let's take a step back and really look at it. Pure and simply, market research is really an ongoing series of conversations with your customers or potential customers. Your job is to ask critical questions and get objective answers.

These conversations can take place in a number of formats. Some take place in person. Others happen online or via paper surveys or questionnaires.

Sometimes, you don't even have the conversation yourself. You can learn a great deal about your target audience by analyzing how they interact with other businesses or the government.

This is all pretty straightforward stuff, and it's all something that the average business owner can do without too much difficulty. In fact, many small businesses do incredibly well without ever taking their market research beyond the do-it-yourself stage!

Four Easy-to-Use Market Research Techniques

Here are four market research techniques you, as a small business owner, can use.

Echo Research

Echo research is market research you conduct in the everyday course of doing business. You simply echo how you connect with your customers on a regular basis, and you then use that opportunity to glean valuable information about your customer base.

This means if you deal with your customers face-to-face in a brick-and-mortar store, you conduct market research by having conversations with your customers within your store. If you engage with your customers primarily online, your market research needs to happen online. If you conduct your business via direct mail or over the telephone, then your market research should echo this format: send a direct mail piece containing a survey, for example, or call up your customers and conduct research.

The benefit of echo research is that it mirrors the way your customers are already used to engaging with you. You're not introducing a new methodology. You're simply bringing up a new topic in an existing conversation: if they're used to talking to you online when they're shopping, it won't seem awkward to fill out an online survey. However, if your customers only see you face-to-face, you'll encounter some resistance when you try to get them to go online and fill out a survey on your behalf. Echoing the established contact method can make conducting research both comfortable and familiar for the business owner and customer alike.

Tools you can use include the following:

- Polls
- Face-to-face interviews
- Surveys
- Questionnaires
- Comment cards
- Question of the week

For example, if you're a clothing retailer who sells online, you can use your website to connect with your customers. When they visit your website to check out the latest, greatest fashions, you can offer them the chance to take a quick and easy poll.

Make the poll simple and fun. You could show pictures of three dresses you're considering offering, and ask them "Which one would you wear?"

Drive participation in your research by offering an incentive: everyone who answers the poll, for example, might qualify for free shipping.

If you're talking to your customers face-to-face, ask them questions. This is a subtle form of complimenting your customers: you're telling them you respect and value their opinion.

Be strategic with your question-asking. Consider having a question of the week. Make this part of your organizational culture: put a sign near the cash register that says, "We want to know what you think: ask about today's question!"

Conducting and keeping track of these conversations while also running your business can offer challenges. It's best to develop an easy technique to capture your information.

Transfer the whole thing to paper. Offer customers the opportunity to complete a short survey for a discount on their purchase, or to enter in a drawing for a prize. Keep these surveys short—no more than two to three questions. For maximum effect and to gain the most customer knowledge possible, make regular surveys part of your organizational culture, so you're always getting a stream of fresh information.

Danger Zone

When you ask customers for their opinions or suggestions, you had better listen, acknowledge, and use their information. Fail to do so and you risk not getting their help in the future.

Finally, comment cards, questionnaire sheets, and "rate our service" postcards all give customers a chance to share what's on their mind while remaining anonymous. This isn't strictly a market research technique, but it can give you great insight into your public's frame of mind and perception of your company.

Make these available to your customer, either to be collected in your place of business or to be mailed back to you. Keep in mind that anonymity makes people vicious: they'll say things they'd never say in person. Take it with a grain of salt, but do listen to what your customers are telling you.

Interviews and Focus Groups

In-depth interviews and focus groups are two tools professional market research companies use regularly. Obviously, trained professionals have a decided edge to getting high-quality information out of a group of people. However, regular people can use this technique, too. Here are the steps to follow to maximize the effectiveness of your interviews and focus group research:

1. Prepare.

To do this well, you will need some organized preparation.

You'll want to have a well-developed plan ahead of time. Write out exactly what you want to learn about the members of your target audience. This list can include *demographic* and *psychographic* information. You can also question what motivates individuals to buy, what they consider to be of primary importance when making purchasing decisions, their previous experiences with a particular product or company, and more.

2. Create a questionnaire.

Put all of the basic, demographic information—address, zip code, gender, income level—into a form a participant can fill in. The rest should be listed as questions you ask during a brief 10- to 15-minute interview.

def•i•ni•tion

Demographics are the physical characteristics of a population, such as age, sex, marital status, family size, education, geographic location, and occupation.

Psychographics take demographics a step further. These include people's lifestyles and behaviors—what they like to buy, where they like to vacation, the kinds of interests they have, the values they hold, and how they behave.

3. Decide who you want to talk to.

Draw up a list of criteria detailing who should be in your interview pool. For example, if you're selling tutoring services, you might want to talk to parents who have children between the ages of 6 and 16.

4. Find participants.

Once you know what you want to discover and who you want to talk to, you need to find participants. There are a number of ways to do this. You can advertise in your business, in the media, or online. In your advertising, you need to make clear what you want from the person—in this case, some time and answers to a series of interview questions—and what you're willing to offer in return. Incentive items can range from a small cash payment to products or services.

5. Arrange the interviews.

If you're interviewing people over the phone or online, that's easy enough. If you want to meet people in person, arrange to meet them either in your place of business or in a neutral third-party location, such as a quiet restaurant.

There's some debate about how many people you need to interview to get a good representational sample of your target audience. Rely on too few interviews, and your sample won't accurately reflect what your target audience is thinking. Too many interviews, and you'll wind up devoting more time, energy, and resources than the information is worth. Strive for a happy medium.

For example, if you have 200 regular customers, you'll want to survey at least 20 people—some of whom can be your existing customers, although if you have the opportunity to interview others who aren't your customers but fit your target market demographic, you should, to benefit from a wider range of perspectives. Ideally, you'll want to get closer to 40 interviews, which represents 25 percent of your customer base.

Keeping your range between 10 and 25 percent will allow you to connect with a meaningful sample without growing your project so large that it will be unwieldy and difficult to manage.

Online Resources

Market research can be as close as your computer. There are a number of online resources that compile and track demographic information.

First and foremost, you want to check out the U.S. Department of Labor's website (www.bls.gov/bls/demographic.htm) This is a treasure trove of information. They compile demographic data by region, state, and larger communities.

The U.S. Census Bureau (www.census.gov) is the largest depository of public information, with data updated regularly. If you sell directly to consumers, check out the information available in the People & Households section of the website. Many communities have their own websites, often providing critical information on who lives and works there. Enter your proposed location's name and "demographics" or "statistics" into any search engine, and you'll get results.

> **Insight**
>
> Google Analytics is a free online facility for obtaining traffic analysis of your website. You can add a tracking code to all pages of your site that you wish to have information about, such as how long people stay on a particular page.

Finally, there are services online that offer customer data tracking and research. There is often a fee associated with these services. However, when you consider the ability to really focus your queries and the quality of the information, not to mention the time you save doing this yourself, it may be well worth it.

Advertising Industry Research

You don't have to reinvent the wheel. A great deal of market research is being done on a continual basis, right in your community. The same thing is true for the town next to yours, and the one next to that, ad infinitum.

This research is being done by organizations that sell advertising. This includes newspapers, both traditional and alternative, as well as community shopper papers, radio stations, television stations, and magazine publishers.

That's not all. Companies that specialize in direct mail campaigns often do extensive market research and demographic analysis.

How do you access this information?

The easiest way can be connecting with the advertising sales representative of a newspaper or radio station. Let them know you're considering advertising with them, and want to know exactly what demographics they reach. They'll respond with a dizzying array of reports, detailing as much information as you want to know, and more.

This strategy is effective on a local level, but what happens if you're hoping to reach a market beyond your hometown?

Magazine advertising can be your best friend. Most major magazines list demographic information in the advertising section of their websites. What you learn from them gives you better insight into what your customers value.

Finally, direct mail companies are a veritable font of information—for a price. If you tell a direct mail company that you want a list of every nurse who lives on Long Island who makes more than $85,000 a year, owns a home, has two kids and a dog, they'll generate a list of exactly who those people are and how you can reach them.

Everything Else You Must Know

We've barely scratched the surface of market research. There are many, many other ways—many of them quite sophisticated—to learn about your customers and what drives their purchasing decisions.

Professional market researchers take a step back and look at not only your organization, but also your industry. Here's a brief overview of services they offer:

Market-share analysis compares how well your organization is doing compared to other companies that offer similar products or services. This comparison can be based on the amount of sales, number of customers, and brand recognition, among other factors.

Public opinion studies analyze the result of one or more polls given to the public. These polls are often conducted over the telephone or online, and are administered to a relatively large group of individuals.

Customer-satisfaction and employee-satisfaction studies are the two most common types of satisfaction surveys. Having a third party administer these studies helps ensure a more objective, unbiased result.

Brand analysis measures the relative strength of one brand against another set of competing brands. Additionally, this analysis can identify the strengths and weaknesses of a given brand.

For example, an image analysis among children's diaper companies might reveal that Huggies is viewed as a pragmatic, practical, and quality choice, while Pampers are the traditional, upscale diaper of choice.

Product positioning analysis looks at the role a certain product or brand occupies within its category. The position a product occupies will help determine which target market it appeals to.

For example, Rolex watches occupy a premier place in the watch market. There is no other watch that even comes close to matching the prestige of the Rolex brand. All other watches must position themselves in relation to Rolex.

Site analysis considers the viability and profit potential of a business location, taking into account a number of factors including foot traffic, parking, neighborhood, lighting, and more.

Trend analysis looks at changes in any given market sector, looking for patterns of growth and sustainability.

Many people are familiar with trend analysis as it is applied in the financial sector: watching the performance of a particular stock over the course of time helps investors identify opportunities where they're likely to make money.

Taking that same concept of watching performance over the course of time under varying conditions and applying it to a market segment, rather than a stock, is trend analysis.

Feasibility studies determine if the project would work. Feasibility studies can be done on new businesses, new products, even on potential upgrades or expansions.

Test-marketing involves marketing and selling a new product in a geographically restricted area in an effort to predict future sales patterns.

Marketing plan development takes all of the information gathered via other methods and uses it to create a series of recommendations and plans you can use to begin making your business better.

Determine Your Needs

The market research needs of any company are going to change over time. If you've got a great location, for example, and have no plans of moving anytime in the foreseeable future, spending money on a site analysis is pretty foolish.

Use your common sense. There are times where it may be well worth bringing in the pros for a specific, targeted task. If you're considering buying a building, you want to know that the location is good. If you're a manufacturer with a product you're not so sure about, it's smart to do some test-marketing before rolling out a national campaign.

Market-share analysis may not interest you on a national or even statewide level—but you very well may want to make sure you're getting the majority of the swimming pool sales made within 50 miles of your business.

Pick and choose. Be selective. At the end of the day, the purpose of market research is to give you a deeper, more complete understanding of your target market.

If you are not reaching your target market and can't figure out why, the objective perspective of a third party can be exactly what the doctor ordered. However, keep in mind that this may be an expensive option.

Continual attention to your customers and your target market is essential to keep things from reaching that point.

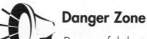 **Danger Zone**

Be careful that you don't get bogged down with too much data. Determine how much information you need to achieve your goals, and limit yourself to collecting that much. Otherwise, you'll find yourself overwhelmed with data!

Bringing in the Pros—Affordably!

Having a market-research team on your side has value, especially when you need continual up-to-date information about your customers, industry trends, and so on. If money was no object, that'd be no problem—but money is an object, and as a small business owner, that can create a problem.

Good market research is expensive. Not rip-your-kidneys-out-and-sell-them-on-the-black-market expensive, but still, quite costly.

If you want to minimize expense and still get what you want, here are three options to consider.

Go Independent

Independent market researchers sell their services on a project-by-project basis. You can post your job on sites like elance.com, Monster.com, or guru.com and let the quotes come streaming in.

This method can offer mixed results. Freelance market research consultants can be very good—but they also could be learning how to do the work on your dime! Ask for references, and don't make your decision based on price alone. If a price sounds too low to be true, stay away!

Look at Data Collection Firms

There are full-service market-research firms, and there are data collection firms. Data collection firms conduct phone interviews or focus groups, and often prepare reports from what they've learned. For less money, they can simply give you the raw data, leaving the analysis up to you.

Before you contract with a data collection firm, make sure you know exactly what you're getting. If you don't know what to do with the 2,500 survey responses they hand you, it's not much good.

Seek Out Schools

Business schools and colleges are a great resource. Seek out marketing professors and ask them if you can have the class work on your marketing-research needs as a project or assignment. Or, far more likely, see if a professor can recommend a few students who would be able to act as independent contractors and conduct the research you need. It's amazing what students will do for course credits.

> **Danger Zone**
>
> Realize that students work on their own time schedules, which are often erratic. And if they decide to drop the course, they probably won't finish your project.

They'll have at least some of the education you need to draw on, and often will work for a fraction of what the pros charge.

The Least You Need to Know

◆ The purpose of market research is to give you a deeper, more complete understanding of your target market.

◆ Use polls, surveys, questionnaires, and comment cards to do your own customer-market research.

◆ Get organized before you start collecting data.

◆ Use a professional market research team when you need more in-depth customer information.

Chapter **6**

Cracking the Code

In This Chapter

- Identifying the "must know" information
- The "D" Factor: demographics
- The "P" Factor: psychographics

Target marketing hinges on the concept of understanding your customers and crafting your marketing message specifically to appeal to them.

In order to appeal to your target customers, you have to know what type of message will resonate with them. You have to know who they are, what their values and beliefs are, and what they think about the world in general—and more specifically, what they think about your type of product or service.

Welcome to the world of demographics and psychographics, the land where you reduce personality and character to measurable traits marked on graph paper. It's not exactly thrilling stuff, unless you're a statistician. The real excitement kicks in when you discover what this information can do for your bottom line.

Introducing Demographics and Psychographics

You can never know too much about your customers. However, to keep from drowning in data, most marketers pick and choose what they want to know about their customer base, concentrating on the most relevant information.

You can divide customer information into two large categories: demographic information and psychographic information.

Demographic information is specific, numeric, and measurable. This includes data such as household income and your customers' age and gender. It's the type of information that doesn't require much interpretation. It's pretty straightforward: you ask a customer how old he is, and he'll tell you he's 45. Mission accomplished!

Psychographic information, on the other hand, is slightly different. When you're looking at a target market's psychographics, you're striving to discover what type of people make up your market. You want to learn how they think, what motivates them, what they consider important—in short, what makes these people tick.

How Much Do You Need to Know?

As we plow deeper into the most essential demographic and psychographic information needed for a target marketer, chances are you're going to ask yourself, "How much of this do I really need to know?" The answer is a definitive "It depends."

Because no two businesses operate in exactly the same way, except perhaps for franchises, each one places emphasis on different things. The level of detail that's critical to one business owner might be completely superfluous information to another.

The "D" Factor—Demographic Essentials

Demographic information, in a nutshell, is the quantifiable data you collect about your target audience. This is nuts-and-bolts information, which is easily enumerated. You can count it, categorize it, and graph it. You look at demographic information to discover the who, what, and where of your target audience.

Demographic information is very black-and-white information: someone is male or female; someone makes $35,000 annually or she makes $350,000.

The value of demographic data is that it enables you to form a measurable, quantifiable snapshot of your target audience. You're identifying specific elements that differentiate your target audience from all other target audiences—and at the same time, it pinpoints groups that they may feel an affinity with.

Groups that share common characteristics often demonstrate similar behaviors. Notice that I said similar, and not identical: at the end of the day, we're still dealing with people here. Not robots. There will always be individual preferences that no one can predict. However, demographic data can help you zero in on a deeper understanding of your target market as a group.

Danger Zone

Demographic data may seem to be cut in stone—but with time, categories change, often expanding to include new definitions. Race was once defined as white and other—now the U.S. Census Bureau recognizes six groupings. This refining of categories will be a great asset to target marketers.

This deeper understanding helps you to be an efficient marketer. You can eliminate the need to reinvent the wheel; if a marketing strategy has been proven, over time, to resonate with groups that share the same demographic data as your target audience, you can draw on that strategy to reach your market.

Conversely, if a strategy has totally bombed with audiences who share the same demographic data as your target audience, you can avoid those choices and sidestep an expensive mistake!

Demographic Essentials

Let's take a more in-depth look at the characteristics that make up the demographic essentials.

Age

How old are your customers? Are they teenagers, young adults, middle aged, or seniors?

Age is a critical component because our decision-making and buying patterns change as we mature. The dress a 17-year-old teen buys is often very different from the dress a 37-year-old woman buys. The investment strategy a 20-year-old favors could spell disaster for a 60-year-old.

Values and priorities change as we grow older. Understanding the age of your customer base gives you at least a primary level of insight as to what is important to them.

Many businesses operate simply by knowing what *generation* their customers belong to, while other businesses need more specific data.

def•i•ni•tion

A **generation** occurs when an age grouping consists of 10 or more years. Generational cohorts comprise large groups of customers who share common life experiences. Examples include Baby Boomers and Generation X.

Gender

Are the majority of your customers male or female? Never make a gender assumption. Many businesses might take it for granted that their major customers are male, only to discover that the real decision-making power in the family is held by the woman.

Bear in mind that some people do not identify exclusively with either gender: in some communities, transgendered or asexual individuals constitute a significant minority position.

Race

Race is one of the most difficult demographic categories to work with. As there is no clear, definitive classification of what race is and is not, a great deal of confusion centers around where to separate race from ethnicity. For example, is someone from Korea, "Korean," "Asian," or both?

Additionally, many people identify with more than one race.

Currently, the U.S. Census race categories include the following: American Indian or Alaska Native; Asian; Black or African American; Native Hawaiian or Other Pacific Islander; and White. There is no category for Hispanic people: they are obligated to choose one of the six main categories and then indicate Hispanic origin, should they so choose.

As you can see, it's a confusing system at best. However, as a small business owner, what's most important for you to know about your target audience is this: "To what race do they see themselves belonging?"

Religion

Religion is often considered a taboo subject. However, religion is a huge, motivating factor in people's behaviors. Understanding the religious affiliation of your target market can help you make better marketing decisions.

For example, racy and suggestive advertising would fall flat in a market where many members are deeply devout and place a high value on women's modesty. That same advertising might not even raise an eyebrow in a market where religion plays no role.

Occupation

What type of work does your target audience do? Are they office workers, or are they on a construction site all day long? Do they consider themselves professional or blue-collar?

Occupation gives you insight into a number of things, including a person's income level.

Education

Education has a direct and measurable impact on income levels and buying patterns. Generally, education is measured based on the highest level of schooling one completed: some high school, graduated high school, some college, graduated college, graduate degrees, post-graduate degrees.

Household Income

What is the average income in your target customer's household?

Income categories can be as narrow or as broad as you'd like. The Pew Research Center, for example, begins at "Less than $10,000 annually" and increases in 10,000-dollar increments.

You may prefer to use a simpler model, especially if you offer high-end products and services. You could draw a metaphorical line in the sand: on one side are people who are able to afford you, while on the other side are people who cannot.

Insight

Consider your target customer's household's income rather than your target customer's income, because your customers may have access to more funds than they themselves earn—or they may have obligations that preclude them from making certain purchases, such as your products or services!

Marital Status

Are the majority of people in your target audience single, married, in a committed relationship, widowed, divorced, or separated?

Each of these situations impacts a person's purchasing decisions and buying behavior. For example, selling life insurance to an individual who has a spouse and dependent children is a very different proposition than selling the same product to a single individual.

Children

Does your target customer have children? How many children? How old are they?

The number and ages of your customer's children tells you a lot about your customer. A family that has six children under the age of 10 demonstrates consistently different buying behaviors than an older couple with one teenager about to leave the nest.

Home Value

Home value measures the market value of your target market's customer. Realize that this number is geographically sensitive: a house worth $250,000, considered a luxury home in some regions, is barely adequate in others. Make sure to always couple demographic information regarding house values with a concrete understanding of house location and the surrounding economic situation. For example, house values in downtown Detroit look very different from those in La Jolla, California.

Location/Region

Where are your customers? Technology has fundamentally altered the way we do business. While we were once limited to serving those customers who were geographically nearby, that is no longer the case.

However, there are some businesses that are largely defined by geography. Retail experts tell us that most customers in a medium to large city will not travel more than seven miles to reach a business. It is reasonable to assume that the same holds true for the majority of service providers, especially those with a more generic offering.

Insight

Most Americans spend just as much time at work as they do at home. Savvy marketers track customer's business zip codes with the same intensity they devote to residential data.

If you provide services or products over the Internet, geography becomes a secondary consideration, if it is even a thought. Still, knowing where your customers live makes marketing to them easier and more effective.

How Do You Get Demographic Information?

There's one really good thing to know about gathering demographic information: you don't have to reinvent the wheel, as there are numerous organizations dedicated to continuously gathering demographic information all across the country.

Best of all, much of this information is free. Every target marketer needs to visit www.census.gov, the U.S. Census Bureau's home page and a treasure house of demographic information.

Another way to get demographic information is through the media outlets that serve your target audience. All media outlets collect demographic information. They need it to serve their advertisers. Investigate advertising opportunities and they'll deluge you with data.

The "P" Factor—Psychographic Essentials

Determining your target market's demographic information is only one side of the coin that helps you segment your group. The other side is a concept known as psychographics.

Psychographic data is concerned with what goes on inside your customers' psyche— literally speaking, what's on their mind. What do they think about? What's important to them?

Psychographic information is useful because it enables you to identify which of your products and services are most appealing to your target audience. It lets you understand the different perceptions about the benefits or value of your products or services that motivate people to buy. You can discover spending patterns, brand consciousness, what influences their buying behavior, and what promotions they respond to most often.

In other words, you can use psychographics to find out what makes your target audience want to buy. The information you gather from journeying into your target audience's brain gives you the essentials to formulate your marketing strategies. Once you have a relatively complete assessment of your target audience's make-up, you now have what's known as a *psychographic profile*.

def•i•ni•tion

A **psychographic profile** is a compilation of all the psychological information you've gathered about your customers, presented as a composite representation of your target market.

Social Status

Social status is often confused with income level. The two are not the same. Social status is a far more nebulous concept than the dollar amount that shows up on someone's tax return. It takes into account what class your customers belong to.

Social status varies greatly by region and cultural group. Just to scratch the surface of the concept, people are often divided as follows:

- ◆ **White-collar workers:** spend their days toiling in an office
- ◆ **Blue-collar workers:** do more manual labor
- ◆ **Pink-collar workers:** make up the largely female administrative corps that accompanies the functioning of white- and blue-collar work

Then, there are people with no collars—the unemployed or overly artistic—and executives, CEOs, and other bigwigs, who conceal their collars under very expensive ties.

Social status can fluctuate. It is one of the few psychographic characteristics where people often have aspirations of grandeur. That is, people who belong to one social class may be very motivated to change positions and attain a higher, more prestigious place in society.

These aspirations create myriad target marketing opportunities. Everything from advanced education to exercise equipment sells as a result of its appeal to people who aspire to change their social status psychographic.

Values and Beliefs

Values and beliefs is a broad umbrella category designed to recognize and measure your target audience's core motivations: the values and beliefs that influence and shape every decision they make.

Values and beliefs may or may not relate to religion. Individuals have personal codes of ethics, moral training, or simply a sense of how things are supposed to be. More often than not, these are based on their upbringing and/or circles of influence.

As a rule of thumb, people make purchasing decisions that reinforce their value and belief systems. They avoid making decisions that run counter to those things they believe to be true. When marketing to your target audience, it is essential that your message aligns with your customers' value and belief systems. That makes it easy for them to do business with you.

Attitude Toward Risk

Risk and reward are intricately linked: the greater the risk, the greater the reward. However, every individual has a cut-off point where the risk outweighs the reward. You need to know where to draw that line for your customers.

In some fields, the attitude toward risk is of paramount concern. Take financial services, for example; understanding the comfort level of a would-be investor as it relates to risk is one of the first things any advisor discusses with a client.

Cultural Position

Are your customers comfortably ensconced in the middle-class mainstream, or do they live on the fringes of society? Are the ideals and values they hold near and dear shared by the majority of the populace, or are they relatively isolated, unique in their approach to life?

Bear in mind that this is not a value judgment. Widely held cultural beliefs are not necessarily better than those only held by a few. Cultural position can indicate the size of a target audience—groups are generally larger in the mainstream of any population, and smaller on the fringes. There may be a relationship between cultural position and income levels, but never assume one. It's always prudent to do further research.

Activity Level

Are you marketing to couch potatoes or go-getters who never sit still? Activity level considers the pace at which your target audience lives life, ranging from totally passive and homebound to cutting-edge extreme adventure.

Activity level influences mindset. A message that appeals to a sedentary type is likely to frustrate and be too slow-moving and complex for people on the go. This means you need to consider your language choices carefully with regard to your target audience's activity levels. Your goal is to emulate their preferred pace.

Comfort with Technology

Technology has become a driving force in our society. However, not everyone is traveling at the same pace on the information superhighway.

It's critical to understand how comfortable your target market is with technology, particularly as that applies to the Internet.

> **Danger Zone**
>
> Never make assumptions about your target audience's comfort with technology based upon age, gender, or ethnicity! Seniors who use the Internet, for example, are online just as much as their younger friends and relatives. There is no correlation between age, gender, or ethnicity and technology use.

Comfort with technology is often viewed as a spectrum: early adopters are very comfortable with and excited by new and emerging technology. Very experienced users interact with technology several hours a day, while occasional users may log on once or twice a week. Some people choose never to engage with new technology.

Financial Values

Money is far more than green pieces of paper that we deposit in the bank or squirrel away under our mattress. In fact, the relationship that individuals have with money is often one of the most telling things you can observe about them.

Some people view money as a goal in and of itself: the more money you have, the better off you are. Accumulation of wealth for them is key. Others view money as merely the means to an end, the medium exchanged to achieve the things necessary to have a "happy" life. Still others are flat-out averse to money, eschewing riches for an ascetic life.

Your customers may have one of these three positions—or they may have another viewpoint entirely. Understanding how your customers relate to money will help you craft more effective marketing campaigns.

Interests/Hobbies

What do your target customers do with their free time? Are they stamp collectors or do they hunt whitetail deer? Will they spend a three-day weekend poring over needle-work patterns or pouring concrete on a new patio?

Interests and hobbies are those leisure-time activities people do purely for enjoyment. They range from passive activities, such as watching television or movies, to more active endeavors, such as rock climbing or mountain biking.

Again, the value in this information is to give you insight into your target market's mindset. Leisure time is scarce; the fact that a sizable portion of your target audience chooses to devote their limited leisure time to a specific activity can provide a deeper level of under-standing.

> **On Target**
>
> Charles Schwab, a financial services company that focuses on the small investor, targets their services specifically based upon their customer's relationship with money. The Charles Schwab customer is someone who views money as an asset to be lever-aged, yet feels insecure in his own ability to invest properly.

Family Structure

Family structure is sometimes referred to as family dynamics. It considers both the size of a family and the roles individuals play within it.

For example, a four-person household could comprise of a husband and wife with two children; a single parent with three children; an adult child, her parents, and her soon-to-be-adult child; a polyamorous triad and their child—the list is endless.

Few target markets are uniformly consistent in regard to family structure. However, understanding how the majority of your target market views the concept of "family," and how the family structure impacts their decision-making, is essential.

Media Engagement

It may seem like we're all plugged in all the time, connected to the media 24/7—but that's a dangerous assumption to make. Media-usage rates and the types of media indi-viduals engage with vary widely by target audience.

Of all the psychographic information you collect, media engagement has the most direct and immediate impact on your marketing efforts. If your target audience is highly literate, and seldom watches television yet spends hours online, then investing time on an effective web presence will give you a better return than devoting energy getting booked on the local newscast.

How Do You Get Psychographic Information?

Psychographic information needs to be gathered directly from your target market. After all, they're the only ones who know what's going on inside their own heads!

Insight

To make psychographic research really easy, there are online applications such as www.claritas.com/ MyBestSegments where you simply enter the zip codes of the neighborhoods you're interested in, and receive a bare-bones psychographic profile within seconds. It's not everything you need to know, but it's a good first step.

Luckily, this isn't very difficult. There are few things that people enjoy as much as talking about themselves. Strategic use of surveys—especially web-based surveys—provide you the opportunity to gather those insights.

There are services you can hire to administer psychographic surveys for you, but a savvy marketer, who knows what information she needs, can accomplish much the same for a fraction of the cost. Bear in mind that most people want some kind of reward for giving up their personal information. Plan on some type of incentive, such as a discount coupon or free gift, in exchange for this data.

The Least You Need to Know

♦ Demographic information is the nuts-and-bolts quantifiable data you collect about your target audience—Who are they? What do they do? Where do they live?

♦ Design marketing strategies based on your knowledge and understanding of demographic information, because groups that share common characteristics often demonstrate similar behaviors.

♦ Psychographic information helps you to identify what it is about your products and services that most appeals to your target audience and what motivates them to buy.

♦ Psychographic information needs to be gathered directly from your target market. Give them an incentive for sharing this information with you.

What Makes Customers Tick?

In This Chapter

- ◆ The essentials of buying motivators
- ◆ Reaching your customers using buying motivators
- ◆ The Super Seven Buying Motivators

When it comes to buying anything from simple services and products to expensive gadgets, buying motivators influence the decisions we make. Understanding what these motivators are and how they make your customers tick simplifies the entire target marketing process.

Luckily, you don't have to reinvent the wheel. Researchers have already identified some of the most common buying motivators. In this chapter we'll outline the Super Seven Buying Motivators—some of the most powerful and universal factors that influence customers' buying behaviors. As effective marketers, your job is first to understand and recognize these incredibly powerful reasons for buying. Then, when you grasp what drives your customers' decision-making, you can better position your products and services to appeal to their wants and needs!

When it comes to buying anything, it all boils down to the power of buying motivators.

What Are Buying Motivators?

"Why did I buy this? I don't even like it!" Have you ever stood at your closet door, pondering the contents and asking that question? Sometimes the choices we make are puzzling and inexplicable, even to ourselves.

Puzzling and inexplicable, that is, until we step back and consider our buying motivators. Perhaps we purchased the offending outfit in question because we thought it would make us look more professional, enhancing our chances for promotion. That's the need for power and control, manifested in clothing. Or perhaps we picked out that outfit with another need in mind: motivated by the need for love and sex, we purchased clothing to make us look and feel irresistible!

Buying motivators are the reasons that we, as individuals, make the decisions we make.

There are a lot of names for buying motivators: they're called motivations, or reasons, or influences. We call them buying motivators because we're concerned about business decisions.

To understand buying motivators, you have to know that what we're really talking about here is simply an expression of somebody's needs. We purchase products or services in a certain way, at a certain time, to fulfill a need—and that's buying motivators in a nutshell.

About the Super Seven Buying Motivators

Maslow's Hierarchy of Needs is a fundamental marketing concept that states we all have needs, and that these can be categorized in levels. First and foremost are the needs tied to survival. Once those needs are met, we progress up the levels to those needs that are of more interest to most small business owners: the needs for emotional safety, security, esteem, and beauty. These are the needs that drive most purchasing decisions.

From Maslow's Hierarchy of Needs, social scientists and researchers have derived almost endless combinations of needs and motivations in an effort to explain why we act the way we do.

From this wealth of motivators, seven are the most universal, powerful buying motivators. Taken alone or in combination, these motivators underlie almost all purchasing behavior.

When you read through the Super Seven Buying Motivators, you might well find yourself pondering exactly what kind of person is driven by a given need. However, this isn't an exercise in value-judgment. This is about understanding your target audience. That's the value in studying buying motivators.

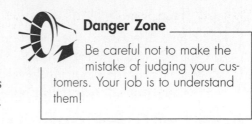

Danger Zone

Be careful not to make the mistake of judging your customers. Your job is to understand them!

You don't have to identify with a motivator. In other words, as a retailer or service provider or manufacturer, you don't have to feel the same way your customers do. There's no law that says a company that caters to people with a strong need to nurture, for example, has to be owned and staffed solely by caregivers! You simply have to understand the buying motivator and make it easy for your customers to fulfill their needs (hopefully with your products and/or services)!

Understanding buying motivators also helps you avoid making mistakes when you reach out to your target audience. When you know what resonates for customers, it's not difficult to extrapolate what will turn those customers completely off. For example, a customer who is driven by the need to belong would not want a product that makes them feel isolated, solitary, or alone.

The Super Seven Buying Motivators

As you read about the Super Seven Buying Motivators, bear in mind that they are not in any order of importance. They are all equally likely to influence a customer. It's your job to discover which of the Super Seven Buying Motivators are the most influential among your target audience.

The Need to Belong and Trust

The need to belong and trust taps into one of the most fundamental aspects of humanity: we all want to be part of something—a family, a team, a club, the cool kids. On a very fundamental level, we're social creatures. We crave connection with others who are like ourselves.

To form these connections, we have to be able to trust. Trust is the glue that makes groups stick together: remove trust from any family, for example, and that family quickly falls apart. If you cannot trust the people who are working for you, do they remain your employees for long?

What Makes Someone Trust?

Sometimes the desire to belong manifests as an urge to join with or be accepted by a group of people different from ourselves. This motivation drives an awful lot of purchasing behaviors, as individuals strive to outfit themselves with the "right" clothes, accessories, shoes, jewelry, electronics, car, house … the list is endless.

Understanding the groups your target audience wants to join or already belong to will help you grasp what values and behaviors are critical to your customer base.

When you're reaching out to customers motivated by the need to belong, you want to emphasize how their purchases will help them achieve, secure, or enhance a position within a desired group. For example, food manufacturers often use images of a smiling family sitting gathered around the dining table in their advertising. Family is the first group most of us belong to, and it remains a powerful force throughout our lives.

> **On Target**
>
> Allstate Insurance's "You're in good hands" motto speaks directly to the need to belong. Insurance customers want to be in a group that's cared for and protected—literally, in good hands.

Coca-Cola's famous "I'd like to teach the world a song" campaign of the early 1970s was a phenomenally successful demonstration of the desire to belong. By giving customers a tangible way to identify with the product, Coke tapped into the desire to belong and expanded it exponentially. It didn't take long for almost the entire nation and the global community to know that jingle!

However, simply belonging is not enough. Tied intimately to the need to belong is the need to trust.

Today's customers are skeptical. The younger they are, the more cynical they're likely to be. Generation after generation of overexposure to advertisements and letdowns by everyone from politicians to sports stars have made it difficult for the average consumer to believe that there is a company they can trust.

Individuals motivated by the need to trust value an organization that keeps its word, that is accountable for its actions, and is transparent in its business dealings. This is especially pertinent as Internet usage has become more common. Industry research tells us that over 90 percent of customers do research online before making a major purchase. They want to know what they can expect—and they don't trust you to tell them! They require external validation of their experience, from rating and review websites, personal blogs, and social-networking sites.

The need to trust manifests in several different ways. Some customers want to know they can trust the merchandise you sell: they want to know that the products are well made and will work as they represent. Others want to know they can trust your prices: are these sale prices legitimately sales prices, or have you artificially inflated all of your prices and then taken token cuts to ape the appearance of a good deal? Still others want to know they can trust you: If they begin shopping with you today, will your store be there a year from now? Two years from now? A decade from now?

Insight

Presenting yourself as the local, hometown option is a great way to reach out to the trust-based customer. For example, a small, regional bank can appeal because decisions are made immediately, without having to check with a headquarters halfway across the country. Being small can be a big advantage!

Fixing Problems Reinforces Trust

If you want to appeal to customers motivated by the need to trust, you have to acknowledge and fix all of the mistakes your organization makes. Jet Blue did a fantastic job of this in 2007, after they responded poorly to an ice storm, leaving passengers stranded for up to 10 hours. Not only did they immediately issue an apology, but they took well-publicized steps to repair the problems and ensure it never happened again.

Another way to market yourself effectively to the customer motivated by the need to trust lies in your return policies and guarantees. You build trust with your customer base when they know they can return items they've purchased, or that you've guaranteed that your service will satisfy.

Danger Zone

When you create return policies and guarantees, think through how you're going to implement them on a daily basis—because if you falter in this arena, you will completely erode any trust your customer may have had in you!

The Need for Excitement and Fun

The need for excitement and fun is becoming more and more influential in the business world. This is true for the culture at large: we're an entertainment-based society. We want the show, the circus, the concert, and the fireworks display, all rolled into one.

People with this motivation want—and more important, expect!—to be entertained every moment of the day. It doesn't matter what type of business you're in, people buy from the people they like. Providing excitement and fun is one way to ensure that your customers like you!

On Target

M & M's, the familiar chocolate candy, brought their product to life with animated characters. These characters feature prominently in their packaging—which kids (and adults!) buy because they're fun.

Insight

There are literally hundreds of places to buy western-themed decor. You can find bucking bronco lamps and lasso-patterned bedspreads all along the Rio Grande—but How The West Was Fun website (www.howthewestwasfun.com) specializes in lighthearted and whimsical western décor. It appeals to those customers who want to have a western accent and a smile.

This motivation dominates even the most staid of transactions: all things being equal, buyers will opt for the purchase that will afford them the most fun. And it doesn't have to be the merchandise or service itself that's fun. It can be the atmosphere the product or service is delivered in, the people selling or providing the product or service, or even the packaging!

Reaching out to customers who have a need for excitement and fun is simple. You simply have to convince these groups that they're going to have a good time! The definition of "a good time" varies by target audience: if you market clothes for preteen girls, an in-store screening of *Hannah Montana*'s newest movie will be fun. On the other hand, the parents of those preteen girls might be far more likely to enjoy themselves at a wine-tasting or book-signing by a celebrity author.

Fun and excitement are highly visible branding concepts. Using fun fonts in signage, upbeat and exciting language in sales copy and advertising flyers, even clever taglines for e-mail marketing, helps convey the impression that your store is an exciting, fun place to be. Don't be afraid of fun: you can do some serious business while having a really good time.

The Need for Easy

In a time-pressed, stress-filled society, many individuals are motivated by a need for life to be easy—or at least easier than it currently is! This often boils down to convenience: these customers seek out products and services that can save them time, money, and effort. These are the people who want merchandise they don't even have to think about: the prepackaged meal they can throw in the crock pot and forget about until it's time to eat; the software that automatically updates itself; the digital video recorder that records all of the best TV shows, a season at a time.

The need for easy is especially prominent in the B2B community. With an ever-increasing number of new and emerging businesses appearing every year, entrepreneurs are looking for any and everything that can make them better business people without having to expend any extra effort.

Making it easy for your customer starts from the first minute you engage with them. Is your advertising easy to read and understand? Keep copy to a minimum, use lots of pictures, and design every marketing piece so questions are answered BEFORE the customer asks them.

If you want to see the master of the Need for Easy, you need look no further than the local Staples store. This office supply chain even features an Easy Button! Every Staples ad prominently features a product, with the product's name, picture, price, and the most relevant benefits. And that's it: easy to look at, easy to comprehend, and with multiple purchasing venues available, easy to buy. A customer can go online, go to the local brick-and-mortar store, or pick up the phone for the products they want. What could be easier than that?

Making it easy also extends to your business location and design. Consider how customers access your store. Are you in a convenient location? Can they park their cars without a hassle? Small factors like a driveway that's difficult to navigate will alienate the shopper driven by the need for easy.

> **On Target**
>
> RingCentral identified a common problem—the difficulty traveling professionals have accessing their phone messages—and responded with an innovative forwarding service that made life easy. Now they have over 40,000 customers!

The Need for Importance

It's good to be the king. Look at the big shot. Who's number one? The need for importance is universal, speaking to a deep-seated longing for status, recognition, and, often, power. People with this buying motivation like to be recognized as special, remarkable individuals, one-of-a-kind superstars in a world filled with regular people. Because they're so special, people with this motivation often like to be in control.

> **On Target**
>
> The best example of catering to the need for importance? Casinos. High rollers get free rooms, special perks, even an escort to their car to make sure they get home safely.

Businesses that provide over-the-top customer service, luxury merchandise and services, and individual attention to the smallest request tap directly into the need for importance by providing some measure of status and recognition.

Insight

The need for importance is not just a high-priced phenomenon. People from every social class and economic strata want to be recognized as special within their group.

An ancillary element of the need for importance is the need to be seen as special by other people—not just the people providing the products and services! This motivation is incredibly powerful.

The need to be seen as important by others is a large part of the appeal behind Ivy League schools such as Harvard and Yale. Simply attending these schools confers a certain amount of prestige upon the students. This gives them one leg up in the race to be seen as important.

Marketing to customers driven by the need for importance means being aware of what's "right" for your customer base. This is a very trend-driven phenomenon: what could be the "right" watch one year could be a career-ending faux pas the next. If you're going to market primarily to this demographic, you need to make a commitment to being not only aware of the trends, but being responsive to them. This may mean immersing yourself in trade publications, attending numerous tradeshows and conventions, and spending time online on a regular basis so you can be clued into what your customer base values—and wants to buy!

It's important to recognize the element of power and control in the need for importance. A significant portion of individuals with this motivation long for control over themselves, their families, their surroundings, their colleagues and peers, random events, and more. Obviously, no one person can have control in all of these areas, but individuals motivated by this need will seek out ways to achieve the most power and control possible.

On Target

Any executive can sign his or her name with a cheap, 12-for-a-dollar ballpoint pen. But many opt to spend hundreds of dollars on a Mont Blanc. These pens have appeal because they are a symbol of power and importance.

While we can't package power and present it directly to our customers, we can appeal to their need for control in two ways: One is with the trappings of power, the merchandise and services traditionally reserved for the person in charge. Another is by selling the products and services that will enable a person to achieve a prestigious position: this is sometimes called positional power.

Finally, when you enable your customer base to do exactly what they want to do, in exactly the fashion they want it done, at exactly the time they want to do it, you're catering to individuals driven by the need for control and power.

These customers want to be able to dictate every detail of the exchange: they know what they want, and they don't want you to change their mind or persuade them to look at something else. Make these customers happy by providing exactly what they ask for—and complimenting their decisions along the way.

The Need to Nurture

The need to nurture is a powerful motivator, especially for people who find themselves in caregiver roles. This includes parents, people who have elderly parents, people who are closely involved with their community and neighbors, and even pet owners. All of these relationships have a certain associated level of responsibility.

Understanding the need to nurture means positioning your products and services so they appear the best and most attractive for an individual to fulfill a certain responsibility. In some individuals, the need to nurture is so strong that it overrides basic self-interest: it is not unusual for a parent to prioritize her child's needs over her own, or a pet owner to buy gourmet food for his cat while dining on ramen noodles himself!

The need to nurture is part of the reasoning behind Crane's line of humidifiers for nurseries. Humidifiers, which add moisture to the air, are generally utilitarian in appearance. However, Crane understood the motivation of their target market—high-income new parents—and designed humidifiers that look like frogs, penguins, bears, and other baby favorites.

The need to nurture drives people to make a wide range of purchasing decisions. Life insurance is, in the vast majority of cases, an expression of the need to nurture: the person purchasing the policy wants to ensure that her loved ones are financially secure after she passes away.

Nurturing Beyond Necessities

While the need to nurture certainly influences the purchases of many of life's necessities—obviously if you're caring for someone, you want to ensure he has food, shelter, clothing—it also drives customers toward other, perhaps not-as-critically-necessary purchases. Toys, jewelry, plasma TVs—more than a few people purchase such items for loved ones, for no better reason than they would make the recipient happy.

Making someone happy is a nurturer's ultimate goal. If you can help the nurturer do that on a consistent basis, you've got a customer for life.

The need to nurture *is not* tied to gender. Both men and women are driven by the need to take care of others. Socially, we're more likely to expect the need to nurture in women, but it occurs in men as well. There are plenty of men out there with this need.

Expanding the Need to Nurture

There are times that the need to nurture extends beyond one's immediate family and friends. A passion for the environment, human rights, the underprivileged, animals, or the community can easily be considered part of the need to nurture. Often termed social awareness, this motivation springs from people's innate desire to care for those around them on a grand scale.

Environmental consciousness is one of the most powerful and visible manifestations of the need to do good. Companies that position themselves as "green," with earth-friendly products, services, practices, and packaging, are appealing directly to the need to do good.

Plum Island Soap Company—which has the absolutely awesome tag line of "Get Dirty, Get Naked, Get Clean, Naturally!"—offers customers the chance to look and smell really good, while being sure that they're using only earth-friendly, environmentally conscious products.

Nurturing and Cause Marketing

An effective way to appeal to customers driven by the need to do good is to offer them an opportunity to positively impact the world without a lot of effort on their part. For example, many people are concerned about breast cancer. Kellogg's cereal has special packaging on many of their cereals with the announcement that a portion of the proceeds of the sales from these products would be used to help fund breast cancer research. Customers were going to buy cereal anyway, but the desire to help a cause they cared about drove many consumers to pick up Kellogg's products rather than any of a hundred other cereals.

The Need for Self-Improvement

The need for self-improvement motivates individuals who always want to do better. This can be on a personal or professional level: some people might want the products and services that make them a better dancer, for example, or they might seek out the software package or training courses to help them be the best accountant in town.

Self-improvement is a type of band-aid for insecurity. We use self-improvement to counter those aspects of our lives we don't feel too good about: if we know we're a bad cook, we buy a new set of pans, hoping that dinner will turn out better. If we know we're not fit, we buy exercise equipment. If we feel incompetent at work, we buy books to make us better at what we do.

Self-improvement addresses insecurity and makes people feel good. On a very basic level, appealing to the need for self-improvement is very similar to appealing to the need for excitement and fun: people are looking for an experience that makes them feel good. When the need for excitement and fun is met, they feel good because they had a great, entertaining experience. When the need for self-improvement is met, they feel good because they now perceive themselves as smarter, sexier, fitter, more efficient, or some other flavor of "Better than I was before I started."

Insight

Competitions and reward programs resonate incredibly well with people motivated by the need for self-improvement: you're giving them something tangible to strive for.

Similar to the drive for self-improvement is the passion for reinvention. Americans are particularly prone to this passion. If you're no longer satisfied with your life, your job, your family, or your career, it's simply a matter of chucking it all and starting all over, reinventing yourself anew!

Appealing to this need involves more than offering your customers the opportunity to improve themselves. You have to understand why your customers haven't already made themselves better. Curves scored a target marketing bull's-eye when they coupled the need for self-improvement with many women's preference for a private, supportive, female-only fitness center.

If you can tap into this drive, and offer your customers the tools and resources to transform their existence, you can have a lucrative business.

The Need for Love

Advertisers say sex sells, and they're right. The drive for love, sex, and passion motivates almost all people at some point in their lives. The sex drive is one of the strongest urges humankind experiences—in fact, it's one of the primary needs on Maslow's hierarchy.

For a long time, people believed that appealing to the need for love, sex, and passion meant creating ads with scantily clad people looking longingly at each other, preferably on a dark and stormy night while dramatic clouds rolled overhead and a red sports car waited in the driveway.

Savvy business owners know that it's critical to expand beyond the visual trappings of love, sex, and romance and really connect with their customers on an emotional level.

> **On Target**
>
> Axe, a line of bodywash and fragrances aimed at young teenage males, markets itself with an overt appeal to the need for love. Douse yourself in Axe, and women will literally fling themselves at you. Even if you're going over a cliff.

When you're appealing to the demographic motivated by the need for love and sex, what you're really selling is hope.

The premise is this: if you have the right product or service, then you can have the love of your dreams. Of course, you can't beat people over the head with that message. Instead, if you're positioning yourself to appeal to this demographic, you need to master suggestive-selling techniques. These customers want to know that someday the dream can come true for them.

Hope is the driving force behind services such as eHarmony, perhaps the world's best-known online dating service. Many companies have applied target marketing concepts to the online dating model, resulting in a plethora of specialty sites. J-date caters to those seeking a Jewish partner, Korean Cupid helps unite Korean couples, and Country Match will help someone lasso the cowboy or cowgirl of their dreams.

Both men and women are motivated by the need for love, sex, and passion. Many people assume that it is only women who want romance, but that's simply not true! Everyone wants to connect with someone, to feel special, to be desired by someone, and to find their true love. The best way to appeal to this group is by tapping into that universal desire and then finding a unique, compelling way to package your products and services so they appear to meet those needs.

The Least You Need to Know

- Buying motivators influence the decisions people make, no matter what they buy.

- Buying motivators are the needs that influence customers' purchasing decisions.

- Take time to understand what makes your customers tick.

- When you grasp what drives your customers' decision-making, you can better position your products and services to appeal to their wants and needs!

Chapter 8

Closing In On a Target: Market Segmentation

In This Chapter

◆ The benefits of market segmentation

◆ The four steps to market segmentation

◆ Selecting the right segment to market to

◆ Determining the value of trends and fads

The world consists of a dizzying array of people. You have probably realized that fact already based on the demographics, psychographics, and motivations that were the focus of Chapters 6 and 7. In a nutshell, there are far more kinds and types of people than you could ever hope to reach effectively.

What you must come to terms with is that you cannot possibly be all things to all people, no matter how hard you try. There are just too many people, and they are all very different from one another.

Enter market segmentation. Rather than take on the impossible challenge of trying to reach an infinite number of individuals, you need to concentrate on identifying and marketing to clearly defined groups. This makes your marketing challenge easier, more efficient, and much more effective. Moreover, it will save you money—always a good thing!

Insight _____

Market segmentation is like a jigsaw puzzle. There are many pieces to put together before you can see the full picture.

Market segmentation is the process of breaking up the existing marketplace (which includes every customer of every customer type, everywhere in the world) into smaller, more manageable groups. Once you identify and assess groups of interest, it's time to select the very best one or ones to market to, and develop strategies to reach them effectively.

The Four Steps to Market Segmentation

Breaking the marketing segmentation process into practical, easy-to-implement bite-size actionable steps will help you understand and, more important, use this dynamic marketing tool.

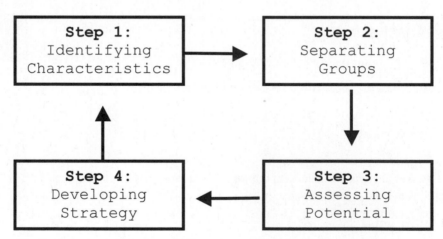

The four steps to market segmentation.

You need to approach in order each of the four steps to market segmentation diagrammed here, as each step builds on the next. For example, you cannot possibly assess the potential of a group until you have identified it and know its characteristics.

You will revisit this process time and time again as your business grows and evolves. Customers are ever-changing. That which is critical today might not even be on the radar two years from now. Market segments reinvent and recreate themselves constantly—some more quickly than others, depending on needs. Your awareness and responsive meter needs to be on full alert at all times.

Step 1: Identifying Characteristics

Begin your market segmentation process by identifying characteristics in your marketplace as a whole. For example, if you are an accountant, what are the identifying characteristics of the people who seek out accounting services?

In this phase, your goal is to identify both the demographic and psychographic characteristics that are prevalent among people who seek out the types of products and services you offer. Additionally, you want to understand the motivations that drive people when they buy these types of products or services.

This should be a relatively large list. Include every demographic and psychographic factor that could contribute to your target audience. Consider every possible motivation.

Step 2: Separating Groups

Once you have pinpointed the identifying characteristics in your marketplace, it is time to use those characteristics to create groups of like-minded customers.

What Makes a Good Group

Not all groups are created equal. Arbitrarily dividing consumers into random segments rarely achieves anything worthwhile. It is merely a mathematical separation, not a qualitative one—one that you can measure.

To create a good, usable market segment, you need groups that meet certain criteria. Ideally, you can measure a group by the following six benchmarks:

- **Internally Consistent:** All members of the group share some identifiable traits that unite them as a whole. For example, vegetarians do not eat meat or fish. Some might also not eat dairy products.

- **Conspicuously Distinct:** A group must have a unique identity that differentiates it from other groups. Take country music fans, for example. They are conspicuously distinct from hip-hop fans. They enjoy different music, wear different clothes, and watch different television shows, and so on.

◆ **Measurable & Identifiable:** You need to be able to secure objective, quantifiable data about your group. For example, knowing the size and location of the group.

◆ **Enduring:** The best groups have continuity even if individual members leave. For example, expectant parents are a group. It is a group with an ever-changing membership, as expectancy by its very nature comes with a time limit. However, because new people are continually becoming expectant parents, the group, and resultant market, can be considered stable.

◆ **Accessible:** As a practical consideration, a group should consist of individuals who are easy to reach. For example, while it is certainly possible to create a group of your favorite movie stars, musicians, and fashion designers, access to them may be more challenging.

If reaching harder-to-access groups is part of your marketing strategy, realize that you will need to devote substantial time, energy, and resources to do so.

◆ **Of a Significant Size:** You can split market segments all day long, refining your target audience until you wind up with six 38-year-old professional women in Chicago who all work out on Tuesdays and listen to Celine Dion and drive Saabs. Chances are that this group would not qualify as a large-enough segment to support your business.

A group needs to be large enough to be profitable. What this means is that the sales realized by reaching out to the group must substantially exceed the costs of forming a relationship with them.

Group Creation Options

There are many different ways to segment groups. The four major ones are as follows:

◆ **By location:** Create a target market based upon the fact that all of the potential customers live or work in the same location. This is an especially powerful strategy if you are in a convenience-based business: dry cleaners, coffee shops, and pharmacies often rise and fall on the relative convenience of their location.

◆ **By demographics:** Returning to all of the information covered in Chapter 6, you can create groups based upon demographic information. For example, your target audience members might have a common gender, age range, type of jobs, or religious belief.

On Target

TRA School Software Solutions is a company created by a former school administrator who had firsthand knowledge and understanding of the technological needs of school administrators. The company thrives by reaching out to a very specific demographic: professionals in charge of administering elementary or secondary schools.

Beautifully Modest, a store that specializes in wedding gowns and special-occasion wear that is not revealing, focuses on a target market that shares many social and religious beliefs.

Eduplay is an Australian company that provides innovative and unique educational programs for expectant parents and parents with children up to pre-school age.

◆ **By psychographics:** Again, drawing on what you learned in Chapter 6, you can create groups based upon psychographic information. All of the members in a target market can share the same set of values, for example. Alternatively, they may belong to the same social class, or aspire to the same goals.

◆ **By behaviors:** You can create groups based on a target market's likely behavioral pattern at a certain time. For example, brides-to-be share a swath of common needs and they tend to exhibit certain predictable behaviors as the wedding date draws near, such as fitness and health concerns. Will they fit into their dress on the big day? Similarly, expectant parents have definable behavioral traits, such as wanting to know as much as possible about the birthing experience.

Step 3: Assessing Potential

Once you have identified a group, it is time to discover if it is going to work for you. Because not every group is the right target market for every company, you want to be selective, and focus on what is the best fit for you.

Assessing a market segment's potential consists of considering how the segment performs or would be likely to perform in four different areas.

Appeal

Does the market segment you are considering have a demonstrated want or need for your products or services? This is a critical question. It may be that no one is selling square-dancing gear to this target market because no one considered it, or more likely, no one in that market segment wants square-dancing gear.

Competition

How many other companies are serving the market segment you are considering? Take into account direct competitors—those businesses, either brick-and-mortar or online, that offer the same products or services you are offering. And don't forget to factor in indirect competitors—products or services that customers view as viable alternatives. For example, a bowling alley offers a wholly different experience than a movie theater, yet both are go-to places on a Friday night.

Too much competition may preclude you from pursuing a market segment. The secret ingredient in a crowded marketplace is differentiation. When you stand out from the crowd because you are markedly different and superior, chances for your survival increase dramatically.

Financial Viability

Financial viability asks the question, "Does this market segment have any money?"

Can the majority of individuals in your proposed target market afford your products and services at the price you want to sell them? Is there enough money in a segment to support your business?

Be realistic. Financial viability often goes hand-in-hand with market growth. Look at the financial viability with clear, objective eyes. Relying on a "hope for the best" prayer is dangerous.

Ease of Entry

How easy will it be for you to reach the market segment you are considering? In business, there is no level playing field.

Danger Zone

If a market segment cannot afford your products/services before you enter it, money is not magically going to appear out of thin air for them to spend it with you.

Some groups are easier to reach than others. Consider social and cultural factors. Are you a member of the group or community you are trying to market to? This often makes it easier to establish yourself as a new business, but there is no guarantee of either immediate acceptance or success!

Each market segment has baseline expectations. No matter what type of business, the market segment comes already equipped with a certain mental picture of what a business like yours is supposed to be like.

For example, conjure up a picture of a women's clothing store on Los Angeles's famous Rodeo Drive. Did an immediate mental picture spring to mind? That mental picture may represent the baseline expectation of what that particular market segment expects.

Meeting your target market's baseline expectations is essential. This is the cost of entry. If you fail to meet those expectations, your business will go belly-up in no time.

Carefully consider what it takes to meet the baseline expectations for a market segment. If you find the cost is too high for one segment, do not despair. There are other market segments to cater to—and you will be far more likely to succeed with the ones where you meet or, better still, exceed baseline expectations!

Personality

Of all the criteria to consider when assessing a potential target market, this one is the most nebulous. Yet it is perhaps the most important.

Consider the personality of your potential target group. Ask yourself if this is a group of people you would enjoy interacting with. If so, would you willingly spend time with them, if being paid to do so were an option?

Life is too short to spend it doing business with people you do not particularly care for.

Authenticity is becoming increasingly important as a marketing premise. As more and more younger buyers enter the marketplace, they bring with them a deeply ingrained skepticism about all things marketing related. They value a genuine, authentic relationship with the businesses they work with. They expect mutual respect. If you cannot bring a certain level of respect to the table when considering a potential market segment, pass it by.

For example, if tattoos and body piercings bother you, do not consider doing business with the market segments who don these accents and accessories.

Picking One

After careful consideration of all of the necessary criteria, you want to pick the group who offers the best potential. This group not only finds your products or services appealing, but also can afford them. Ideally, this will be a group who is easy to reach and whom you will enjoy working with.

All of these factors are important. However, because none of us lives in an ideal world, it's important to be flexible and willing to compromise.

 Danger Zone _____

Beware of marketing to the wrong target markets. Invest time in finding the right audience for your products and services. It will pay dividends.

Step 4: Developing Strategy

After identifying the market segments that have the most potential, the next step is to develop a strategy to reach that target market.

A number of target marketing strategies are covered at length in the next chapter. It is important to find a strategy that most effectively resonates with your target market.

While developing your strategy, keep the following questions in mind:

 ◆ What will grab this group's attention?

 ◆ What will make this group feel an emotional connection to my business?

 ◆ Where does this group like to spend time?

 ◆ What would persuade this group to buy from me?

You will find the answers to these questions, in large part, from the work you did in identifying the key characteristics of your target market.

What's Hot and What's Not

Society is constantly changing. That means your customers' wants and needs vary over the course of time—sometimes permanently, while other times just for a short while. The stability of the change is the difference between trends (long-term change) and fads, crazes, and hype (short-term change).

These changes affect the market segmentation process. While you're in the process of identifying a target market, with a particular focus on the long-term viability of that segment, you need to make sure that you're making your assessment on information that will either always be true or at least has a reasonable expectation of remaining true.

What does that mean? There are some basic facts that will always be true. For instance, people will always need health care. Individuals who have money want to make the best use of it, and those who do not have any money want to get some. Parents will always need to care for their children, and someone, somewhere, will be in the market for a drop-dead pair of high heels that cost more than a small home on the Jersey shore.

Other things either cease to be true due to changes in technology or the marketplace. Typewriters and typewriter repairs were once an essential part of doing business. Today you will probably find more typewriters in antique stores than in offices.

Still other things are only true for a very brief period in time: Beanie Babies, those small stuffed toys, were both highly collectible and valuable for a brief period in the mid-1990s. Today, they are neither collectible nor valuable.

It all boils down to the need to understand the difference between trends and fads.

Understanding Trends and Fads

A trend has the potential of becoming a long-term influence on the future of a market. It occurs when a change in customer demand is permanent, or has the potential to become permanent. For example, the push toward green, environmentally friendly products and services started in the early 1970s, and demand has grown steadily ever since.

def•i•ni•tion

A **fad** is a short-term trend. A temporary, short-lived style, type of clothing, notion, game, behavior, or event that is propelled by popular momentum.

Danger Zone

Due to the short-lived nature of fads, you should be aware of fads and factor them into your business decisions, but you should avoid making business decisions based entirely on them.

A *fad* and a trend may resemble each other. For example, the use of lime-green wall paint may be a fad, but using designer colors in home décor is a trend. Fads have a short, intense life span. Customer demand may be high—but it is also fleeting.

A fad can certainly influence your business decisions. When Harry Potter was all the rage, you'd better believe savvy bookstore owners were carrying J. K. Rowling's books!

If you are a retailer, sensitivity to what is hot at any given moment can make you a superstar. Some retailers market themselves very effectively by having the latest fad-merchandise, particularly in apparel, toys, and electronics. It's important to remember that supplying your customers with the of-the-moment merchandise is a strategy, but that your brand, in and of itself, should not be tied to any individual fad.

Be a Trend Spotter

You certainly want to consider trends when determining your target audience. A trend can create an entire market: the trend toward both parents working outside the home led directly to an explosion of products and services designed to make life easy: convenience foods, daycare, even pet-sitters for those who have "children" of the furry persuasion.

A trend can even serve as one of the factors you use to define your target market. Keep your eyes and ears open to what is happening around you both locally and globally. Change happens all the time. Your job is to become an astute and savvy detective who can sift through and separate that passing fancy from the next important long-lived trend.

Market Segmentation Checklist

Complete this sheet for each of the target markets you are considering. After you have completed a sheet for each market segment, compare your results and pick the one that looks to be the best fit for you.

Step 1: Identify Group Characteristics

What are the demographics of this target market?

- ◆ _____
- ◆ _____
- ◆ _____
- ◆ _____
- ◆ _____
- ◆ _____

What are the psychographics of this target market?

- ◆ _____
- ◆ _____
- ◆ _____
- ◆ _____
- ◆ _____

What are the behaviors of this target market?

- ◆ _____
- ◆ _____
- ◆ _____
- ◆ _____
- ◆ _____

continues

continued

Step 2: Separate the Groups

What makes your group internally consistent?

_____

What makes your group conspicuously distinct?

_____

What makes your group measurable and identifiable?

_____

What makes your group enduring?

_____

What makes your group accessible?

_____

Step 3: Assess the Potential

Has your potential target market demonstrated a need or want for your products/services?

_____

How has it demonstrated that need or want?

_____

What companies, products, or services do you consider your competition—direct and indirect?

_____

Does your potential target market have money to spend on your products/services?

_____

How easy will it be for you to reach your potential target market?

_____

On a scale of 1 to 10, with 1 being the lowest and 10 being the highest, rate how you feel about working with your potential target market.

_____

Step 4: Develop a Strategy

Answering the following questions will help you determine which marketing strategy will resonate most effectively with your target market:

What will grab this group's attention?

_____

What will make this group feel an emotional connection to your business?

_____

Where does this group like to spend time?

_____

What would persuade this group to buy from you?

_____

Would you consider your products/services a trend or a fad?

_____

The Least You Need to Know

- Market segmentation is like a jigsaw puzzle. There are so many pieces to put together before you can see the full picture.

- Identify your target audience's demographic and psychographic characteristics and understand their motivations to buy.

- Pick a market who finds your products or services appealing and affordable and can offer sustainability for your business.

- Recognize the difference between a trend and a fad before investing time and energy in your marketing efforts.

Pick Your Path: Target Marketing Strategies

In This Chapter

◆ Recognizing the need for a target marketing strategy

◆ The role of your strategy in decision-making

◆ Target marketing strategy options

Are you fired up and ready to go? Are the car keys jingling in your hand, signaling it's time to get the target marketing show on the road? Are you ready to start realizing all the benefits target marketing has to offer?

After all, you know who your target market is. That's half the battle, and by all accounts, by far the largest half. But, hold your horses; you're not quite ready to hit the highway yet.

Before you get started, you have to know how you're going to reach your target market. That's the strategic element in target marketing: the careful planning and plotting part that enables you to connect on a meaningful level with your target audience.

There are many routes up the mountain—but not all climbers will pick the same one. Target marketing is the same way: there are many routes to success, but they won't all be equally appealing to all business owners. In this section, we'll explore the available options and how to select the target marketing strategy that's right for you.

What Makes a Great Strategy?

Let's start with some definitions. A strategy is an elaborate and systematic plan to accomplish predetermined goals. Therefore, a target marketing strategy is no more than a plan to help you achieve the goals and objectives you've defined for your business, using target marketing tools.

Having a strategic plan helps you to identify how you want to reach your customers, when you want to reach them, and in what locations. You'll need to be proactive rather than reactive. This means that you can proceed with a clear, orderly plan to strengthen your target audience bond, rather than flailing about, continually guessing what next right thing you should be doing.

A great target marketing strategy should do the following:

1. Focus directly on the group of customers you want to reach

2. Appeal to those customers on multiple levels, hitting both logical and emotional buttons

3. "Fit" with your existing branding efforts

To be effective, a target marketing strategy must take into account the audience you want to reach. Once you've identified your target market, explore the best ways to reach this group.

Great Strategies Match Your Target Audience

In addition to being effective, a target marketing strategy has to do more than just reach your customers. Your message needs to resonate with them. You want your customers to identify with the products or services you're presenting. They should be able to put themselves into the story.

For example, if you plan on marketing your products and services to stay-at-home mothers, you want to take into account how this group views itself, what messages they identify with, and what messages will entice them to buy.

A portrait of Mom as an unsung hero, overworked and underappreciated in the midst of noisy children, nonstop chores, and harried husbands worked very well for Calgon, suppliers of water softeners. When they offered mothers a chance to be "taken away" with a luxurious soak in blissfully quiet surroundings, the message resonated.

Where did they present this message? In places where you find stay-at-home mothers. They used daytime television commercials, *shelter magazine* advertising, and aggressive placement in grocery stores to help transform simple bath salts into a best-seller.

The Calgon campaign worked because Calgon understood who they were trying to reach. They presented a marketing message that their customers identified with. They showcased the "overworked, overwhelmed, and longing for momentary relief" message in locations their customers already were.

This didn't happen by chance. The executives at Calgon didn't wake up one morning and spontaneously latch onto the "Take Me Away" campaign. A great deal of thought, research, and strategic planning went into the process.

def•i•ni•tion

Shelter magazine is a publishing-trade term used to indicate a segment of the U.S. magazine market—specifically referring to aspirational lifestyle magazines about the home, décor, furnishings and gardens. Many catalogs in these categories are also moving to become more like magazines.

Great Strategies Are Flexible

A crucial element of the strategic planning process is the weighing of options. Not all target marketing tools work equally well with all audiences. It's during the strategic planning phase that you take an objective look at the tools available to you and decide what will work best with your target audience.

Having a target marketing strategy helps make decision-making easier. When presented with a marketing opportunity, you decide if it's a wise use of your time and resources. Checking the opportunities against your plan is vital. If the opportunity moves you closer to achieving your defined goals and objectives, it's a good option to explore further. If it doesn't, let it go and realize that it's not right for you.

 Insight

A target marketing strategy serves the same purpose as an outline for a book: it lets you know what you want to do and when you want to do it!

Danger Zone

Select a target marketing strategy based upon what's best for your business. Don't be swayed by popular theory and business fads: do your research and pick what's right for you!

The fact is, marketing is not an exact science. Even the largest organizations in the world make mistakes. Remember New Coke?

Savvy target marketers make regular assessments part of their promotional strategy. Be objective when you consider a campaign to see how it's working. Don't be afraid to make necessary adjustments when you realize you're not on the right track. Obviously, if you find that you're exactly on track to meet your goals and objectives, stick with it!

Why Do You Need a Target Marketing Strategy?

Every smart business owner has a business plan. This plan is your road map that provides guidance as you run your business. With that in mind, having a target marketing strategy is equivalent to a fully customizable GPS system guiding your way!

Not only will you know where you're going, but it's possible to make your journey in the most efficient way possible. A target marketing strategy enables you to journey toward success along the roads you most enjoy. To do this, you adopt the strategy that fully reflects the best, most appealing aspects of your company's personality. You then leverage them to attract more customers.

This can be a fun process, as most small business owners enjoy self-expression and creativity, elements that come with effective target marketing efforts.

Elements of a Target Marketing Strategy

A target marketing strategy has six distinct steps. Each one of these steps is critical, and each step builds on the step before it. As you go through the following, don't skip a step. If you do, you'll have a shaky, incomplete plan that's difficult to implement.

Step One: Set Goals and Objectives. What do you want your target marketing campaign to accomplish? Set specific, quantifiable, and measurable goals, such as: "I want sales to increase 15 percent over the next two weeks."

Set a deadline for each of your goals. If you set very long-term goals, such as "I want to grow my business 200 percent in two years," it's a smart idea to set benchmark goals to be met along the way to help keep you on track.

Step Two: Identify Groups. Who will you be marketing to? Clearly identify your target audience. Spell out in as much detail as possible who these people are, where they live, where they work, and all of the other demographic and psychographic information you've read about in Chapter 6.

Step Three: Pinpoint Needs. What makes your target audience tick? Explore your target audience's primary motivators. Make sure you have a good handle on what values they hold dear, what criteria they consider most important, and what will make them buy.

Step Four: Craft Your Message. Each target marketing campaign should have a specific message, designed to resonate with your target market. There's no cut-and-dried definitive model to follow, but most effective marketing messages contain these three elements:

- ◆ **A hook:** Captures the customer's attention. Often this states a common problem your target market faces that your products or services will solve.

- ◆ **An emotional connection:** Helps your customer to identify with your offering. Expert marketers refer to this as your benefits statement. Will doing business with you make your customers happier, smarter, more efficient?

- ◆ **A call to action:** Gives your customers something to do once they've read your message. Do you want them to visit your business, book an appointment, log on to your website, place an order?

Step Five: Select Your Delivery Method. What is the best method to reach your customers? Do they respond well to media appearances, or do they prefer in-person contact? Do they research online or trust what they hear from family and friends?

Once you've identified the delivery method your target market values most, use that route to bring your message to your customers.

Step Six: Assess Effectiveness. Compare the results of each and every target marketing campaign with the goals and objectives you've set. Did the campaign perform as expected? Did you meet your goals or did you fall woefully short?

This assessment helps determine if you should continue the campaign as designed, or if it requires some form of adjustment.

Niche Marketing vs. Target Marketing Strategies

Is niche marketing a target marketing strategy? Often confusion reigns between these two terms. So let's set the record straight so that you understand how niche marketing differs from target marketing.

Plain and simple, niche marketing concentrates its efforts to reach a small, well-defined subsection of a larger target market. What this really means is that you could take your target market and divide it up into much smaller chunks or niches. You then concentrate your efforts and plan a strategy to market to one chunk, or niche. For example, if your target market is professional women ages 35-55, a niche market might be professional women ages 35-55 who work in health care.

There are several strategies available to reach customers in your niche. You need to pick the one that most closely matches your customers' expectations of your company.

Choosing the Right Strategy

You're now ready to select a target marketing strategy. Armed with who your target market is, it's now time to focus on reaching them in the most effective way possible that's within your budget.

Remember, this is marketing, not bricklaying. While it's important to proceed carefully, maintaining some element of flexibility in your decision-making process is vital. Unfortunately, finding the exact target marketing strategy involves some trial and error. If you begin using one strategy only to discover it falls flat, you must be willing to readjust and try another route to success!

What Are Your Options?

There are countless target marketing strategies, each one designed to appeal to a particular market segment. Most, however, are variations on three major options: buying behavior strategies, generational strategies, and relationship marketing strategies. Let's take a look at each one of these so that you better understand them.

Buying Behavior Strategies

Buying behavior target marketing strategies look closely at the influences exerted on customers by many forces, such as their family, their employer, and/or their community. It also takes into account their hopes, such as where they aspire to be a year from now.

To use a buying behavior strategy, you must know what type of purchase your product or service represents to the customer. Let's address the four types and a customer's possible reaction.

The four types of purchase are as follows:

◆ **A minor new purchase:** Something the customer has never purchased before, but one he is not likely to put lots of thought into. For example, a ballpoint pen with a rubber grip for the fingers to rest on.

◆ **Minor repurchase:** Routine purchases. This is something the customer buys over and over again, largely without much thought. Brand loyalty plays a large role in minor repurchases. For example, a Pepsi drinker automatically picks up another Pepsi.

◆ **Major new purchase:** Something the customer has never purchased before, and is nervous or uncertain about buying. Often, this purchase requires a substantial investment of resources. The customer is likely to do some level of research before making a decision. For example, a large-screen high-definition television set.

◆ **Major repurchase:** The customer has purchased this type of item before, and is reasonably confident about her decision-making process. For example, buying the same make of car she has purchased previously.

Influences Your Customer Faces

A number of forces influence customers. Each one will steer their buying decisions in one direction or another. These influences include internal forces, which are the customer's own values and ideas; external forces, which includes the customer's cultural background, role in society, and their current socio-economic situation; and marketing, which is the only one of these three forces you can control.

A buying behavior strategy takes all of these factors into consideration and tries to identify the points where internal and external forces meet to create a marketing opportunity.

On Target
French's Fried Onions uses a buying behavior strategy by promoting their product to middle- to upper-class young women with families, who want to have a traditional Thanksgiving side dish. They use aspirational shelter magazines during the fall period to feature their product.

Being in the Moment

Buying behavior marketing often hinges on understanding the purchasing situation. Not all buying opportunities are created equal. Savvy target marketers realize high profits when they take advantage of some of the particularly unequal ones.

For example, a baby's pacifier normally costs a few dollars. They're available at almost every grocery and department store. Most parents pick one up without a second thought.

However, if that same parent is in a hotel room in an unfamiliar city in the wee hours of the morning with a screaming tot who has lost her beloved binkie, that same parent will spend $15 for a pacifier without a second thought. That's the power of being in the moment, having your product or service available in different locations where your customer might need it.

Recently, a famous movie personality was staying at a fancy resort in the Adirondacks. At midnight she started experiencing incredible cramps in her legs and called the front desk for a massage therapist. Not exactly a convenient time to offer your service. However, the therapist who took the job was able to charge a hefty fee for the treatment.

Being Outside of the Moment

Without a captive audience, a buying behavior marketer must understand his target market's decision-making process.

Generally, the customer decision-making process includes five steps. These steps remain consistent, although the speed at which one moves through them will vary by purchase type. For example, minor repurchases move the fastest, and major new purchases move the slowest.

Step One: Recognize Need. During this stage, the customer acknowledges that she wants or needs something. This can range from a simple, "Boy, I'm thirsty" to a more complex, "I think it's time to redo the kitchen."

Step Two: Search for Information. Now the customer gathers the data necessary to make a satisfactory purchase. This search can be a quick trip down memory lane— "Boy, I liked Brand X pretzels last time I had them!"

Alternately, the search for information could be prolonged when the customer solicits family and friends for opinions, or does Internet research and more.

Step Three: Evaluate Options. During this stage, the customer weighs the relative merits and benefits of the products and services she's researched. Realize that internal and external factors weighing on the customer will influence the decision.

Step Four: Purchase. Based upon the evaluation process in step three, the customer will select a product or service for purchase.

Step Five: Post Purchase. This stage encapsulates the moment where the customer considers the experience she had engaging with your products or services. The post-purchase phase is very important, as it will directly influence your customer's decision the next time she needs to make this type of purchase. The last thing you want is a feeling of "buyer's remorse," where she regrets the purchase made.

Generational Strategies

"Pepsi: The Choice of a New Generation!"

"Not your Father's Oldsmobile."

"Play Beyond."

Each of these slogans—from the height of The Cola wars, the heyday of Buick, and the launch of Sony's Playstation 3, respectively, represents a generational marketing strategy. Each message is crafted specifically to resonate with a target market composed of members of a specific generation.

These customer groups, called generations, are defined largely by their age. Customers are shaped by the times they live in. The cultural environment and economic circumstances one experiences directly impact buying behaviors.

Loosely defined as a period of 20 or so years, the five marketing generations are as follows:

- ◆ **The New Generation/The Silent Generation:** Born in the late 90s and early 2000s, the New Generation has yet to find a universally accepted name for itself.

- ◆ **Millenials/Generation Y:** Born between the 1980s and the end of the century, Generation Y is often referred to as the Internet generation, the Google generation, and the MySpace generation.

- ◆ **Generation X:** Born between 1965 and 1980, Gen Xers grew up in the shadow of the Baby Boomers, their predecessors. They're often referred to as the Latchkey Generation and Slackers.

◆ **Baby Boomers:** Born between 1946 and 1964, Baby Boomers are the most documented, researched generation in history.

◆ **Mature Citizens/Seniors:** Born between 1909 and 1945, mature citizens are now either retired or planning to soon leave the work force.

Targeting with Generational Marketing

A generation is a long time. It's a very broad category. When you think of all the people born between 1965 and 1980, you're thinking about 49.1 million people in the United States. Gen Xers appear as a midget when compared to either the Baby Boomers or Generation Y!

An effective target marketer can choose to target one generation.

You can refine a generational marketing strategy, taking age and sensibilities into account when crafting products and services. Curves, for example, thrives because they offer their fitness program specifically to older, often fuller-figured women. This appeals to a wholly different generation than the women who attend a gym like Bally's Fitness. Both groups of women want the same thing: to work out and get fit. However, the older women at Curves value the private atmosphere and supportive environment, often hard to find in the competitive, upbeat, exhibitionist experience at the Gen-Y-oriented Bally's.

> **Danger Zone**
>
> "What about the next generation?" Increasingly savvy consumers are growing cynical toward marketing targeted toward an entire generation. It's time to get smarter!

> **On Target**
>
> Jitterbug Cell Phones designs and markets its products to older customers: aging Boomers and Mature Citizens who want the convenience of a cell phone yet can't handle small buttons or hard-to-follow instructions.

What Do You Need to Know About a Generation?

There's far more to a generation than the time it started or stopped. If you're considering a generational marketing strategy, it's vital to understand the social and economic events that shaped your target market.

For example, Baby Boomers were dramatically impacted by the events of the Vietnam War. That conflict shaped their attitude toward authority, government, and personal responsibility. The civil rights movement and the first tentative steps into space happened during their formative years, inspiring the generation to think and believe that anything was possible.

Insight

Every generation has its own set of pivotal moments that impact every member. Know and understand these moments for the market you're targeting.

Relationship Marketing Strategies

"One Client at a Time."

"We Try Harder."

"Benefit from our experience."

Each of these slogans—which belong to Morgan Stanley, Avis Rental Cars, and Buchwald Tax Firm, respectively, illustrate relationship marketing in action.

Relationship marketing is the art of attracting customer attention, to begin and maintain an ongoing, profitable relationship over the course of time. This is a powerful and highly effective target marketing strategy, based on the revolutionary concept that people like to do business with organizations they know and trust!

Relationship marketing works best when you offer a product or service that a customer needs on a regular, on-going basis. As a rule of thumb, the more often you see your customers, the stronger the relationship needs to be in order to be effective.

Think about it. Who do you know better: the clerk at the coffee shop where you stop for your daily latté or the sales professional at the car dealership you visit every time you're due for a new set of wheels?

What's important is to know the true value of all the purchases your customer makes now and in the future. This is called the *lifetime value.*

def•i•ni•tion

The **lifetime value** of a customer refers to the total amount a customer will spend with your business over the course of your relationship.

A Change in Focus

Most small businesses conduct target marketing campaigns in an effort to continually attract new customers. In a relationship marketing strategy, while you definitely still want to bring in new business, the majority of time, effort, and energy is spent retaining the customers you already have.

Customer satisfaction is one of those terms that's been bandied about since the dawn of time. How often have you heard businesses say that they provide the ultimate in customer service? Probably more times than you can remember!

In a relationship marketing model, customer satisfaction simply isn't enough. With all the choices and options available to your customers, being satisfactory or adequate is tantamount to being invisible.

Customer service is a controllable factor that you can use to differentiate yourself from the competition. This works equally well for service professionals, from the accountant who e-mails his clients when changes in the tax law affect them, to the hairdresser who drives out to the wedding site to make sure the bride's up-do is perfect before she walks down the aisle.

Insight _____

Small retailers compete with megachains who can outspend them on advertising and promotion, while offering lower prices and a wider selection. The small retailer can outperform the chains when they provide superior customer service in an effort to keep the customers coming back. Customer service is a form of relationship marketing.

Why Relationship Marketing?

Relationship marketing is a popular target marketing strategy because it is effective and efficient. The cost of marketing to your existing customer base is far lower than attempting to reach new customers. Additionally, because your customers already like your business, you don't need to sell them on your business. What you must do is convince them to come back. This strategy is infinitely easier than attracting someone who's never been to your place before!

Relationship marketing concepts are often integrated into other target marketing strategies. Combining multiple strategies enables savvy business owners to have it all: attracting new customers and holding onto them!

The longer your customers do business with you, the more products and services they buy from you. It's that simple!

The Relationship Marketing Process

Organizations that adopt a relationship marketing process have to go through a four-step process. Each of these steps builds upon the previous step, and each one is critically important.

Step 1: Identify Who You Want to Have Relationships With. Pinpoint your target market. Generally, if you pursue a relationship marketing strategy, you need a target market that enjoys some level of stability. It's hard to develop relationships with people who aren't around!

Stability can be defined in terms of geography, income level, or life stage. Parents of young children, for example, are a relatively stable group.

Step 2: Evaluate Customer Value. According to the experts, 80 percent of most small business's profits come from 20 percent of the customer base. Identifying that 20 percent is critical. When your marketing and promotion budget is limited, you want to make sure you're directing it toward the most valuable customers.

Step 3: Focus on Retention. Relationship marketing hinges on identifying your most valuable customers and devoting considerable resources to keeping them.

This involves a regular, precise campaign to keep in touch with your customers, and delivering marketing messages designed to bring them back—perhaps far more frequently than without any friendly reminders from you.

Customer retention is a key element in relationship marketing. You can read more about it in Chapters 18,19, and 20.

Step 4: Create Advocates. The final step in relationship marketing involves transforming your customers. Don't worry! You don't have to borrow Harry Potter's wand—even though the results are almost as magical!

Successful relationship marketing encourages long-term, loyal customers to tell their family and friends about their experience with your business. Remember, word-of-mouth is the single-most powerful influence most people encounter. If you have a cadre of loyal customers talking about how great your place is, you're going to get more business.

Advocates are often referred to as evangelists, influencers, cheerleaders, secret sales-men, and more. It doesn't matter what you call them … it's what they do promoting your business that matters most!

The Least You Need to Know

- ◆ Savvy target marketers make regular assessments part of their promotional strat-egy. They aren't afraid to make changes to stay on track to meet their goals and objectives.

- ◆ Niche marketing differs from target marketing because it concentrates its efforts on reaching a small, well-defined subsection of a larger target market.

- ◆ There are countless target marketing strategies, each one designed to appeal to a particular market segment. The three major options include buying behavior strategies, generational strategies, and relationship marketing strategies.

- ◆ Numerous forces influence customers' buying decisions. These include the cus-tomers' own values and ideas, their cultural background, role in society, and their current socioeconomic situation.

Part 3

The Whole Nine Yards

In this part, we're going to delve right into the nuts and bolts, the tools and techniques that make target marketing work.

There are thousands of different types of businesses, and each one of them has their own distinct target market. Not every technique you find here will work equally well for everyone; it's time to capitalize on your knowledge of your target audience to identify those strategies that will resonate with your ideal customer.

View this as a smorgasbord of techniques, with the very best of eight effective winners displayed for your choosing!

10

Start the Ball Rolling

In This Chapter

- ◆ Understanding target marketing approaches
- ◆ Focus and flexibility to get started in the right direction
- ◆ Three routes to target marketing success

Remember your childhood? I want you to go way back to those teenage years, when someone—probably your mother or a teacher—shared these immortal words of wisdom with you: "It's not what you say; it's how you say it!"

In other words, delivery is everything. You can have the best target marketing message in the world, but if you're not communicating it in an effective tone, it's going to fall on deaf ears.

To strike the right tone, you need the right *target marketing approach*. In this chapter, we'll look at the concept of the target marketing approach and present three of the most powerful, effective approaches for you to consider using.

Starting on the Springboard

Now that you've contemplated the many target marketing strategies available to you, it's time to pick an approach.

def•i•ni•tion

A **target marketing approach** is the strategic, planned way you implement your target marketing strategy.

On Target

Hebrew National's "We Answer to a Higher Authority" campaign effectively pinpointed them as the kosher, all-beef alternative in the hot dog section. This saves time. Shoppers no longer have to read the label on a half-dozen hot dog packages!

Consider it this way: if the target marketing strategy is comparable to a road map or outline you use to guide your actions, the target marketing approach you adopt is the choice of vehicle you take on your road trip or the prose you use to pen your opus.

The approach is all about style. Your target marketing approach conveys valuable information about your business to your customers. They sense what kind of experience they're going to have long before they ever do any business with you.

As customers are increasingly pressed for time, effective communication of your target marketing approach helps your customers make more informed decisions.

You can use your target marketing approach as a major differentiator from your competition. This enables you to spring into view, positioning your organization in the most ideal location possible, that is, directly in front of your customer's eyes!

How to Determine Which Approach Is Right for You

When contemplating potential target marketing approaches, consider the following four points.

1. Consider Your Target Market

What are the expectations your target market has for your type of business? Every customer has a mental picture associated with your industry. Consider how your target marketing approach meshes with those expectations. There are two divergent routes you can take:

The first approach is where your target marketing approach is in alignment with customer expectations. For example, a financial planner who chooses to pursue a target marketing approach of "Be the Expert" will focus time and energy on becoming a highly respected professional who teaches seminars and workshops, and has a very visible media presence. This appeals to a certain segment of clients, who expect and value expertise from their financial advisor.

The second approach is to position yourself counter to customer expectations. Let's revisit our financial planner. The same professional could consider an exclusive, "We're Not for Everyone" strategy, limiting their practice to only extremely wealthy individuals. Some potential customers might be alienated when they discover they don't make enough money to merit this planner's attentions. However, that disappointment is more than offset by the resonance this approach has for the small, niche group of clients who do qualify.

2. Consider Competition Within Your Industry

Your target marketing approach should set you apart from the competition within your industry. The only way an organization will thrive in the incredibly competitive marketplace is to differentiate itself from its peers.

Consider your major competitors. How are they target marketing? What approach are they adopting? How can you position yourself as an attractive alternative to what they're doing? Is there a microniche begging for attention? Customers don't want more of the same old, same old. Adopt a strategy that enables you to be enticingly different.

3. Consider Competition Outside Your Industry

Customers have a finite amount of time and resources, and an almost endless amount of ways to spend both. Consider your positioning in the marketplace compared to other businesses that serve the same function as you.

For example, a movie theater isn't only in competition with other movie theaters. They want to attract customers in search of a few hours of entertainment. This then pits them head to head with the local bowling alley, dance club, concert hall, shopping mall, fitness center, and more!

Be open to adopting successful target marketing approaches that work well in other industries. If you share the same target audience, you may benefit from the same techniques!

4. Consider How You Want to Run Your Business

The final consideration is seldom discussed, but is critically important, especially to the small business owner.

When determining which target marketing approach you'd like to adopt, consider how you want to run your business. There must be a clear, positive, and direct relationship between your business vision and the target marketing approach you adopt.

Danger Zone

Resist the temptation to adopt a target marketing approach simply because it is hot or trendy. If your approach doesn't mesh with your business vision, implementing the approach will create problems.

As customers age, authenticity and sincerity become increasingly important. Younger consumers are incredibly media savvy, and tend to be skeptical of any and all marketing messages they receive. They're very sensitive to anything that seems fake or forced. Avoid coming across as insincere by picking a target marketing approach that accurately reflects your business vision.

Adopt and Adapt

As we've mentioned throughout this chapter, successful target marketing is all about the approach. You want to connect with your target audience on a deep, fundamental level.

This would be so much easier if all target markets behaved in the same way. Many small business owners long for a simple formula, such as, "If we say X and do Y, customers will beat down the door."

But the truth is, it's not that simple. Each target market consists of unique, dynamic individuals, and no one approach is the absolute perfect way to connect you to your customers.

Selecting an approach requires two critical components:

◆ Knowledge of your customer base.

◆ Knowledge of your business.

The ideal target marketing approach will resonate with your customers and accurately represent your business.

You're not going to find that approach ready-made. Truly effective target marketing approaches are custom-made, created by each small business owner in response to what he's learned about his target market.

Keep that in mind as you read this next section. Use the information you find here as a starting point, but feel free to tweak the concepts until they suit your needs!

Learn from the Masters: Three Routes to Success

How many target marketing approaches are there? Well, how many businesses are there? How many target markets are there? Once we have those numbers, we can come up with an exact figure—but until then, trust me, the total is somewhere between staggering and stratospheric!

Luckily, most of these hundreds and thousands of target marketing approaches fall into three general groups. Each individual approach is simply a variation on an underlying theme.

There are, of course, target marketing approaches that aren't based on one of these three themes. However, this trio does make up the vast majority of successful target marketing approaches.

1. Be the Expert

This approach hinges on showcasing how much you, as the business owner, know. This is ideal for businesses where customers come searching for solutions to their problems.

2. Make It Fun

This approach centers on our culture's endless appetite for entertainment. This is ideal for business owners who have customers in search of a good time.

3. Exclusivity

This approach works by limiting access—or creating the perception of limited access—to products and services to a select, deserving group of customers. This is ideal for businesses that have customers who are strongly socially motivated and who want to be in the know.

Let's look at each of these approaches more closely.

Someone Has to Know It All

The world is a complicated place—and it seems to get more confusing and challenging every day. This makes for a stressful situation for the customers who have needs they don't know how to fill.

Enter the experts! By showcasing an extensive knowledge of complicated subjects, businesses that adopt the "Be the Expert" strategy reassure their customers that they'll be taken care of. All of the worry and stress melts away from the transaction—which makes it worth every penny of the high price tag that expertise commands.

> ### On Target
>
> ExpertTire understands the "Be the Expert" approach. They've even integrated Expert into their name! This full-service auto care chain touts its ability to understand a vehicle from bumper to bumper.

Key Concepts

There are three key guidelines you need to be aware of when promoting yourself as an expert:

◆ Publicize your expertise. Knowledge and insight give you a competitive edge— but only if your customers know you have them!

◆ Build credibility with regular, prominent media appearances.

◆ Save the customer time and money by doing the job right the first time.

What Audience Are You Appealing To?

A range of customers are drawn to the "Be the Expert" marketing approach. What attracts them is the reassuring message implicit in this approach: "Here, at last, is someone who has the answer to all my questions!" This customer type values security and trust.

At the same time, a large part of the appeal of the "Be the Expert" approach appears to save the customer time. By going to the professional who's regarded as the expert in her field, customers assume they will get quick results, eliminate costly mistakes, and enjoy some peace of mind.

These customers tend to be older, more educated, and earn a higher-than-average salary. As a rule of thumb, the more expensive the product or service, the more customers value your expertise.

Who Does This Work Best For?

Being the expert works best for those small business owners who need their customers to trust, respect, and especially, refer them. Expertise works very well as an element of word-of-mouth advertising. If you embrace the "Be the Expert" model, you want to be the business everyone's talking about when someone asks, "Who's the best for …?" or "Who would you recommend when I need …?"

This model serves service professionals extremely well. Everyone from accountants to violin teachers thrive when they attract customers willing to pay for their expertise. Retailers who handle specialty merchandise also benefit from embracing this model. Customers seek out expert retailers because they want to make wise purchasing decisions.

On Target

Ace Hardware capitalizes on the "Be the Expert" concept with their highly targeted "Ace is the place with the helpful hardware folks." The message combines expert appeal with a friendly, welcoming, we-know-you're-not-a-pro approach, which is reassuring to customers who aren't sure what they're doing!

Just Like a Barrel of Monkeys

Girls just want to have fun—and they're not alone. For a significant portion of the marketplace, the entertainment value any situation offers plays a critical role in the decision-making process. Customers pick the option that appears to offer the most fun.

On Target

Having a colonoscopy isn't most people's idea of a good time. However, Dr. Patricia Raymond, of Rx for Sanity, manages to merge gastroenterology and mirth—attracting those patients who want great care with some fun. She combines top-notch professional skills with jokes designed to "crack up" the patients; indulging in some bathroom humor puts her patients at ease.

Then there's the surging popularity of Internet retailing, which has put an additional burden on brick-and-mortar operations. It appears that every product on the planet is only a click away. What this means is that you need to give customers a reason to buy from you. Often, that reason is that a visit to your store offers extra entertainment value.

Fun games, events, signage, and marketing materials significantly add to your brand. You become the fun place to go.

Insight

Entertainment comes in many forms. Seminars, classes, and in-store workshops draw crowds, as do celebrity appearances!

On Target

Jordan's Furniture, New England's largest furniture retailer, advertises that it's not a store, but rather, it's an experience. They call it "shop-pertainment." One of their stores includes a 3D IMAX theater. In addition, as one of their monster promotions they offered a full rebate on certain items if the Boston Red Sox won the World Series.

You can make it fun without going to extremes. The standards of fun vary from industry to industry and from target market to target market. Many specialty yarn stores "make it fun" by providing places for their customers to knit and chat—capitalizing on this strategy is simply devoting some space to tables, chairs, and conversation!

Key Concepts

There are three key guidelines you need to be aware of when employing a "Make It Fun" strategy:

- Be bold: if you're going to make it fun, don't be afraid to laugh and be silly. Look at Google: they change the text on their home pages to celebrate random days just because.

- Involve your team. Making it fun is an organization-wide choice. It only works if everyone's on board.

- Stay tight with your target market: fun is a dynamic force. You want to stay ahead of the curve!

Danger Zone

The experience and the expectations have to match. Only promote yourself as "The Fun Place" if you really offer your customers a great time. Authenticity matters!

What Audience Are You Appealing To?

Customers who are drawn to the "Make It Fun" approach place a high value on the experience. They want the good times, the memories, the special moments they can look back on and laugh about.

These customers are generally members of Generation X or Y. They're younger, tend to be middle to higher income, and move often.

Saving time and money is important to these customers, but price and convenience are not their paramount concern. They'll pay higher prices to secure the products and services that they want while having a good time.

Insight _____

The more you know about your target audience, the easier it is to provide them with a good time. Take a good look at what types of entertainment your customers enjoy and emulate the best of what they already like!

On Target
Even the driest, most staid professions can adopt a "Make It Fun" strategy. Coda, Agresso, and CIMA—who respectively sell accounting software, enterprise resource planning solutions, and management accounting services, none of which are inherently giggle-worthy—created Extreme Accounting video games like "Ski Sumday" and "Book Balance Dive" to capture the interest of their target market!

Never overlook the power of the web to add a fun element to your business. Social networking, virtual environments, text-messaging, and other web-based connections help the small business owners begin building or reinforcing relationships with their customers.

Who Does This Work Best For?

"Make It Fun" is a fantastic strategy for business owners who thrive when they see customers often. If you're a service provider who values the once-a-week customer or the retailer who loves the regular shopper, "Make It Fun" can work for you.

Moreover, any business that is experiential in nature could consider the "Make It Fun" strategy. This includes the obvious choices, like restaurants, taverns, and clubs, as well as service providers ranging from salons to stockbrokers. My editor likes going to her bank because they always have treats, whether cupcakes, apples, or candy. It makes banking more fun (not to mention fattening!).The more fun it is doing business with you, the more often customers will come back. We're simple animals: if an experience is fun, by and large, we want to repeat it.

Start the fun early. Research indicates that the more often a business owner sees a customer early on in the relationship, the longer and more profitable it's likely to become!

It's Not for Everyone

Exclusivity appeals especially to those customers who want something that others don't have. Groucho Marx may have said it best when he said, "I don't want to belong to any club that would have me as a member!"

Adopting an exclusivity-based target marketing approach means setting your products and services distinctly apart from the mass market. There's an overt acknowledgement that only a small, select, presumably superior class of customers will value and appreciate your offerings.

> **On Target**
>
> Volkswagen capitalized on the exclusivity approach with their very successful campaign, "Drivers Wanted." The message was clear: not anyone was worthy to get behind the wheel of a Jetta. You had to earn that right, by being a true "driver."

> **Insight**
>
> Exclusivity is not limited to the diamonds and caviar set. The motivation to be in the know extends to every level of society. There are "It's Not for Everyone" lawn mowers and tractors.

Customers who respond to exclusivity-based target marketing approaches enjoy being an insider, someone in the know, who is judged cool enough, or smart enough, or stylish enough, to have access to the "right" products and services.

Exclusivity caters to the need for power and prestige. Often, having the right piece of "It's Not for Everyone" merchandise or using the services of the right "It's Not for Everyone" service provider provides a type of social currency, a tangible demonstration that the customer is, in fact, part of the in crowd.

The use of exclusivity among a product or service's customer base can create a sense of community. For a great example of this in action, look at Mac computers. There's a huge—sometimes seemingly uncrossable—canyon separating Mac users from PC users. Mac users glory in being different. They take pride in their group identity. The whole phenomenon has lead to a wildly successful marketing campaign featuring the Mac guy vs. the PC guy. With less than a dozen broadcast television commercials, the differences between the two computing options have become part of mainstream consciousness.

Key Concepts

There are three key concepts to keep in mind when employing the "It's Not for Everyone" approach:

- ◆ An exclusive product or service can't be for everyone: there must be some criteria determining who's "appropriate."

- ◆ Create a community around your products and services. Customers want to belong! Online options abound.

- ◆ Every market has room for an exclusive option: this is not a strictly high-end strategy!

Insight

Social networking sites, chat rooms, and other online community-building tools can serve as the virtual manifestation of "It's Not for Everyone."

What Audience Are You Appealing To?

Customers who respond to exclusivity-based target marketing approaches place a high value on what other people think of them. They tend to be very social, highly involved in community and faith-based organizations. Income levels vary, but most exclusivity-motivated customers tend to be in the high end of their particular income bracket.

"It's Not for Everyone" is a concept that works for all age groups. Exclusivity's appeal begins in grade school, where young children want to be in on the "secret" and have the exact, right toys and clothes. This carries right on through adulthood, resulting in the quest for the secret vacation hideaway only the best people know about.

There is an interesting crossover effect, where the "It's Not for Everyone" effect dovetails neatly with the socially conscious consumer. Never underestimate the power of peer pressure on the socially conscious customer: they don't just want to be green, they want to be the right shade of green!

Who Does This Work Best For?

"It's Not for Everyone" works best for those small business owners with customers who want to be part of a select club—the insider's group of people in the know.

For service providers, this means the customers who feel that they can gain an advantage by securing your services. Even though all the money gets invested in the same stock market, some customers are drawn to a financial advisor with a limited clientele, who only accepts those customers he deems "adequately serious" about financial planning.

High-end tattoo shops often turn away customers who want run-of-the-mill ink work. They don't want to diminish their brand, and only take those jobs that showcase their talents to the max.

The concept is a little more difficult to apply in the retail world. Niche and specialty retailers are often forced into this strategy almost by default, which renders exclusivity almost moot as a point of differentiation. In these instances, merchandise selection is not enough: you need to cultivate an atmosphere that's only welcoming to the right type of customers. This often means very high-end merchandise, which often only certain groups can afford.

The Least You Need to Know

- Your target marketing approach conveys valuable information. Customers sense what kind of experience they're going to have long before they ever do any business with you.

- Considerations for your target marketing approach include knowing your market, your competition in and outside your industry, as well as how you want to run your business.

- The three most common target marketing approaches include "Being the Expert," "Making It Fun," and creating exclusivity with "It's Not for Everyone."

- With all three approaches you must know and understand the target audience you want to appeal to and who it will work best for.

Chapter 11

Here, There, and Everywhere: Web Marketing 101

In This Chapter

◆ Learning how to make the most of your website

◆ Connecting to your target market with blogs

◆ Understanding the power of podcasting

◆ Informing and influencing your target market with online education

It's a wired world. Anything and everything we want is online—and that includes our target audience! Hours spent online have recently eclipsed hours spent watching television in some markets.

This is good news and bad news for the target marketer. On the positive side, establishing an effective web presence is relatively easy and inexpensive. The downside? The low barriers to entry mean that the web is an increasingly crowded place. You have to be strategic and selective, adopting only the web-based target marketing strategies that will work best with your audience.

Your Home on the Web

Every small business needs to have a website. There is no two ways around it: for today's customer, if you do not have a website, you are not in business.

Nearly 90 percent of all buyers who are planning to make a major purchase go online to see what their options are and how much they should expect to pay. Service providers receive equal scrutiny. Before customers trust you with their health, finances, or even hairdo, they want to see how you position yourself online.

Luckily, looking good online can be both easy and affordable. While it is certainly possible to spend thousands of dollars on website design, most small businesses do not need to do so to connect with their target audience.

Understanding the Purpose of Your Website

To realize maximum value from your website and use your online presence effectively to connect with your target audience, your website must be built with a specific purpose in mind.

That purpose will be different for each organization. Consider the specific purpose to be the primary driving impetus behind your website. In it should be the main reason you want your organization to be online in the first place.

Common reasons companies go online include these:

♦ To communicate with customers

♦ To present goods and service offerings

♦ To expand business and increase sales

♦ To enhance customer service

Your own reason may include any or all of these factors. Be specific when setting goals. For example, say, "By creating this website, I want to build my brand awareness and really get my name out in the community. I'll know that the website's working for me if I get three new customers a month from the site."

Knowing How Much Website You Need

Not all websites are created equal. Some are simple: a few pages, with some text and a few pictures, contact information, and that's it. Others are far more complex, with embedded video, flash animation, searchable catalogs, e-commerce functionality, and more.

Which one is better? It depends on two things: your specific purpose for the website and what your target audience wants and values.

If the specific purpose you have in mind for your website is to simply inform the public that your business exists, where it is located, what hours it is open, and what products and services you provide, you can get by with a very simple website and still establish an effective online presence and maintain your brand.

However, if you want to sell products online, have a searchable catalog, 24/7 tech support available via live chat, and other cutting-edge features, then you are going to need a lot more website.

There are four tiers of business websites, beginning with the most elementary, and advancing in sophistication:

◆ **Tier One: The Online Brochure:** The simplest tier, this is a simple, informative site that does not have e-commerce functionality. The online brochure is basically a virtual business card: you tell people who you are, what you do, and a little bit about how you do it.

◆ **Tier Two: E-Commerce for Beginners:** At this point, you add some e-commerce functionality to your website. You can sell your products and services online, there is a great deal of information about your company, and you engage in both *data collection* and search engine optimization.

def•i•ni•tion

> **Data collection** is the process of capturing customers' e-mail addresses and other critical information while they visit your website.

◆ **Tier Three: Advanced E-Commerce:** This is the stage where a significant portion of your business is conducted online. At this point, web-based marketing, promotion, sales, and service are required.

   Most small businesses, upon reaching the third tier, require extensive help from third-party providers. This is the highest level of website attainable without a substantial investment of time and resources.

◆ **Tier Four: The Big Time:** Here is where you will find companies like Amazon.com, Zappos, and Shutterfly. These large organizations have a major Internet presence, and have their own IT and web-marketing departments to keep it that way!

While most small businesses cannot compete with Tier Four level companies, it's often possible to form profitable relationships with them. Companies on this tier should be viewed as a model and as a resource.

Target Marketing with Your Website

Begin with the right domain name. Your domain name is your website address. While this can be the name of your business—www.nelsonsflowershop.com will bring you to Nelson's Flower Shop—it does not have to be.

Domain names should be short, snappy, and memorable. If you have a great tag line, consider using that as your domain name. You want customers to be able to find you the way they remember you. That is why www.wetryharder.com will bring you to Avis Rental Cars.

> **Danger Zone**
>
> Customers don't always spell things correctly. To avoid losing customers because they can't find you online, buy the most common misspellings of your domain name and have them redirect to your main site.

About Search Engine Optimization

Where is the best place to be on the Internet? Listed as the number one result on a Google search, that's where.

def•i•ni•tion

Search engine optimization is the art and science of creating content and arranging your website in such a fashion that your company's website consistently shows up as number one in the search engine results.

Overwhelmingly, customers and would-be customers click the first result any search engine provides when they enter a query. Second- and third-place finishers get some clicks as well, but after that ... well, you're pretty much out of luck.

That is the logic and driving force behind *search engine optimization*.

Any search can have only one number one result—and a lot of sites want to be there. That is why an entire industry has sprung up around search engine optimization techniques.

This industry splits into two schools: organic search engine optimization and paid search engine optimization.

Organic search engine optimization works, in part, by filling your site with content that gets the search engine's attention. This is trickier than it sounds. Any time there is a marketing opportunity, people find a way to take advantage of it. Deceitful practices designed to "bump up" a website's rankings (known as Black Hat SEO) have led major search engines to continually change the algorithms they use to determine rankings.

As mentioned, there are legions of professionals who devote their lives to understanding the intricacies of search engine optimization and will help you enhance your site for a fee.

However, there is quite a bit of search engine optimization you, as the business owner, can do on your own.

The Three Keys to Do-It-Yourself SEO

Pick Keywords. Keywords are the terms or phrases web users type into search engines in an effort to locate relevant websites. Your keywords should reflect how your customers are likely to look for you. For example, an educational toy retailer in Pittsburgh might consider the following keywords:

- ◆ Educational toys
- ◆ Home school
- ◆ Early education resources
- ◆ Pittsburgh toys
- ◆ Best toys in Pittsburgh

Online tools can help you assess the relative popularity of each keyword; there is no sense writing content that contains a certain phrase if no one searches for that phrase!

Most small businesses need three to four keyword phrases to increase their chances of attaining high search engine rankings. It is very difficult to attain top ratings with only

Insight

Wordtracker.com helps website owners and search engine marketers identify keywords and phrases that are relevant to a particular business and most likely to be used as queries by search engine visitors.

one keyword, and trying to incorporate more than five keywords gets cumbersome and problematic.

def•i•ni•tion

Meta tags are tags inserted into documents to describe the document. These are used by browsers and search engines to identify the pages. Their importance has been significantly reduced as search engines have become more sophisticated.

Optimize your pages. Every page on your website should incorporate your keywords, featured often and prominently. Use keywords in your headlines! Additionally, make sure the keywords show up in all of your site's *meta tags*.

Get quality inbound links. Quality inbound links is a fancy way to say, "Other sites that think this site's pretty cool!" Online, this means inbound links, where other blogs and websites comment on or talk about your content, with a link connecting their site to yours.

One strategy to create lots of inbound links is to submit articles relevant to your target audience to online media sites, content distribution sites, and more. Each article should include a link back to your main site. Every time the article is published, you get an inbound link, bumping up your search engine ranking.

Other routes to generating quality inbound links include link swapping with other business owners and listing your site on directory websites.

Just Put Bacon on the Cat: Blogging

The blogosphere (the online community of individuals who read or maintain online journals, generally called *blogs*) is a strange place. You can gain visibility by writing regular posts filled with critically valuable information, poignant insights, or life-altering wisdom the entire world needs to know.

def•i•ni•tion

Blog is short for web log. Blogs are publicly available web pages, with personal views and links expressing the opinions and observations of a particular person, on a specific topic or theme, and are usually updated regularly reflecting the personality of the author.

Or, conversely, you can tape bacon to your cat, which is what science fiction writer John Scalzi did one day when he desperately did not want to work on what he was supposed to be working on. The picture of the infinitely displeased cat has become an icon of the blogosphere, and now random people send bacon-themed pictures to him on a regular basis.

It's a fairly reasonable expectation that more than a few people who were first exposed to Scalzi via his blog—which contains a lot that's actually not about cats with pork products on them—have enjoyed his writing and gone on to purchase his novels.

Not a bad result, although we have yet to have the cat's definitive word on the situation.

Blogging as a target marketing tool requires maintaining a regularly updated online journal with content that will be of interest to your target market. Blogs were steadily escalating in popularity for many years and now have stabilized as an effective strategic target marketing tool.

Insight

The most recent target marketing trend in the blog world is microblogging. Programs like Twitter enable users to post super-short (140 character!) entries.

Creating Your Blog

Starting a blog is as simple as going to a blogging website and setting up an account. There are a number of well-known and user-friendly sites to choose from, from Blogger to Wordpress and LiveJournal.

Most blogging programs go out of their way to make blogging easy. They offer a number of templates and tools that even the least-computer savvy person can navigate.

Choose a design that positively reinforces your business's image. This is a great way to connect with your target audience: color scheme, graphics, pictures, and even layout can be used to project exactly the image that will resonate with your market.

As a practical aside, blogs are pretty useless if no one can read them. Pick a design that is easy on the eyes of your target audience. This means if you are catering to 14-year-old girls with a high tolerance for Hello Kitty and J-Pop, you can use pink text, flashing floral elements, and sparkly rainbow animation. Other audiences are likely to appreciate a more readable format!

Blogging requires as much time and effort as you would like to devote to it. Some business owners do quite well with a short entry once a week, while others update their blogs several times a day. You decide what is best for you.

But What Do I Write About?

The hardest part of blogging is knowing what to write about. While you can blog about anything and everything, if you are using a blog as a promotional tool for your business, it is a good idea to keep focused on the type of information your customers turn to you for.

This means if you are in apparel, you can blog about the latest styles, what celebrities are wearing the labels you carry, or the best outfit to wear for an interview—or a rave, or rock climbing! It all depends on your target audience.

Danger Zone

Avoid using professional jargon or acronyms, which might alienate readers. No matter what your business is, use language that is easily understood by the average layperson.

Information that will entertain, inform, and enlighten is always appreciated. Never forget, blogs are a great platform to display your business's personality: add a little "behind the scenes" content and let your readers feel like they really know you.

Generally, blog entries are short: a paragraph or two on a given topic.

Understanding Comments

The comments feature on most blogging platforms can be your best friend. Comments enable your readership to talk back to you, telling you exactly what they think.

That might seem absolutely terrifying! However, having a direct conversation with your readers is great for target marketing purposes. You are getting firsthand demographic and psychographic research: blog commenters are not shy about explaining themselves.

Insight

Your blog can do double duty: connecting you with your target audience while raising your position on search engine results. Simply write entries that incorporate your keywords!

Be prepared for a few flies in the ointment. People who have way too much time on their hands, generally called trolls, enjoy making random obnoxious, inflammatory, or disturbing comments on blogs. That is not the type of thing you want your customers reading. To control the types of comments, turn on the comment-moderation feature, which enables you to view comments before the whole Internet does. If they are horrid, delete them.

Promoting Your Blog

Tape bacon on your cat in isolation, and you are really strange. Tape bacon on your cat and tell the world about it, and you are suddenly a marketing genius.

The best blog promotion strategy in the world is to write absolutely fantastic entries regularly. Quality, like cream, always rises to the top, and along the way, you will develop a loyal readership.

Barring that, which is admittedly a rather time-intensive method, you can actively promote your blog. Strategic ways to do this include registering with blog ranking sites, such as Technorati, Digg, and Stumbleupon, which enable readers to vote for your posts and expose them to a wider readership.

Additionally, you can link to your blog from your website, mention it in your podcast and advertising, and register with blog search engines.

Making the Most of Your Blog

More than a few bloggers have looked at a year or two years' worth of entries and realized that without even trying, they have written a book! A book can be a great target marketing tool. You can read more about that in Chapter 14.

Giving Voice to Your Ideas

Did you ever wonder what the commuter on the train is listening to so intently on his iPod? Or what plays through the earphones a local CEO wears while she works out at the gym?

Sometimes it's music. But increasingly, people are taking advantage of MP3 technology to listen to *podcasts*.

Podcasts can be on any topic and any length. Some are a few minutes, while others go for over an hour. Check out iTunes.com to see the variety that is available for a fee and for free.

def•i•ni•tion

Podcasts are audio files distributed over the Internet. Listeners download the files, and either play them on the computer or a listening device, such as an iPod.

Podcasting offers the ultimate target marketing tool to connect and talk directly to your customers about what they are interested in. Talk about reinforcing the relationship!

What Do You Talk About?

Podcasting is a powerful tool for small business owners who want to develop a strong, ongoing relationship with their clientele.

The trick to effectively using podcasting as a target marketing tool is to talk about topics that are of interest to your customers that they can't get any place else. This might mean displaying your knowledge and expertise, or it could mean talking about the events of the day; great books; or clever ways to train your pet, child, or spouse to do what you want ... the list is endless.

> **On Target**
>
> Schaeffers Investment Research uses daily podcasts to connect with customers who want up-to-the-minute financial insight.

Consider podcasting as your opportunity to talk directly to your customer. In a way, this is a customer service opportunity. What can you do, in the course of that conversation, to make their day easier, help them achieve their life goals, or make them feel better? Achieve one of those three ends consistently, and you will build a loyal corp of listeners—many of whom will be more than amenable to purchasing your products and services.

It Is Not Just What You Say ...

The delivery of your podcast is just as important as the content. Tone, language choices, and other factors can help endear you to—or alienate you from—your target audience.

MSNBC's financial guru, Jim Cramer, for example, has a particularly loud and over-the-top style, no matter how he delivers the content. His personality comes ringing through, in text, in person, on screen, and when you listen to his podcast, Wall Street Confidential.

Your podcast delivery style needs to be representative of the way you do business. All great podcasts are ...

- ◆ **Concise:** Each podcast should have a clear focus. Pick one point you want to concentrate on and select your material to support and illustrate that point. It is better to offer several short, clearly focused podcasts than one, long, rambling, self-indulgent diatribe.

- ◆ **Conversational:** Make your material engaging. That might be difficult, especially if you are talking about estate planning or tax avoidance strategies, but it is necessary. Use real-life examples and simple language to communicate your points. Listeners will tune out jargon, dry statistics, and "academic-speak."

♦ **Clear:** Once upon a time, politicians and actors used to train by speaking with a mouth full of pebbles. The thought was that if they could make themselves understood even under those circumstances, clear speech would present no problem when speaking unimpeded by pebbles. Don't run out and put rocks in your mouth; however, make an effort to speak clearly. Listeners won't value what they can't understand.

♦ **Consistent:** You can podcast monthly. You can podcast weekly. You can even—if you are brave and have the time—podcast daily. It does not really matter, as long as you pick a schedule and stick to it. Blow off your listeners at your peril. If there is no material when they expect it, they will not come looking twice.

The Logistics of Podcasting

The process of creating podcasts is pretty basic and straightforward. It takes a little bit of time to get acquainted with all of the steps, and a minimal investment in equipment, but after that, podcasting is as easy as having a conversation with your best customer.

There are four steps to creating a podcast:

1. Design and create your content.

2. Record your content in a digital format. This is when you will need your microphone and recording software.

   If you have a mixer, you can add background music and sound effects to your podcast.

3. Upload your podcast to the web. You can post your podcast to your website or blog. If you need help, this is the time to ask someone knowledgeable—teenagers can often be a big help, as this is second-nature to them.

4. Connect with your target audience now that you have a podcast.

Insight

Many free or low-cost recording software packages are available online. For example, www.audacity.com is one of the free tools available.

Danger Zone

Most commercial music is protected by copyright! Do not use copyrighted material on your podcast! Check out www.musicbakery.com for license-free music.

Promoting Your Podcast

Your podcast does not start working for you until customers and potential customers hear it! It is essential to promote your podcast heavily, and let the world know it is out there.

Insight

List your podcast in online podcast directory websites, such as Podcast Alley and iPodder or iTunes.

Ways to do this include linking your podcast on your website or blog, mentioning it in e-zines and e-mail correspondence, and in print advertising.

There are topical podcast directories. Type your podcast topic and "+ podcast" into a search engine to discover what the options are in your field. While you are doing that, keep an eye out for podcast review sites. These offer a great opportunity to draw attention to your podcast!

Educational Marketing + Webinars

Online education is an incredibly powerful lure for selected target markets. Individuals who are time pressed, geographically isolated, or perpetually hungry for knowledge value the ability to attend educational events without ever leaving their computer, office, or home.

The most popular format for educational marketing is the *webinar*.

def•i•ni•tion

A **webinar** is a web-based conference in which participants log into a website, where they are presented with a video or slide-show style presentation, with live or recorded commentary.

Many webinars feature live chat functionality, which enables participants to ask questions throughout the event.

Webinars have such value that many business owners charge admission to them. The admission helps offset the cost of hosting a webinar—as the logistics of creating a webinar on one's own are quite challenging, most small business owners turn to a third-party provider, such as Gotowebinar.com, Webex.com, or Confertel.net.

If you are positioning yourself as the expert resource for your target audience, webinars are a powerful tool. Additionally, because webinars offer the ability to restrict access, they entice buyers who value exclusivity.

The Logistics of Webinars

To realize maximum value from a webinar, you need to identify a topic that is of immediate and overwhelming importance to your target audience. Here are examples:

- Making Your Business Thrive in a Tough Economy

- How to Sell Your House at Lightning Speed

- Six Strategies to Make Your Kids Smarter

The possibilities are endless.

Once you have selected a topic, you will want to contact a third-party provider to find out what their requirements are. Generally, these include a PowerPoint or short video presentation, along with your ability to be on a conference call during the scheduled event.

Like any educational programs, webinars need heavy promotion. Reach out to your existing customer list and ask them to help you promote the event. While a webinar is a great way to sing to the choir and remind your existing customers that you are an expert resource, you also want to capitalize on the chance to attract new and repeat business.

Most webinars are recorded. Consider using this recording as a premium item for your customers, a free download on your website, or as the basis for other articles or products you might have mentioned during the program.

Putting It All Together

As you can see, there are many, many web-based target marketing strategies. Here is how to incorporate those strategies when you are positioned to.

As the Expert

Blogging and podcasting are natural choices for expertise-based business owners. Additionally, webinars allow the opportunity to provide valuable education to your target audience.

Making It Fun

Focus on those topics that make your target audience laugh out loud, smile, or participate. Incorporating games, puzzles, and contests into your blog or website is a great strategy.

Exclusivity

Make customers register to see your site, access your blog, or listen to your podcast. Create the impression that this information is only for those people "in the know."

The Least You Need to Know

◆ Make your website a powerful addition to your marketing arsenal.

◆ Blogging is a powerful online communication tool and is here to stay, so learn how to use it to connect to your target market.

◆ Use podcasts to build a more personal relationship with your target market.

◆ Webinars enable you to share your expertise through various educational programs.

Chapter 12

12

Here, There, and Everywhere: Web Marketing 201

In This Chapter

- ◆ Getting a vision of the viral world
- ◆ Social networking strategies
- ◆ Using YouTube
- ◆ Marketing on the go: making the most of mobile phones
- ◆ Tech and trends: what's the relationship

Establishing an effective online presence is the first step to target marketing on the web. However, there's so much more that can be done online, and the options expand exponentially every day.

The web is wide-open territory. New communications platforms emerge regularly, each with a new way to connect you with your target market. One offers video, another, the chance to generate virtual editions of your business for customers to while away the hours.

One thing is certain. Target marketing online means shifting your message from a medium you control—your blog, your website, your podcast, or webinar—to one where others take charge. You're entering the wild side of the web where others control the conversation and you are merely a player in it.

It's scary, but the risk can pale dramatically when compared to the reward. Viral campaigns have launched careers and transformed everyday businesses into cult brands. It's a matter of knowing what you've got to say—and to whom.

The Power of Viral Marketing

Viral marketing is word-of-mouth 2.0—the type of buzz that could only happen on the Internet. At its simplest, viral marketing consists of crafting a marketing message so engaging, so wonderful or funny or powerful, that people feel compelled to share it with everyone they know.

> **On Target**
>
> The first company recognized as a viral marketer was Hotmail, the e-mail service that attached advertising to every outgoing e-mail message sent. Today, Hotmail has over 23 million active users.

Generally this sharing happens via e-mail forwards: someone passes along a message to everyone in his address book. Viral marketing also occurs when people independently blog about a marketing message, post about it on social networking sites, or discuss it in their podcasts or video blogs.

Viral marketing gets its name from the process of the message being passed from one user to the next. Much like a cold sweeps through an office, a funny video clip or shocking story can travel through a workplace at record-breaking speed.

What Makes a Message Viral?

The first tricky part of viral marketing boils down to answering one simple question: what is going to make someone, anyone, take time out of her day to share your marketing message with everyone she knows?

There is no definitive rule. People are funny creatures: there are countless goofy or informative or shocking videos online that never capture the public's imagination, and linger, ignored, in a dusty corner of the web. Other items are like popcorn kernels. They pop here, there, and everywhere, so much so, they wind up hitting the mainstream media!

Generally, however, three types of messages have a greater-than-average chance of becoming viral.

The Funny

Humor is the undisputed king of viral marketing. Everyone, everywhere, likes to laugh—and everyone, everywhere, likes to be the person in the know with a funny message to share.

Bear in mind that humor is subjective. What's hysterically funny to one group could very easily offend another—or worse, fall absolutely flat.

When considering what humorous content to include in a viral marketing campaign, make sure you know what makes your target market laugh. They're the people you want the forwards to go to. They're the ones most likely to value and remember the message.

> **On Target**
>
> Geico, the car insurance giant, hit a homerun with their series of commercials featuring modern-era cavemen. The spots were so popular that Geico created The Cavemen's Crib, an online space where web users choose to interact with the prehistoric spokesmen.

The Powerful

Rhonda Byrne picked up a 100-year-old book and discovered wisdom within that would change her life. And once she, and a talented team of marketers, decided to spread news of that wisdom online, Byrne had a phenomenon on her hands.

Her book, *The Secret*, is an international best-seller, topping the charts in many categories. A huge part of the book's success is directly attributed to the huge online push it received. Readers blogged about what they'd learned, quoting entire passages. There were online discussion forums devoted to the book, and clips from the movie version were watched on YouTube long before the movie was officially released. In essence, this was an absolutely brilliant target marketing strategy.

Because the information in Byrne's book was perceived as high value—it was informative and effective—people were highly motivated to share it with others they cared about. The value deeply connected to the emotional reaction people had to Byrne's book. They felt so strongly about what they'd read or heard that they wanted the world to hear about it.

The Informative

Educational material is amazingly popular online. People value how-to information and are willing to make it viral.

Viral marketing experts say that this trend reflects how most web users search for information. For example, if you're someone who wants to learn how to make broomstick lace, you might enter the words "How to make broomstick lace" in a search engine window.

> **Danger Zone**
>
> Understanding viral marketing means understanding authenticity: web users are cynical to the core. Be genuine—because if discovered as a phony, this could easily wreck your reputation!

One of the first results might direct you to a YouTube video with the catchy title, "How to make broomstick lace." It's short, so you watch it—and wind up following the links through to the sponsoring online yarn shop, where you find exactly the hooks, yarn, and instruction books you need to make the shawl of your dreams!

Your Place on MySpace

MySpace is the most prominent, well-known social networking site on the Internet. There are other social networking sites, ranging from the professional connection site, LinkedIn, to more fringe-oriented sites like Friendster. Facebook is rapidly gaining ground in the social networking world, but with just under 30 million users, they're still a good distance behind MySpace.

What Is Social Networking?

Social networking creates communities on the web. Websites invite members to post profiles, blogs, photos, song lyrics, commentary—pretty much whatever they'd like—as part of an ongoing community conversation.

> **Insight**
>
> Nielson Online, the web-measuring equivalent of the well-known television ratings system, reports that approximately 60 million people use MySpace.

Social networking sites like MySpace are very broad by nature—but communities form within larger social networks. For example, on MySpace there are over 4.4 million smaller communities called groups currently running. Each group focuses on a specific topic. There are groups for beach lovers and Red Sox fans, and there are groups that want to stop animal cruelty and promote free-range chickens.

No matter how small or esoteric an interest, there's a home for it on a social network somewhere.

This is music to the ears of the savvy target marketer, who salivates at the thought of connecting with their audience where they are.

Ning is a relatively new addition to the web, and it enables you to create your very own social network. For the right company, this novel target marketing strategy will certainly differentiate you from the competition.

Insight

Second Life is an Internet-based virtual world that enables its users, called Residents, to interact with each other through avatars. Residents can explore, meet other residents, socialize, participate in individual and group activities, and create and trade virtual property and services with one another.

What You Need to Know

The number one rule that applies to MySpace and other social networking sites is simple: keep it real.

In other words, be authentic. Say what you mean, and own up to what you do. Authenticity is very important to the demographic that hangs out on MySpace and other social networking sites. By and large, these people are very used to being marketed to. They've been exposed to commercial messages from their cradle. They don't believe any of it, anymore—and more important, there's a very conscious parsing of MySpace and other social networking arenas as self-limiting networks with their own codes of behavior.

What does all that mean? It means that the same old, same old marketing shtick won't work on MySpace. If you're trying to sell something, say so. At the same time, you'd better have something else to bring to the conversation, or MySpace won't have a place for you.

How It Works

Joining MySpace or any other social networking platform is a simple matter of logging onto the site, filling out a brief registration form, and you're ready to start participating.

Realistically, however, you want to put a little more thought and care into the process. Begin by understanding what you want to accomplish by participating in social networking sites. Set quantifiable goals and objectives.

Common goals for social networking participation include these:

- Increasing awareness of your brand.

- Introducing new products and services.

- Identifying likely customers.

- Creating a network of evangelists—customers who are so fanatically loyal to your products and services that they tell everyone they know about them.

> **Danger Zone** _____
>
> MySpace and other social networking platforms all have friend functions, where readers, fans, and others publicly declare their connection to you. Be cautious when befriending people. Take a moment to look at the profile of whomever you're friending. There are a lot of spammers and adult-oriented sites that you may not want to ally your business with!

Assessing Opportunities

Participating on social networking sites can take a lot of time—creating a profile, posting messages, updating your status, and collecting friends and connections. All this activity takes time out of your day, which means that you must assess the reward to determine whether it's worth your time and energy.

> **On Target**
>
> Toy manufacturers like Hasbro, maker of the Littlest Pet Shop line, are integrating social networking into their toys: teaching young consumers to interact online with the brands they love.

Social networking does not work equally well for all audiences. Generally, you want to embrace social networking, particularly if you're in a referral-driven market, that is, dependent on selling the next hot item or being the go-to expert.

Social networking as a marketing tool is still in its infancy—and so is much of the target market.

You're on YouTube

YouTube, the major online site for video content, gets more viewers than network television. Currently, experts say that more eyes are on YouTube, checking out what friends and neighbors are doing, than tune into the major television networks.

That's pretty impressive—especially if your target customers are among the 20 million people who are logging on. The vast majority of YouTube content is entertainment only. However, that could depend on your own personal definition of entertainment. Watching college kids surf mattresses down the dorm stairwell isn't exactly the same as watching *Masterpiece Theater*.

Insight _____

YouTube is so influential, in fact, that *Time* magazine voted it "Invention of the Year" in 2006.

However, surprising numbers of businesses are doing very well by marketing themselves via YouTube. Blendtec, a relatively unknown company in the small-appliance world, gathered an almost cultlike following with their regular YouTube feature: Will It Blend?

Will It Blend does more than present Blendtec's products' abilities to mix up a mean milkshake. GPS systems, iPhones, hockey pucks—they're all demolished in the Blendtec.

That demonstration of Blendtec's power, seen on hundreds of thousands of computer screens, many hundreds of thousands of times, has sold a boatload of blenders.

What You Need to Know

While YouTube might resemble television, there are some fundamental differences critical for the small business owner to know.

You can save money. Establishing a presence on YouTube is infinitely more affordable than showing up on network or even cable television. Posting video is free; your only cost is creating video content.

Better still, the culture of YouTube means you don't have to spend $8 million producing your video. This is not the place for highly polished, super-slick videos. YouTube is very much a do-it-yourself environment. The typical video shown on YouTube is often recorded on a $300 camera.

Content counts. You can't just throw up a copy of your latest commercial on YouTube and expect to get any kind of positive result out of it. People don't tune into YouTube to watch commercials. They tune in to see "something" different that they would not normally see elsewhere.

This "something" can come in a number of flavors: some people come for entertainment, others for education, and still others for information they just can't get any place else.

This makes YouTube a great vehicle for anyone pursuing a target marketing strategy of "Being the Expert" or "Making It Fun."

Bear in mind that YouTube is hardly the only video-hosting platform on the web. However, at this point, it is the giant in the room, dwarfing all other competition.

How It Works

Before using this dynamite target marketing tool, find out if your target market visits YouTube. You might be surprised who watches YouTube; there is no typical YouTube user.

Determine what type of content your target audience searches for. The easiest route may be to ask yourself, "What questions does my ideal customer have?"

For example, if you run a garden supply shop, your customers may want to know how to control grubs, or plant rosebushes, or trim the hedges into the shape of circus animals. If you're a professional organizer, your customers want to know how a scene of absolute chaos can be turned into a beautiful office space, with everything filed and functional.

> **Insight**
>
> YouTube works best when every video links directly back to your web page. Then, make sure you have a landing page that encourages visitors to linger—and better still, become customers!

Informational and powerful videos are often easier to make than humorous ones. That being said, don't shy away from humor. If you can make your customers laugh, they'll keep coming back and spending time on your website. Look at Blendtec. It shouldn't have to be rocket science.

Promoting your YouTube videos is critical: you want to be part of YouTube communities. Additionally, making your videos available on blogs and social networking sites helps spread the message about your business.

Understanding YouTube as a Target Marketing Tool

It's often difficult to see the direct connection between posting funny videos online and realizing greater sales in your business. There isn't necessarily a direct relationship.

In many cases, YouTube serves as an effective marketing tool showcasing the distinctive personality of your business. Bear in mind that in the current marketplace, consumers value the relationship they have with your business more than anything else.

Another route that YouTube serves the target marketer is to help you share your expertise directly with your target audience. This consideration is essential if you're in a niche market. Being the only business with a video online that details how to handle a specific problem can certainly drive a lot of business your way.

Celling Yourself

Mobile phone marketing is a rapidly emerging trend. Cell phones are everywhere, with increasing numbers of people opting to use cell phones exclusively.

It seems logical that because people have their cell phones with them continually, mobile phones represent the marketing platform of the future. Some companies—specifically those in the entertainment and communications industry—are rapidly and aggressively moving into cell phone advertising.

The appeal of mobile phone marketing is twofold: one, you have a way to reach a customer who may not be online or engaging with traditional media. Second, companies can specifically target prospects using mobile phone marketing. Cell phone companies not only know who is using their phones, but they know their usage patterns and other demographic information.

Currently, traditional advertising, delivered via banner ads or short video clips, are being used with mixed results. As this trend matures, you'll see new and exciting strategies evolve. So keep your eyes open!

More successful, and of more interest to the target marketer, are mobile marketing campaigns that directly engage the recipients and invite them to participate.

This means contests and accessing social networking sites. Key to this emerging marketing method is inviting interactivity and strengthening the relationship you have with your customers.

 Danger Zone

Mobile phone marketing can only do so much. Even the most fervent advocates consider it only one tool in a successful target marketer's toolbox.

What You Need to Know

As of this writing, there are two routes of mobile phone marketing available to the average small business owner.

The first, and probably easiest, way to take advantage of cell phones' omnipresence is to integrate cell phone number collection into your database marketing and customer retention program. More about this in Part Four.

The next option to consider is creating contests and promotions where customers call in. Trivia contests and puzzles are incredibly popular and can generate tremendous word-of-mouth buzz around your business. They can also add a fun cachet to a brand.

What's Hot and What's Not

According to the experts, new technology appears online approximately every two and a half seconds—and theoretically, every new application has the potential to transform your business.

How do you know what's worth your time and what's a total time-waster? That's a serious question, when you only have 24 hours in a day and still have a business to run.

Save time and minimize frustration by adopting this six-step process for approaching new technology. Followed consistently, this process enables you to identify viable promotional opportunities, discern which ones appear to have sticking power, streamline the learning process, and adopt best practices right from day one!

Step One: Don't Believe the Hype

Enthusiastic, cheerleading-style articles touting the latest tech tool as the solution to all of your marketing challenges are fun to read, but they seldom provide enough information to make a solid business decision!

def•i•ni•tion

Twitter is a free social networking and microblogging service that allows its users to send and read other users' updates (known as tweets), which are text-based posts of up to 140 characters in length.

Put yourself on a short rein, and don't let enthusiasm for the flavor-of-the-week be your only guide. Do your research. Discover what demographics are adopting the touted technology. For example, the audience for *Twitter*-powered microblogs is different from the crowd downloading podcasts onto their cell phones.

Longevity is definitely a relative term in this environment, as Internet trends move at the speed of light. However, longevity is key in determining when a fad has staying power. For example, blogging has been around for years now, and has proven business applications, while other, newer tech applications have yet to prove themselves.

Consider if you want to be on the cutting edge, taking the risk to try out the new technology and benefit as an early adopter, or if you'd be more comfortable going with a known and proven platform.

Step Two: Seek Out Reputable Resources to Serve as Guides

While you're doing your due diligence and researching this new technological tool, pay special attention to where your information is coming from. Not all resources have equal value. Look to those individuals who are consistently cited as an expert by others. It's wise to have a rule of three for this. If three disparate sources all reference the same individual or work, there's a better than fair chance that resource has some real value that can be of benefit.

Remember, you don't have to limit yourself to online research, although that's often the quickest and easiest way to find information these days. Check print media: if a tool is well established enough to have books devoted to it, chances are it can be used to help you promote your business effectively.

Step Three: Identify What You Want to Accomplish

Set a clear goal for yourself. This goal needs to be specific, quantifiable, and realistic. Rather than saying, "I want to be on YouTube because everybody's there!" consider, "I will post four videos a year to YouTube, each one focused on a different segment of my area of expertise."

Knowing what you want to do is essential. Having an end objective helps you to understand what skills you need to concentrate on and which ones are irrelevant. For example, if you want to build your business through blogging, focus on learning how to write a great blog entry, how to promote your blog, and strategies to raise your blog's visibility.

This step helps you to save time and be more efficient.

Step Four: Learn the Vocabulary

Make life easy for yourself! Before you start diving into the hows, whys, and how-comes of any new area of study, take an hour to familiarize yourself with the much-needed vocabulary. Every technology has a specific language you need to understand so that you can be more efficient.

Consider this vocabulary similar to the professional jargon you use when conversing with colleagues. It's likely that your conversation might be unintelligible to the average listener, unless you took the time to define and explain the terminology you're using.

Chances are you don't have someone on hand to explain confusing terms or unfamiliar language. If you forge ahead, hoping to pick up the meaning in context, you're likely to be very frustrated, and no closer to achieving your goals. It may seem like wasted time to focus on vocabulary early in the process, but language makes comprehension possible.

Step Five: Don't Reinvent the Wheel

No matter what your goal or objective, there's a better than fair chance that someone else has already done it before you. Look for examples that resonate: a blog you'd like to emulate, podcasts that inspire you, YouTube videos that have you green with envy.

Study these examples carefully. What is it about them that works? Make a list of those things you'd like to adopt for your own message. Obviously, you don't want to make a carbon copy of someone else's work, but there's nothing wrong with modeling yourself after people who have done a great job communicating their message effectively!

Step Six: Ask Questions and Embrace Expertise

You don't have to do it all yourself! Small business owners often fall into a common trap. They convince themselves that because it's their business, they have to do it all—marketing, selling, filing, hiring, firing, and so on. As a corollary to this, there's a common misconception that one should know everything possible about running a business from day one and never need any help!

You need to put that attitude behind you! Save time, energy, and effort by asking questions! There are a number of platforms to do this online. Entire web communities exist for individuals who want to build a better blog, create great YouTube videos, and more. Find a community you're comfortable with—this might require a few minutes with Google—and ask questions. This is often the quickest way to find information and, as an added bonus, start forming relationships with potential colleagues, clients, and peers.

Putting It All Together

Target marketing opportunities on the web appear every single day, changing and evolving as online communities morph and adapt to the dynamic expectations of web users. The advantage to this is that small business owners must be both forward-thinking and critical. Pick and choose those opportunities that enable you to connect effectively with your target market and build your brand.

Here's how to do this.

As the Expert

Social networking and YouTube offer prime opportunities for you to showcase your knowledge. Focus on answering your target market's most common concerns. Make sure through your various communications that you bring them to your website, where there's enough information to ensure they know you're the expert source!

Making It Fun

YouTube was made for you! Enjoy making your target market laugh. Take advantage of inclusive platforms, such as cell-phone-based contests, to get customers reaching out to you.

Exclusivity

Pay careful attention to what social networks you join. You want to appear on the premier social network for your market. For example, top bridal retailers know they have to be on TheKnot.com, because this is where the best bridal businesses gather. The key is to understand and know what your target market's expectations are.

Also, exclusivity can be served by using cell phone communication as part of your client retention strategy. Well-timed calls to let your customers know of a special sales event can add to the luxurious, "in the know" feel your clients enjoy.

The Least You Need to Know

- ◆ Target marketing online means shifting your message from a medium you control to one where others take charge.

- ◆ When using viral marketing, answer the question: what is going to make people take time to share your marketing message with everyone they know?

- ◆ The number one rule when using any social networking site is to keep it simple, real, and authentic.

- ◆ YouTube, as a target marketing strategy, enables you to share your expertise directly with your target audience.

Chapter 13

It's All About the Buzz

In This Chapter

- ◆ Understanding the power of word-of-mouth marketing
- ◆ Learning the best ways to create buzz
- ◆ Capitalizing on networking techniques

You might have a great business. You might have the best business in the world. That's not going to matter, unless your customers know you're there.

The most effective and powerful way to spread the word about your business is *word-of-mouth marketing*. Inspiring and generating conversation about your practice will generate more sales, bring in more customers, and sell more products and services than any advertising you can do, any promotion you can run, or any price cuts you may take.

Understanding what gets people talking and how to capitalize on that conversation is the essence of strategic marketing. In a target marketing capacity, you want to focus on starting conversations among groups of individuals already predisposed to value your products and services.

The Power of Word-of-Mouth Marketing

Word of mouth is the Holy Grail of small-business promotion. It's the pot of gold at the end of the rainbow, the silver lining in the dark cloud, the free parking space in a rainstorm. Every smart small business owner wants positive word of mouth.

What is word of mouth, and why does everybody want it?

In short, word of mouth means getting your customers to talk about your business. The purpose of all marketing and promotional efforts comes down to creating word of mouth.

Word of mouth is so coveted by small business owners because it is so valuable. The average customer trusts and responds to what their family, friends, and colleagues tell them about a business far more than any marketing message they might receive from that same business.

> **def•i•ni•tion**
>
> According to the Word-of-Mouth Marketing Association, **word-of-mouth marketing** is the art and science of creating genuine customer enthusiasm, amplifying it, and sharing it with future fans.

After all, when was the last time you ate at a restaurant after your best friend told you about the bad food or service?

At least half of all customers value word of mouth more than any other source when they have to decide where to spend their time and money. In particular segments, such as B2B sales, health care, and professional services, word of mouth is even more important.

How Do You Create Buzz?

Buzz is word of mouth of the moment. Not only are people talking about a certain business, but they're talking about it right now.

Buzz is a fast and fleeting phenomenon because it is very difficult to sustain an ongoing public discussion of your products and services for an extended period of time.

There are a number of routes to creating buzz. They all boil down to one central concept: if you want people to talk about your business, you have to give them something to talk about.

You can do this by virtue of being new. You can do this by having something fundamentally different and unique about the way you do business. You can do this by being the best in your field. There are almost an infinite number of ways to get people talking about you.

Technology has given us an almost equally infinite number of platforms for people to have these pivotally important conversations. The Internet, of course, is the most influential technology here, which is why we've devoted two chapters (Chapters 11 and 12) to effectively positioning yourself on the web.

In this chapter, we're going to take the old-school method and discuss the first and still most powerful way to create word of mouth: networking. To create conversations among your target audience, you need to talk to your target audience. Here's the face-to-face way to do it.

> **On Target**
>
> When Sir Richard Branson launched his own airline, Virgin Atlantic, there was a tremendous amount of buzz surrounding the event. Frequent flyers were talking about the new airline, the media was talking about the new airline, and the Internet was ablaze with speculation about Branson's latest business venture.

Making the Most of Networking

Networking is easy. All you have to do is walk into a crowded room and convince everyone in there that you're the best thing since sliced bread!

Okay. Relax. It's not that bad.

Networking starts with a conversation. These conversations can take place in a formal setting, such as a business event, or they can take place spontaneously, while you're watching the local soccer team kick the ball around and strike up a conversation with the person next to you.

def•i•ni•tion

Networking is the art and science of beginning new relationships, strengthening existing relationships, and being available to those people who want to have a relationship with you.

Seven Guidelines to Being a Successful Networker

Here are seven guidelines you need to know to be a successful networker.

Relax. Small-business success is a marathon, not a sprint. Every conversation doesn't need to lead directly to a sale. Take the time to focus on the moment and enjoy the conversation you're in.

If you're nervous or shy, take some time to meditate, center, or do whatever you need to do to calm yourself before attending networking events or attempting to start a business conversation in a social setting. Nervousness shows, and it's not appealing.

Listen more than you talk. There's nothing in this world people love more than talking about themselves. At the same time, there's nothing rarer than a good listener. Stifle the impulse to talk, talk, talk, and instead focus on being a good listener. Ask the people you're with about themselves: what they do, where they went to school, and so on. Keep it personal and light—you don't want to come off like you're conducting an interrogation or wanting to sell them something.

Remember your manners. No matter where you are, you want to remember and use your best manners. This isn't about using the wrong fork to eat your salad. Instead, make sure that you're unfailingly nice to everyone you meet, including wait-staff, service personnel, and others who happen to be around while you're networking.

People judge you by how you conduct yourself, and this includes your treatment of others. You never know if the investment banker you desperately want to invest in your company made his way through college waiting tables!

Danger Zone

Watch your table manners, common courtesies, and the like. More than one deal has gone sour because of the way a prospect ate a meal!

Be in the moment. Your intention when networking is to get to know the people you're with. You want their time and attention. That means it's a good idea to shut off your cell phone—there's nothing ruder than constantly interrupting a conversation to answer the phone and expecting them to hold on while you chat.

Skip the gossip. Bad-mouthing your competition is a sure sign of an amateur. Avoid the temptation to dig up dirt on your industry colleagues or indulge in idle gossip. It's far too easy to pick up a negative reputation for indulging in this kind of behavior—not to mention the risk of alienating peers and colleagues you might someday need on your side.

Leave the literature behind. Don't bring brochures, catalogs, or samples everywhere with you! A simple business card is enough. If it turns out, during the course of conversation, that the people you meet are interested in learning more about you, you'll have plenty of time to supply them with sales materials afterward. It's a great excuse to reconnect by either sending or hand delivering your sales materials.

Pick up the tab. The best way to get something from someone is to give them something first. Don't be afraid to pick up the tab, especially if you just happen to run into someone at the coffee shop.

Sometimes you'll run into guests who can't accept your generosity because their employers forbid them from accepting free meals or other gifts. Government employees fall into this category, so it's best to just follow their lead. However, pay when you can. It's a nice gesture that shows you value the relationship.

Who Should You Talk To?

There are an estimated 6.7 billion people on this planet. Even if you started right now, there's no way you're going to be able to talk to them all!

It's a good idea to be friendly and warm with everyone you meet. However, there are individuals who, because of their own extensive network of professional and personal connections, are extremely influential. These people are sometimes referred to as "king makers."

You'll want to identify the king makers within your community and within your industry. These are good people to know, and it's often well worth the effort to seek them out. They may turn out to be a potential customer, or a mentor, advisor, or friend.

Insight

Never underestimate the influence of a partner or spouse on someone's opinion of you! Make a point of being genuinely nice to the better halves of everyone you meet.

Where to Network

You can network anywhere—some of the most profitable business relationships known to humanity had their genesis sitting in airplanes!

Different settings require different approaches. Generally, you can split networking opportunities into two categories: professional and community.

Professional Networking

Professional networking is the art and science of capitalizing upon the relationship you have with your colleagues and peers. This is essential if you're in a referral-driven business, where customers seek out your services after consulting with other professionals they know and trust.

It takes a village to raise a child—and it's just as accurate to say it takes a village to build a business. No one business can be all things to all people. No one store carries every type of merchandise, and no one service provider can handle every case. That's where the referral model plays its role. When you can't help your customers, you want to send them to someone who can.

There's an implied expectation that these relationships are reciprocal: if a colleague sends you tons of work, you're expected to return the favor, when appropriate. If the local dress shop sends every lady with narrow feet in town to you for shoes, then when some slim-footed lass asks where she can get a great dress, you know where to send them.

All of this sounds great, but first you have to know whom to refer your customers to. As the owner of a small business, the lion's share of your time is consumed by running your business. Meeting your colleagues and peers and learning enough about them— and letting them learn enough about you—is essential to forming profitable referral relationships.

Insight

Business Networking International (BNI) is the largest business networking organization in the world. They offer members the opportunity to share ideas, contacts, and most important, business referrals. It's based on a proven concept by BNI Founder, Dr. Ivan Misner, called "Givers Gain." If I give you business, then you'll give me business, and we'll both benefit as a result.

The Old Boy's (and Girl's) Club: Networking at Professional Associations

Every industry has a professional or trade association. Generally, each sizeable segment within a field has professional associations as well.

A jeweler, for example, belongs to the American Gem Association. They can also belong to the National Chinese American Jeweler's Association, the Women's Jewelry Association, and, the Jewelers of America, the retail trade association.

There are any number of professional associations you might be eligible to join. Becoming involved with a professional or trade association is a great way to meet colleagues and peers. These organizations collect the very professionals you may want to refer your customers to.

When considering what professional associations may be best for you to join for networking purposes, consider the following:

♦ **The organization's reputation:** You want to ally yourself with the best, most prestigious association that you can.

♦ **The benefits of membership:** Every professional association offers some level of benefits, from a subscription to the association publication and an annual conference to health insurance plans and professional advocacy. Obviously, the more benefits you can secure, the better.

♦ **Costs of membership:** Consider how much it will cost you, in terms of dues and time commitment, to join a given professional association. The benefits of membership and the networking opportunities need to meet or, at best, exceed the expense.

Insight _____

To get the maximum bang for your membership buck, become actively involved in whatever association you join.

Danger Zone _____

Simply joining an association won't achieve many networking opportunities. You need to be involved to truly gain networking benefits.

Capitalizing on Your Professional Association Involvement

Joining a professional association is the first step. Then it's time to get involved. The primary way to get involved in the workings of any professional association is through volunteering.

Professional organizations continually look for new and enthusiastic volunteers. There's a perpetual need for someone to actually do the work of running the association, especially as more established members retire or take a less active role.

What types of jobs need to be done within a professional organization? There are a whole range of tasks, from organizing conventions and events to producing the association newsletter to recruiting new members. The list is endless, and there's always a need for someone to do the work, especially someone who's eager and enthusiastic.

It is often easier and more immediately rewarding to join local professional associations first, and then, if necessary, work your way up to state, regional, and national level organizations.

The benefit of doing this work is that you're demonstrating your value to your colleagues and peers. If you impress them during professional networking opportunities, they'll be far more likely to send business your way.

Danger Zone _____

Doing volunteer work can eat up a lot of your free time. Keep your commitments in check. Don't agree to more than you can handle. Practice saying "no" politely!

Networking at Industry Events

Professional and trade organizations generally hold annual or semiannual meetings, for the purpose of educating their members, facilitating networking opportunities, and disseminating industry-specific information.

Insight _____

According to *Tradeshow Week*, there are approximately 5,000 independent tradeshows held every year in the United States, attracting over 50.6 million attendees and 1.4 million exhibitors.

There's often a tradeshow affiliated with these industry events, during which companies exhibit their latest goods and services. Generally, these industry-specific events are closed to outsiders, which means the general public can't come in.

Both industry events and tradeshows offer superb professional networking opportunities. In many instances, you may find yourself at a tradeshow even if you don't belong to any professional associations. These are prime buying opportunities, and are often the very best place to see what new products and services are being unveiled for the coming year.

Attending Industry Events

Tradeshows at industry events are often the best buying opportunity of the year. Manufacturers wait for tradeshows to unveil new merchandise; if you want to know what's new, what's hot, and what's coming, you need to be at your industry convention and tradeshow.

A substantial part of the networking opportunities at a tradeshow take place away from the show floor. Walking the show and visiting exhibits is certainly a good way to get a feel for who the industry players are and what options are out there, but the fast pace and intense crush of the crowds make developing meaningful relationships difficult.

With that in mind, many tradeshows offer programming tracks as well as networking opportunities. You'll learn about these either from the show website or in the information you receive when you register for the show.

These are prime networking opportunities. While there may be 2,000 individuals on a tradeshow floor, it's not at all uncommon to attend an educational seminar with 25 or fewer people. In these quieter settings, there's a greater chance of connecting, not only with the presenter, but also with the other participants who are interested in the seminar topic. Generally, people who are actively interested in improving their business are good people to know.

Networking events come in many flavors: dinner-theater evenings, sports events, outings, cocktail parties. These events give you an opportunity to connect with colleagues and peers, theoretically without any sales pressure. Some events are by invitation only, when sponsoring vendors allow entry only to their existing customers and most likely prospects.

During networking events, remember that the focus is on getting to know people. It might look like idle chitchat, but often that idle chitchat is what profitable relationships are built upon.

> **Danger Zone** _____
>
> Alcohol often flows freely at networking events. Go slow or stick to soda: you want to have your wits about you and avoid making a bad impression! "Loose lips sink ships!"

Exhibiting at Industry Tradeshows

If your target audience is comprised of other companies, either manufacturers who use the raw materials or components you provide, or retailers who market your products directly to customers, you need to exhibit at tradeshows.

No other medium offers the direct face-to-face marketing opportunity that tradeshows do, and frankly, if you're looking for this type of buyer, you need to be where they go shopping. That means tradeshows.

Exhibiting at a tradeshow is a special combination of sales technique and theater. You need to have a great exhibit: the booth space you occupy at the show has to be visually engaging, completely unique, and representative of your branding. At the same time, you need superlative people skills to begin meaningful relationships with potential customers, who you only get to talk with for four to five minutes, tops!

Exhibiting at a tradeshow requires extensive planning. This is not an inexpensive option. Exhibiting can run you a few hundred dollars if you're at a small, community-level show, on up to thousands and thousands of dollars for large, national events.

However, the potential rewards are great, especially when you're at the right show, in front of the right target audience. As part of your research, take the time to discover what shows attract the largest percentage of attendees likely to be interested in your products and services. Then learn what other successful exhibitors have done at that show to make the most of their exhibiting experience.

Insight

Tradeshow organizers often make attendee demographic information and tips for successful exhibiting available on their website. Check it out!

Industry events offer some unique target marketing opportunities. These include speaking opportunities and sponsorships.

Speaking Opportunities

Speaking opportunities abound at most industry events. In addition to the keynote speech opportunities (which are hard to secure and usually reserved for either professional speakers or industry gurus), most events offer several educational presentations.

If your target audience attends the event in sizable numbers and your target marketing strategy is to present yourself as the expert resource, presenting an educational program is a must-do. Contact event organizers well ahead of time to secure a slot. These opportunities are highly prized and often get planned as far as 12 months in advance of the event.

Capitalize on speaking opportunities by presenting your audience with a dynamic, engaging performance that makes them think, informs them of something new and useful in the field, and entertains them. Yes, that's a tough order—but if you attain it, not only will you have successfully started or reinforced your relationship with the audience, but they'll tell their colleagues about the great presentation they just saw. It's a way to create buzz at the event!

Tradeshow Sponsorships

Sponsorships require a financial investment in order to have your organization's name and logo displayed in multiple ways such as these:

- Show signage
- Tote bags

- ◆ Event collateral materials
- ◆ Networking dinners
- ◆ Educational programs

This is one area where you'll really want to consider the cost-benefit relationship. In a highly targeted event, where you want the attention of a very large percentage of the target audience, sponsorship can be a smart move. Otherwise, save your money.

def•i•ni•tion

A **sponsorship** is a gift for which the donor receives a predetermined benefit, such as advertising.

Community Networking

Networking on the community level means focusing on relationships with people who probably don't share any professional background with you. They may own businesses of their own, work for local employers, or simply share the same zip code you do.

Approaching these relationships requires a slightly different approach than professional networking. When you're in the professional venue, you're very clearly there to do business. In the community sphere, that straight-forwardness is not always appreciated. People want to develop genuine relationships with the organizations in their community, not simply be viewed as a potential market.

That means getting involved, sometimes on the grassroots level, in what's going on in your community. There are a number of ways to do this, but the three most prevalent are sponsorships, community events, and the rapidly emerging practice of cause marketing. Let's take a quick peek at each one of them.

Community Sponsorships

The stockcar careens around the track, so fast you can barely see the Pulaski Lumber and Egglefield Ford logos plastered on the side. Across town, a little guy steps up to bat, "Bernie's Toyshop" emblazoned proudly across the back of his uniform. The local senior center bus runs regularly through town, courtesy of Hometown Pharmacy.

All of these are examples of sponsorship, where a company financially supports an activity wholly outside the normal course of their business. Generally, sponsorships can be divided into three main areas:

- ◆ Entertainment (sports or cultural events)
- ◆ Youth (sports or educational activities)
- ◆ Other special interest groups (the elderly, ethnic, or religious groups)

In a sponsorship relationship, you provide the funding, and your logo shows up all over an event. The more money you donate, the more prominently your name gets featured.

This can be a very smart target marketing strategy, when you sponsor those activities that are of extreme importance to your target audience.

Assessing Sponsorship Opportunities

As a business owner, you very rarely need to search for sponsorship opportunities. People will be knocking on your door every single day, looking for money for every good cause that comes along.

You cannot support everything. Even Bill Gates doesn't do that, and he has way more money than you!

You need to be selective. Develop a sponsorship strategy. If you're going to sponsor something, it should be an activity or cause that is of prime importance to your target audience. Ideally, it should also be something you and your staff have a great deal of enthusiasm for; it's hard to generate much team spirit for the local football team if you can't tell the difference between a quarterback and a quarter pounder!

Once you've identified an opportunity that you believe will resonate strongly with your target audience and appeals to you, determine how much you're going to commit to the sponsorship. It's far more effective to throw all of your sponsorship energies into one area than to give small amounts of support to multiple organizations.

That means if your target audience is into stock car racing, commit to one team, preferably one driver. If the ballet's your crowd's thing, do what you can to make the ballet thrive, and let the opera take care of itself.

Mention your sponsorships in your advertising, on your website, and in your signage. Don't be afraid to mention it on social networking sites and your blog. If you're proud of how well "your" Little League team did, there's no harm in letting the world know. Put pictures of your team, your car, or your ballet company up in your business, so your customers can see them.

Insight

Sponsorships of this nature are a concrete demonstration of your commitment to the community.

Community Events

Community events are the local version of industry events or tradeshows. They often appear as Business Expos, Home Shows, RV Fairs, Wellness Fairs, Pet Walks … there's as many types of community events as there are types of communities.

During a community event, companies set up booths, very similar to what one would expect at a tradeshow. But often, that's where the similarities end. These events are open to the public. Some events are strictly informative, while other events allow selling on the floor. Educational and entertaining "extra" programming is nonexistent or minimal, and while tradeshows can and do go for days and days, community events last only a few hours, perhaps extending over a weekend.

The primary opportunity in community events lies in exhibiting. The fees for these events are generally pretty low, especially compared with the costs of industry tradeshows. However, you still need to turn in a top-notch performance, presenting yourself as professional, appealing, and personable.

Community events can take up a lot of time and energy. Depending on your community, there could be a LOT of events in any one time period. Rather than trying to participate in all of them, you want to be selective.

It is better to pick one event that has a strong appeal to your target market and commit to that one wholeheartedly than to "phone it in" at numerous smaller events.

Cause Marketing

Doing good is good business. Cause marketing, sometimes known as community involvement, involves throwing your financial resources behind a charitable cause.

Generally, the causes companies select to support are those that resonate or "make sense" to their target audience.

Strategies that work on the national level can certainly work on the local level. Numerous pet stores have strengthened their relationship with their customer base by supporting no-kill animal shelters.

When picking a cause to support, it is essential to do your research. First, you want to make sure that the cause really resonates with your target market. The best way to do this is by talking to your best customers about what they're passionate about. Second, you want to research the organization you're considering. Make sure they have a good reputation for being honest and ethical before you ally your brand with them!

Don't hide your light under a bushel. If your business supports a cause, let your customers know! Hang signs in your business, mention it on your website, and include it in your newsletters. In fact, consider having a special sales event or promotion specifically to raise funds for your cause of choice!

Putting It All Together

Word of mouth is too powerful of a tool to be ignored. Every small business owner needs to focus on creating some buzz around his or her practice periodically.

Here's what that means if your target marketing strategy is one of the following.

As the Expert

If you want to create buzz as the expert source, you need to position yourself front and center of every relevant newsworthy event. If the stock market crashes and you're a financial advisor, you need to be right there telling your target market what they need to know. A toy recall endangers local kids? As a children's retailer, you want to be on the front page, proposing alternatives and sharing safety guidelines.

Making It Fun

Making it fun is a great strategy to create word of mouth. People love to have a good time, and they love to tell others about the good time they had. Staging fun promotions and events, participating in community events, and staging zany competitions and stunts can create a great deal of word of mouth around your business.

Exclusivity

Create word of mouth with an exclusivity strategy by capitalizing on the power of secrets. Limit access to something: a website, a newsletter, an event. By making it invitation only, you're going to enhance the aura of "This isn't for everyone"—and get people talking about what it takes to be involved and what they are or aren't missing out on.

The Least You Need to Know

◆ Word-of-mouth marketing is the most effective way to spread the buzz about your business, products, or services.

◆ Plan a networking strategy in your professional and local community.

◆ Check into speaking opportunities at industry events.

◆ Look out for the right sponsorship opportunities that impact your target market.

The Power of the Pen

In This Chapter

- ◆ Understanding the value of the written word
- ◆ Using language to connect with your target market
- ◆ Creating content that works for you

The pen is mightier than the sword. Embracing print is one of the easiest, most cost-effective ways to put you directly in front of your target market. Moreover, the credibility gained from being in print far outweighs any other marketing tool available to you. Plus print retains longevity not available in any other type of media.

The Benefits of Print

While there are no silver bullets in the target marketing gun, appearing in print regularly can build your business quickly. Here's why you might want to consider picking up your pen—or sitting down at the computer!

You Look Really Good

Being in print—whether it's an "Ask the Doctor" column or an article on the perfect gift for hard-to-please in-laws—showcases your expertise and skills directly in front of your target audience. No matter what field you're in, there's a publication geared directly at your target audience. Appearing in it enhances your credibility. There's a very clear perception that someone who shows up often in the editorial section of a publication (as opposed to advertising, where anyone who can pay can play!) is a superior source.

Amazing Ability to Reach Your Target Audience

No matter what your target market, there is a publication catering to exactly that customer. Speed metal musicians? Environmentally friendly quilters? People who consider their cats children? High-tech collectors?

Every target market has at least one publication. The larger target markets have multiple titles. Really large target markets even have their own sections in general newspapers or general interest consumer magazines. For example, *Popular Photography & Imaging*, a monthly publication aimed at professional and amateur photographers, runs a regular column called "Digital Toolbox" and "Picture Doctor."

> **On Target**
>
> Organizing expert Donna Smallin is the author of seven books on uncluttering, organizing, cleaning, and simplifying life that have sold nearly 750,000 copies worldwide.

Targeted publications are read by people who belong to your market segment, people who either actively do business with you now or potentially will in the future, given the opportunity. It's also a self-selecting audience. For example, few people pick up *Cats & Kittens* if they're not interested in cats!

It's Cheap

Various aspects of marketing can be expensive. One look at an advertising rate card, for instance, no matter what medium, could make your heart skip a beat.

Writing, on the other hand, is pretty close to free. Yes, you have to make an investment of time and energy. However, writing doesn't require expensive, specialized equipment. You don't have to take any courses to learn how to write well (you certainly can if you want to, but it's not a requirement!)

What about making money with your writing? Some people do it. Generally, these are people who make a substantial commitment of both time and energy to writing. That's time and energy you're already using to run your business, so don't sweat it if you're not making big bucks with your prose. Some publishers may pay for content, but many won't. Your payoff is the exposure you gain by positioning yourself front and center before your target market.

Writing Articles

If you want to use print to achieve target marketing aims, writing articles is the place to start. Articles, which are simply short text pieces that appear in newspapers, magazines, and online publications, enjoy the largest readership of any printed form and are relatively easy to produce.

Don't freak out about what you can write about! When writing to appeal to your target market, make them happy by providing useful, factual information in an easy-to-read style. Tell someone how she can make her life easier, how she can perform a given task better or get more joy out of it, and you've more than delivered.

The First Step

The first step in writing articles is determining where your target audience is likely to see them! This is trickier than it might sound.

Discovering which individual titles, among thousands of options, your target audience reads can challenge even the best detective. However, the two best ways to discover what your audience reads are as follows:

Method one: ask them directly. Set up a survey on your website, ask customers in person, or create a poll in your business where people can fill out a brief questionnaire to claim a prize. You want to know the top three periodicals (newspapers and magazines) they read.

Method two: sneak in through the back door. Every publication, from the smallest community newspaper to *The Wall Street Journal*, keeps detailed information about their readership. The larger the publication, the more detailed the information available.

Insight

There are over 1,000 companies in the United States publishing magazines, with over 10,000 titles in circulation. There are approximately 1,400 daily newspapers, and thousands more that appear weekly.

Who is this information for?

Frankly, it's compiled for the benefits of potential advertisers, who want to make sure they're shelling out their money wisely. This is one of the key concepts of target marketing: advertise in the locations where your target audience spends their time.

That same information is vital when you're looking to place articles. Request advertising information from the publications you're interested in and study the demographics. You will find the necessary details in the "Readership Overview" section on the website. For example, this is the information you will uncover for *Computer* magazine:

> *Computer*'s readers are highly educated, visionary individuals who drive technological change in the global computing industry. They are active, committed industry professionals whose technical expertise is essential to their companies' purchasing decisions.
>
> Readers depend on *Computer* for current, unbiased, and thoroughly researched information on the newest directions in computer technology.

While this isn't the detailed demographic information target marketers prize above all else, it definitely is a start in the right direction.

Ideally, you'll use a combination of method one—asking your customers—and method two—accessing the publication's demographic information—to compile a list of places you'd like to appear.

The Second Step

After that, it's simply a matter of contacting the editor (you will find this information on the publication's website or masthead) and asking them how open they are to having you contribute some articles.

Insight

You will find the details of a publication's article requirements by searching the following sections on their website: Submissions, Editorial, Editorial Calendar, and For Writers.

You will increase your chances for placing content with a clear, well-thought-out proposal. Focus on what would best serve that editor's needs. Recognize that they are always in search of interesting and topical content for their readership.

Make a note of what type of content the publication is already running, and propose more of the same. For example, *Massage Magazine* features 15 "news brief" articles per year, each of which runs between

200 to 800 words. If you want to be in *Massage Magazine*, you'll increase your chances by proposing a short, 500-word news brief article because the format fits what they're already using.

The Third Step

Once you have an indication of interest from the publication's editorial staff, it's time to write the article.

The best articles for target marketers hoping to establish their credibility and build their audience contain short, concise tips and techniques that reveal some measure of their expertise.

Pick one main theme, and stick to it. Use lots of stories to illustrate your points, and make sure that every fact in your article is verifiable.

Always echo the format of other articles in the publication you are writing for.

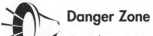

Danger Zone

Avoid any type of self-promotion in your articles. Educating your target audience should be your primary goal. You will gain credibility as an expert as you begin to publish more articles.

The Final Step

Don't miss the chance to realize the maximum value of every article you write. For example, archive articles on your website, include photocopies of your work in your media kit, post short articles on a bulletin board in your business location, and leave duplicate copies in your place of business for customers to take and read at their leisure.

Also, consider compiling all the articles you've written into a book, further enhancing your credibility and building your brand!

Assessing Opportunities

New business owners spend a lot of time and energy trying to break into print. The first time you get published, there's a big thrill: there's your name, and your business, front and center in the appropriate section of the local paper, or in the trendy, of-the-moment magazine.

It does not take long for the requests for articles to start coming to you, especially when you gain a reputation for great content, delivered with a minimum of hassle. However, writing articles takes time and energy. So, make sure you focus your time and energy on those publications that actually appeal to your target market.

Writing Columns

Columns are articles, generally between 500 and 850 words, that appear on a regular basis in a consistent location within a publication. They may be formal and strictly informative, or they might have a more casual, conversational tone.

Columns are particularly powerful for those business owners who provide products or services to other business owners. Regular columns appearing in a trade publication can generate business as well as open the door to other marketing opportunities, such as speaking engagements or consulting work.

> **On Target**
>
> Tracy Coenen, a forensic accountant, writes a regular monthly column for the *Wisconsin Law Journal*. Even though she advertises in the publication, she discovered that more business derives from the column.

Columns also work well in newspapers and some general-interest magazines. The column form presents a unique opportunity to highlight your brand's personality. In addition, it gives the readership an opportunity to develop a relationship with you through your words.

How It Works

Writing a column is a substantial commitment, and you'll need an established record as a writer before an editor will trust you with a column.

With that in mind, start to create a small portfolio of six to eight sample columns, representative of the type of work you'd like to have appear on a regular basis.

The best types of columns respond to topical and timely events. For example, if you're a massage therapist writing about wellness, have columns about "stretching to reduce stress" ready and available for those days when the headlines have everyone on edge. Be aware of the calendar, and time your content appropriately, such as "7 Tips For Stress-Free Holidays."

Remember that a column can't be blatant self-promotion. However, you do want to demonstrate enough of your expertise and insight that readers who have need of your products and services will want to seek you out.

Assessing Opportunities

Columns make for a powerful and highly valued target marketing platform. What this means is that opportunities to secure a column present themselves fairly infrequently. Generally, if a publication has a columnist covering a topic, it will rarely be open to a second. (Although it never hurts to ask!)

Be selective about where your columns appear. You want your name and brand to be aligned with the best publications catering to your target audience. When applying for a columnist position, make a list of all potential publications, ranked in order of prestige. Begin by looking for opportunities at the very best and work your way down the list. Bear in mind that you want to work with those publications that will enhance your image.

Tip Sheets, Checklists, Booklets

If your target audience is short on time and they value convenience, consider providing them with *tip sheets*, *checklists*, and *booklets*.

These short forms offer the ultimate in convenience. By stripping away all extraneous information and presenting only the essentials, you're catering to those who want quick access to facts, tips, and techniques.

A great example of checklists in action is the regular appearance of back-to-school supply lists that appear in every office supply store once August rolls around. Consider what variation you could create: Back-to-school time for Mom? Back-to-school beauty supplies? Time to take your finances back to school?

The hidden value of booklets is that people tend to hold on to them to refer to again and again. Make sure that each of these short-form pieces is emblazoned with your name and logo. When people turn to you for assistance via print, it reinforces the idea that you are the go-to source (the expert) for a particular area of expertise.

def•i•ni•tion

Tip sheets are bulleted lists of points, with a sentence or two explaining each point. **Checklists** are bulleted lists of points, formatted in a way that ensures someone takes all the steps needed to complete a task. **Booklets** are minibooks, delivering in a succinct format the most critical information about a topic.

How It Works

Tip sheets, checklists, and booklets are generally self-publishing projects. You create them yourself, and then either head off to the local copy shop to produce as many as needed, or turn them into a downloadable *Portable Document Format (PDF)* file.

The trick is to use tip sheets, checklists, and booklets to build your brand. This means getting them in front of your target audience members.

Places to show these include the following:

- In your store or office

- In media kits

- At community events: home shows, wellness fairs, etc.

- For distribution if you teach a class

- At speaking engagements

- In your packaging when shipping a purchase

- Sent to community groups that cater to your target audience

- Offered as a free download on your website in exchange for information such as a name and e-mail address

def•i•ni•tion

Portable Document Format (PDF) is a file format that lets you capture and view robust information—from almost any application, on any computer system—and share it with virtually anyone, anywhere.

Assessing Opportunities

Creating tip sheets, checklists, and booklets involves costs. Copying, printing, and postage make up your largest expense.

Ideally, you want to use these materials for information that your target audience will always want. For example, if you're a lawn care specialist and you know that grubs are a recurring problem in your area, a tip sheet on "The Five Best Ways to Avoid Grubs" would be a prudent use of your time and resources.

Design your tip sheets, checklists, and booklets with an eye to answering the most common questions or challenges your customers face.

Always include a call to action on your tip sheets, checklists, and booklets, such as "For more information on this subject, make sure to visit (your website)."

Book 'Em!

A book is the ultimate credibility enhancer. Authoring a book lends the writer a certain weight and authority. If you want to be considered an authority in your field, writing a book is the way to go.

Ideally, your book will offer a solution or series of solutions to the most common problems individuals in your target market have.

For example, if you sell sporting and exercise equipment, consider writing a book on whole family fitness, covering how to motivate everyone in the family to get off the couch and start using the equipment.

A dance instructor could pen a volume to inspire ballerinas-in-training, while a financial planner would profit from creating a "The Best Way to Protect Your Legacy" title.

Books written for target marketing purposes must demonstrate that you are aware of and have insight into common problems relevant to your business. Readers want information that will make their lives easier, more efficient, lucrative, and fun—in short, a problem-free existence.

Use your book as a platform to explain how you'll help your customers achieve that end!

> **On Target**
>
> Michel Brown, a financial planner, wrote a book titled *The IRA Winner's Circle* to help his clients as well as to enhance his credibility as an expert in the field.

How It Works

Writing a book is a highly individualized process. Everyone does it differently. This is one instance where the methodology doesn't matter as much as the result!

Every book needs one main, driving idea. The main, driving idea behind this book is "Use creative strategies to reach a carefully defined group of customers effectively and your business will grow."

Every idea, thought, and example that goes into your book needs to support your main idea.

Choose a structure for your book. The ideal recipe consists of something informative and easy-to-read in a style that appeals to your target market.

Keep the focus on educating, entertaining, and informing. A book, in this instance, is a very subtle form of target marketing: you're demonstrating your expertise or personality, and that's the hook. Pushing your actual products or services will come later.

Assessing Opportunities

How do you get your book published? The two primary ways are traditional publishing and self-publishing. The primary difference between the two comes down to who pays for the production of the book, and who has the final decision over editorial content, book design, and more.

Traditional Publishing

Traditional publishing, considered by many as the gold standard, offers the ultimate in credibility. Another company has paid the bill for your thoughts to be shared with the public.

Working with a traditional publisher involves creating a book proposal, which is a sophisticated sales piece selling your publisher on the idea of the book. You then write the book to the publisher's requirements, it goes through an editing process, and finally it's time to sell and market the book.

While working with a traditional publisher helps access to bookstores, you still have a tremendous job to promote your book. Make no mistake: this is hardly all your publisher's responsibility. The more promotion you do on an individual basis, the better your book will sell. In fact, most publishers require that you have a detailed plan explaining how you, as the author, plan to market and sell your book.

Self-Publishing

When you self-publish a book, you retain total control over your project: from the content to the cover design to how you're going to promote the book. It's your baby to do with what you want.

The trade-off for complete autonomy is that the financial burden belongs to you and you alone. Self-publishing means paying for the layout, design, cover design, printing, binding, and shipping of your book. Recent significant advances in print on-demand technology helps make self-publishing more affordable than at any point in history, but it is still fairly expensive.

Be aware that marketing the book is your responsibility. As you would with traditional publishing, spend time putting together a marketing strategy for your book.

Getting a self-published book into traditional brick-and-mortar bookstores can be challenging. However, self-publishing companies that offer distribution and fulfillment service exist, but like everything, for a price.

Make It Easy

Creating a book sounds overwhelming—and sometimes it is! If you're busy running your business, finding the hours necessary to sit down and craft a book might be impossible.

You can try, but before you know it, you'll find yourself staring at the computer screen at two o'clock in the morning, cursing yourself for having taken on such a gargantuan project.

Relax. There are a few ways to make it easier for you. Here are a couple of options to consider:

- **Embrace compilations or anthologies.** Compilation books are created by having a group of like-minded professionals each contribute an essay on a topic reflecting their particular expertise, centered around one common theme.

  You can take on the role of organizing the book, add an introduction and summary, and voilà, here's a book you can use to build both your credibility and standing within your professional network.

- **Hire a ghostwriter.** Ghostwriters work behind the scenes, putting together books for their clients for a fee. Many times, journalists and freelance writers double as ghostwriters to supplement their income.

  Each ghostwriter-client relationship is different. You'll want to interview several candidates before committing to one: you want someone who is prepared and knowledgeable about the subject matter you'll be covering, who can produce copy quickly and efficiently, and is willing to do so confidentially. Bear in mind you still have to give the ghostwriter the material to write about: from raw research to lengthy interviews, the time commitment is still pretty considerable.

Putting It All Together

Integrating print as an element of target marketing is cost-effective and powerful. Realize the maximum value of your efforts by aligning the use of print with your target marketing strategy. Here's how to use print.

As the Expert

Informative, content-heavy articles, tip sheets, booklets, and books are great. Generally, customers value an authoritative voice—"The Best Way to Do X" or "Seven Insider Secrets You Must Know About Y."

Making It Fun

Let your personality come out and have some fun in print. Quirky humor and conversational styles resonate with target markets who value fun and entertainment. Don't be afraid to have an offbeat point of view while still conveying accurate, useful information. Insider language and appealing directly to your audience is really effective here— "The Girlfriend's Guide to Picking Really Great Wine," for example.

Exclusivity

If you're adopting an exclusive strategy, you have to be very selective about where your written work appears. This is one instance where you'll be very judged by the company you keep.

So if you're an upscale business, you need to be only in upscale publications. If you're getting along by catering to an alternative target market, you need to be in alternative media—which might mean forgoing traditional newspapers, for example, in favor of more cutting-edge publications.

The Least You Need to Know

◆ Writing enhances your credibility as an expert.

◆ Make writing your friend. Start off with small, easy projects: checklists, tips, or articles.

◆ Check out opportunities to get articles into the publications your target market reads.

◆ If writing a book is an overwhelming task, consider hiring a ghostwriter to help you.

Chapter **15**

Fear-Free Media

In This Chapter

- ◆ Understanding the role of the media
- ◆ Learning to cultivate relationships
- ◆ How to look good on TV
- ◆ Finding out the essentials for radio

The media is one of the most powerful forces in our culture today. It can make or break careers, raise one company up and destroy another. The media is like the ocean, uncontrollable and overwhelming.

With careful planning and strategic thinking, you can navigate the waters of the media and establish a commercially profitable presence upon it. Like a small sailboat in a surging sea, it's possible to attain great things. You just need to work a little harder and plan things carefully to get where you want to go.

Television and radio offer a number of target marketing opportunities for the small business owner. Focusing on the local marketplace is relatively easy, cost-effective, and can generate sales and build credibility.

Not too shabby for a few minutes of screen time!

Cultivating Relationships

The media has a large presence, but it consists of a relatively small community of professionals. This is especially true on the local level, where a television station may have a staff of no more than twenty people and a radio station a fraction of that!

To break into TV or radio, you need to appeal, first and foremost, to the small community that is the media. Chronically on deadline and under a tremendous amount of pressure to please both their audiences and their advertisers, media pros place a high value on sources who have proven their reliability and are easy to work with.

There are a number of ways to start a relationship with the media: sending press releases, contacts made through networking, or doing something so incredible the media seeks you out.

Once that relationship has started and the TV or radio journalist has decided to give you a shot, do what you can to make life easy for them. Remain professional, and stay calm even if things do not go exactly as you anticipated.

Here are five guidelines to help ease your anxiety working with television:

- **Be prepared.** Be prepared for your time on TV or on the radio. Know what you want to say, and plan on more than one way to say it. Every minute matters, so get to the point quickly.

- **Don't be a prima-donna.** This is not the time to make demands of the show's producer or host. When you have won an Oscar, appeared on *Oprah*, and sold 18 million copies of your book, then you can make demands. (Even then, being a high-maintenance guest will not do great things for your career!)

- **Be friendly and engaging.** A conversational style will serve you well 99 percent of the time: few TV or radio shows favor a dry, pedantic style that runs the risk of turning the audience off.

- **Send a thank you.** After you appear on TV or on the radio, send the show's producer and host thank you cards. Its common courtesy—and it will make you stand out from the crowd.

- **Value their work.** Make a point of giving shows you have appeared on special notice when you have something newsworthy to share. Again, this is a demonstration that you value their work.

Fifteen Minutes of Fame on TV

Television is a pervasive, omnipresent force in our lives. Two thirds of American homes have more than three televisions, and on average, those TVs are on for nearly seven hours.

Cable and satellite programming is very niche-oriented, which is a real coup for the target marketer. For instance, there are at least four stations targeted at people who value their homes, home decoration, and repair: DIY Network, HGTV, Fine Living, and Discovery Home.

All of these stations need a tremendous amount of content. Running programming 24 hours a day, 7 days a week is a huge job. This is particularly true for news stations, which do not have the luxury of running reruns!

Insight

According to a Nielsen study, the average home receives 104 stations. This total includes roughly half a dozen broadcast networks, and dozens and dozens of cable or satellite stations.

Getting Booked On TV

The first thing you need to know about television is stolen directly from a bumper sticker: Think globally, act locally.

If you have never been on television before, you want to start with your local broadcast stations. Local stations are generally affiliates of larger broadcast networks (ABC, CBS, NBC, and Fox), which means they receive the majority of their programming from the parent network. Still, a small and important percentage is produced 'in-house,' and that is where your opportunities lie.

Generally, most local stations have their own news show. Many also have local business, environmental, and home shows.

Begin by getting in touch with the producer of the appropriate show, and telling them why you would be a great guest. This is called your pitch, and it is very important. You want to let them know who you are, what you have to talk about, and most important of all, why it is a great idea for them to have you on now. Relevance matters: you want to have your segment reflect issues people are thinking about right this minute.

Insight

The more often you appear on local TV, the better! Not only are you building your brand and appealing to your target market, but you are also becoming more comfortable on screen.

That means if you are a financial planner, you want to pitch "saving for college" stories right around back-to-school time, when classes start. That may not be the ideal time to start thinking about how you are going to pay for Junior's college, but it is when most people start thinking about it.

If a producer likes your pitch, they will be in touch, and you are on your way. Make sure to get a copy of your appearance: this is your demo piece you will need to show to producers of larger, national shows before they will consider booking you.

Appearing as a Guest

TV is a very visual medium. You are going to be judged based on what you look like far more than on what you have to say!

With that in mind, here is what you need to know about appearing as a guest.

Your Appearance Has to Match the Expectation

Choose your clothing, hairstyle, and accessories carefully. They need to reflect the image you want your target market to see. If you are appealing to environmentally conscious, socially progressive parents, for example, you do not want to show up in leather pants and wearing ivory bangles.

Danger Zone

Don't wear colors that clash with the studio backdrop. Also, avoid clothing with heavy patterns, as the busy pattern will distract the viewers, who will pay more attention to what you are wearing than what you are saying.

Be as attractive as you can. Not all of us are stunningly beautiful, but do the best you can with what you have. Dress neatly and keeping with the current fashion helps.

Check with the producer ahead of time for clothing recommendations. For major appearances on national television, hire a stylist. It will be well worth it.

Be Engaging

Watch the show before you appear on it! Pay attention to how the host interacts with the guests. You will want to echo that style: if a show is chatty and conversational, à la Regis and Kelly, you want to be able to banter with the best of them. On the other hand, if a show has a more formal feel, with a host asking questions of an expert guest, you want to be prepared to convey a lot of information in a semiformal setting.

Entertain

TV audiences love stories and examples to illustrate your point. Because television is a visual medium, consider using physical examples of what you are talking about. For example, it is one thing to discuss the perfect purse for the office—and another entirely to show that purse!

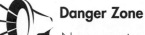

Danger Zone

Never surprise a show's host or producer with a demonstration, prop, or example. Clear *everything* ahead of time: surprises are not a good idea!

Having Your Own Show

If you discover that you are great on television and that you are reaching your target market effectively on the small screen, you may want to consider having your own show.

This is a substantial commitment. However, many local TV stations and public access stations have a strong commitment to locally produced content. The opportunity may be there, and it is well worth exploring.

On Target

Dave Ratner, of Dave's Soda & Pet City, a four-store chain in Massachusetts, for years has hosted a show *Dave's Pet Show* on the local ABC affiliate. It draws a pretty doggone loyal viewership. They have even beaten Letterman, on occasion!

Putting It All Together

Target marketing on television means remaining mindful of the target marketing strategy you have chosen. Your appearance needs to be consistent with your branding.

Here is what that means for each strategy.

As the Expert

Television abounds with opportunities for experts. If this is the strategy you have chosen, focus on appearances that will allow you to showcase your knowledge. Roundtable discussion shows (common on some PBS stations) are great for this, as are local news shows.

Making It Fun

Bringing the fun to television sometimes happens spontaneously: if you are having a fun and newsworthy event at your business, perhaps the local network will cover it.

You can interject humor and a light element into most television appearances. Point out the lighter side of what you are talking about (even if it is pet grooming: there is humor in hairballs!)

Exclusivity

Exclusivity is the hardest concept to convey on television: you are using a mass-market media to market to people who do not want to be part of the mass market.

However, you can capitalize on your exclusive appeal by appearing on "The Best of …" type of shows. Oprah Winfrey's "My Favorite Things" shows raise exclusivity to an art form: while she showcases a few affordable options on occasion, there are many profiles of fabulous merchandise most mere mortals cannot even afford to look at.

Did You See Me on the Radio?

Radio is going through a renaissance. A medium recently thought to be dying has made a surprising comeback, largely by adopting new technology. That is great news for target marketers, who now have a wider range of options to explore.

Radio comes in three flavors now: There is conventional radio, with the AM and FM stations we all grew up listening to. There is streaming or Internet radio, in which content is delivered via the web and listened to through a computer's sound system. Finally, there is satellite radio, in which a digital signal is transmitted via satellite to the listener's receiver.

Each format has its own unique set of advantages and disadvantages, as well as its own potential for effective use in target marketing.

Conventional Radio

Nearly three quarters of people who listen to the radio everyday listen to conventional radio. They average 80 minutes a day, much of this time in their car.

Here are some advantages of conventional radio:

♦ It's familiar to most people: 247 million people in the United States report listening to conventional radio.

♦ It's free to listen to.

♦ Its wide range of station choices and formats allows some measure of target marketing—because country music listeners tend to have different motivations, demographics, and psychographics than hip-hop listeners.

♦ It's available almost everywhere.

Here are some disadvantages:

♦ Conventional radio listening rates are on the decline.

♦ Its geographically limited format: a station's range is limited by the strength of its signal.

The potential of traditional broadcast radio for target marketing is limited. While stations do offer some kind of rough targeting by varying the types of music they play and the format they follow, there are generally not many choices. You may have a rock station, a country station, an alternative station, and a pop music station in one area, but seldom more than one or two of each flavor.

 Insight

Public radio is steadily gaining in popularity, and has a well-defined (and potentially hugely profitable) target audience. Appearing on public radio can build credibility and help you start forming a relationship with your target market.

Streaming or Internet Radio

Internet radio is the new kid on the block, having snuck onto the media scene in the past few years. A combination of conventional stations streaming their traditional analog signal broadcast online and stations that never bothered with traditional broadcasting, Internet radio is steadily growing. Most listeners to Internet and streaming radio are between the ages of 25 and 54. Prime listening times, not surprising, are during traditional office hours. People listen to streaming radio at work.

Here are the advantages of Internet radio:

♦ It has a wide geographic reach: the signal goes wherever the Internet does.

♦ Its self-selecting target audiences. Audiences listen to Internet stations because that is what they want, not because that is what is available.

♦ It's generally free to listen to.

♦ More talk-formats on Internet radio, which means a larger need for guests!

Here are the disadvantages:

♦ It's not as well known as traditional radio.

♦ Your listeners can be all over the world—which means if you are offering products and services of a local nature, people outside of your area will not be likely to use/purchase your services even if they like what you have to say.

The potential for using Internet radio for target marketing is surprisingly high. Given both the prevalence of talk shows on streaming radio and the fact that listeners have the whole of the internet to search for exactly the right radio station, if you select opportunities carefully, you can talk at length to an audience predisposed to hear you.

If you are appearing on a conventional radio station that streams its content, you are getting an added bonus from your appearance!

Satellite Radio

Satellite radio may be the target marketer's perfect tool. The large number of highly targeted stations (Sirius radio boasts 198 stations as of this writing, including both The Catholic Channel and The Playboy Channel) means you can position yourself directly in front of listeners who will be interested in the products and services you offer.

Additionally, satellite radio offers highly niched content: if you are concentrating on a small, well-defined target market, satellite radio may be the only outlet that affords you the chance to reach your audience.

Here are the advantages of satellite radio:

♦ It's rapidly gaining in popularity.

♦ It comes preloaded in some cars and electronic devices.

- Its wide range of highly individualized stations allows for highly effective target marketing.

- It's favored by higher income consumers.

Here are the disadvantages:

- Compared to both conventional and streaming radio, satellite radio has the smallest number of listeners.

- Listeners have to pay to access satellite radio content.

The potential for target marketing is good, and getting better. Satellite radio has a relatively small market share now, but this is changing as the public adopts the technology. The highly defined nature of the stations makes target marketing a snap.

Appearing as a Guest

When a radio journalist contacts you for an interview or a producer asks you to appear on a show, it is time to do your homework.

The first thing you want to know (before you agree to appear!) is the name of the station and what show you are being contacted for. Get the host's name, and then do your research. You want to know as much as possible about the show and the host before you agree.

You also want to know about the station's listeners. Who are they, and where are they from? What challenges are they facing and why do they turn to this station for answers?

The more you know about a station's guests, the better you will be able to talk about what is important to them. Remember, this may be the audience's first encounter with you and your company. You want to come across in a positive way.

Know Your Material

Keep on point during an interview, and know what you are talking about. Radio listeners, especially those who listen to talk radio, tend to be fact-driven. They value accuracy and will want verification of your statements. If you use statistics, tell the listeners where those numbers come from.

Stand Your Ground

Some radio shows thrive on conflict. Whether it is a polite but heated discussion among booksellers about Shakespeare's writing, or a down and dirty free-for-all about local politics, with image consultants weighing in, audience's love to see the sparks fly.

This atmosphere draws many listeners, but it is easy to misstep and look foolish. If you go on a confrontational show, it is essential you hold your ground regarding your position. Appearing to change position will diminish the value of your brand. At the same time, you do not want to lose your temper.

Be Current

Radio is driven by current events. Even if your business is not topical, you will want to find some way to tie your commentary and thoughts to the events of the day.

The very best example of this I have ever seen was a wedding planner who was able to explain how a series of tropical storms might affect floral choices available to brides.

Speak in Sound Bites

Radio is a fast-paced medium; you do not have time for long, detailed explanations. Speak in brief, content-rich bursts. That way, no matter when listeners tune in, they will hear you saying something of real value.

Have a Call to Action

What do you want listeners to do after they have heard you on the radio? Do you want them to visit your website, call a toll-free number, buy your book? Whatever your objective is, you want to create an easy way for listeners to move toward it.

> **Danger Zone**
>
> Do not overdo the sales pitch! Appearing on a radio show as a guest is a brand-building opportunity. You need to be subtle. Certainly encourage people to seek out your business, but don't hit them over the head with promotional offers.

If you can, structure your interview to engage listeners early and often. Tell them "You'll want to write this down!" For maximum effect, you may want to consider making a free offer. For example, "E-mail me at (your web address) for a copy of a special report." They will already have a pen or pencil in hand due to your earlier prompting.

Also, always ask the host if listeners can call the station or access the station's website for your contact information. If they can, that is an added plus—make sure to mention it!

Be Prepared

Have everything you need or might potentially need on hand before you start the interview. This includes a glass of water, a single sheet of talking points, and a pad of paper and pencil to make notes if you need to. This last point is especially critical if you are taking listener calls during the segment—you will want to make note of the caller's name so you can use it during your response. Additionally, create a sheet detailing who you are talking to, what you are talking about, and where the station is located.

Most radio interviews take place over the phone. A few take place in the studio, but those are the vast minority. So before you call in, make sure you are in a location that is quiet and free from interruptions. You will sound better if you stand up while speaking. Do not forget to shut off your cell phone, other lines, and other electronics—they always ring at the wrong time!

Hello, Caller: Having Your Own Show

Regular appearances on radio shows, particularly call-in shows, can lead to a show of your own. Radio listeners are a particularly loyal bunch: if they like what they hear, they are not shy about letting the station know.

On Target
Dr. Patricia Raymond combines humor and knowledge of gastroenterology (her medical specialty). Her wry, insightful commentary on health was a big hit on her local public radio station, and now she's the host of NPR's phenomenally popular program, *House Calls*.

Putting It All Together

No matter what type of radio show you appear on, you need to remain true to your marketing strategy. Here is how to capitalize on radio, if your strategy is one of the following.

As the Expert

Experts shine on radio. Seek out call-in shows, where you can respond to listener's questions. Lengthy interviews also work very well, as they illustrate the depth of your knowledge.

Making It Fun

To make radio fun, you need to be very selective about your appearances. Seek out those hosts and shows that will give you the latitude to let the fun side out. Fun and humor also do really well at drive time, when listeners want to tune in to something that makes the drive go by more quickly—but nothing too, too heavy.

Exclusivity

Exclusivity works phenomenally well on radio, particularly Internet radio and satellite radio. Limit your appearances to the very best station for your target market. You want to appear as a trendsetter!

The Least You Need to Know

◆ Preparation is the key to your success for TV or radio appearances.

◆ Talk in sound bites and have a call to action when interviewed.

◆ Relevance matters. Make sure you reflect issues listeners or viewers are currently concerned about.

◆ Think globally; act locally!

Chapter **16**

The Different Faces of Advertising

In This Chapter

◆ Understanding the smart way to advertise

◆ Recognizing the multiple advertising options available

◆ Choosing the right advertising medium

◆ Applying targeted advertising strategies that work

Sometimes you have to spend money to make money. That is the concept behind advertising: guaranteed placement and exposure in order to capture your target audience's attention.

Advertising has a bad reputation, and that is frankly because there is so much of it—and much of it stinks. However, few small businesses can survive without mounting some form of advertising campaign. The trick is to keep your advertising efforts in perspective: they should form a part of your overall marketing and promotion strategy, not the entirety of it!

Being a Smart Advertiser

Half of all advertising works. The trick is to know which half.

Considering the cost, that sentiment should make your skin crawl! Advertising is a powerful and established tool in the marketing arsenal, but most small business owners do not know how to make advertising work well for them. As a result, they place ads here, there, and everywhere, hoping beyond hope that something will work.

There are two approaches to advertising: you can use a broad, mass-market approach, trying to reach everyone and anyone; or you identify a target audience, learn where they congregate, and reach them there.

The first method is very expensive. The second method has the benefit of being highly cost-effective, capable of driving sales, and building brand awareness. Which one would you choose?

Key Concepts for Smart Advertising

There are three key concepts that will help make you a smart advertiser.

Letting the Message Lead

To create the best advertising, decide first on what message you want to convey to your target audience. Identify your offer and your call to action—what you'd like your customers to do. Then, and only then, begin the design process. You want to have a clear concept in mind before you start talking to an ad representative. Too often, small business owners are responsive to an ad rep's pressure to buy space. That's backward! Begin with the message.

Danger Zone

Just because your target audience congregates in one area, such as a social networking site or blog, does not mean they want to see advertising there.

Choosing the Right Medium

To be an effective target market advertiser, you have to know where to find your target market. More important, you have to understand how they view advertising in that medium.

Survey your customers. Ask them what magazines they read, what newspapers they read, and what social networking sites they hang out on. This is where you need to be advertising!

Insight _____

A strong target audience of upscale, literary, eclectic professionals gathers on the social networking/blogging site LiveJournal—but when Six Apart, the parent company, decided to start hosting advertising on the site, the cognoscenti were not amused. There was a loud, impassioned backlash against the ads, which destroyed any hopes the advertisers had with connecting with their target audience.

Measuring Results

Every single time you conduct an advertising campaign, you want to measure the results objectively and quantifiably. This will help you judge if the money you have spent is a wise decision or if you need to try another method.

Ways to measure your advertising results include these:

Insight _____

At the heart of all advertising is the ability to deliver what you promise your clients. No matter how clever or memorable your marketing is, if you fail to deliver on that promise, you will fail.

- ◆ Include a code or keyword customers need to use when ordering your products or services.

- ◆ Use coupons in your advertising. Track how many are redeemed.

- ◆ Compare sales numbers before and after you begin an advertising campaign.

Targeted Advertising in Print

There are endless opportunities to advertise in print. Newspapers, magazines, and direct mail all utilize the power of print to capture customer attention, drive traffic, and deliver sales.

However, perhaps because print is the oldest and most established advertising medium, it is also the most crowded. It is hard to create a print ad that will stand out from every other solicitation on the page.

Each form of print media requires a unique target marketing strategy. Here is how to best approach target advertising in newspapers and magazines.

Newspapers

Newspapers, once the go-to source for all of the day's vital information, are declining slowly and steadily. While most major papers still produce a paper edition, many of them now complement it with a web-based edition. The day when newspapers only have a virtual existence is fast approaching.

Insight

Newspaper readership is strongest among people over the age of 35. Hartford, Connecticut, Cleveland, Ohio, and New York, New York have the highest percentage of daily newspaper readers. High income and older people read the newspaper most regularly.

Danger Zone

Forego "business card" or "holiday celebration" pages, where you can buy an approximately 2"×3" space in a whole page ad. They are seldom effective unless they are incredibly focused, for example, "Everything you need for Prom."

That said, some target audiences still read the newspaper faithfully on a daily basis. Additionally, alternative papers, catering to specific target audiences within a community, tend to have fanatically loyal readerships.

If your audience reads the newspaper, either traditional or alternative, then you will want to explore print advertising opportunities. Further, refine your campaign by pinpointing the page or section within the paper you want to advertise.

Small two- or three-line classified ads are a very affordable way to maintain a consistent level of visibility in the community. Rick Segel, a retail expert and proprietor of The Retailer's Advantage, advocates what he calls a specialty ad: the name of your business, your tag line, and your phone number.

When you commit to a newspaper campaign, always ask how much it will cost to have your ad also run on the newspaper's website. Sometimes you can get more exposure by negotiating a multiplatform package deal.

Magazines

At the time of writing, magazine publishers are currently waging an aggressive campaign to prove that advertising within their glossy covers is actually worth the expense. Considering the top-flight prices of an ad in a national publication, they have their work cut out for them.

However, certain target markets are very responsive to magazine advertising. Bridal and special-occasion dresses, for example, have long been marketed very effectively in publications like *Bride's Magazine*, *Elegant Bride*, and *Modern Bride*.

National publications often produce zoned editions, distributed to a specific state or region. Advertising in the appropriate zone is often markedly more affordable than placing an ad in the nationwide edition. Another way to get exposure in a national publication without the full cost of an ad is to buy in to a listing ad. This is where manufacturers partner with a group of retailers to highlight a product. Store owners "buy in" to the opportunity to have their store information listed on an advertisement with the featured product, generally under the heading "Available at these fine retailers …."

Insight

Advertorials, in which an advertisement masquerades as editorial coverage, have been used successfully by some small businesses who capitalize on the credibility-enhancing aspects of these ads. Other consumers resent the implied deceit in the medium. Proceed with caution!

Direct Mail

Direct mail is print advertising sent specifically to either your existing customer base or in an effort to attract new customers. We devote quite a bit of time to reaching your existing customers via direct mail in Chapter 20. Here, we focus on what is a very effective strategy for some small business owners.

Valpak and other specialized direct mail companies send envelopes containing multiple direct mail pieces, generally including coupons, to highly targeted groups of people.

Individual businesses can "buy in" to the Valpak concept and have their coupons distributed. Whether this is a good strategy for you comes down largely to your target audience. If your target marketing includes the middle- to high-income bracket, largely female, within specified zip codes, a Valpak could work very well for you.

The trick is to design a very careful type of offer for this type of campaign. Valpaks are often used to introduce a new customer to your business; design an offer that will entice customers to come in and see what you have to offer. However, these campaigns can attract "cherry picker" customers who will come to see you to redeem the offer and never return. That is a cost of this type of advertising.

Targeted Advertising on TV

Americans watch a lot of television. Two thirds of homes in the United States have more than three sets, and on average, they are on for seven hours every single day.

Many small business owners never explore the idea of television advertising, based on the assumption that it is too expensive. That is not necessarily true. While prime-time high-profile commercial slots, such as those aired during the Super Bowl, cost hundreds of thousands of dollars, the vast majority of commercial time is far more affordable, especially if you know how to locate the bargains.

What Are the Options?

Television advertising comes in two varieties: broadcast television and cable.

Broadcast television—which includes the stations in the ABC, NBC, CBS, and FOX networks—offers limited advertising opportunities to the small business owner.

These stations broadcast over a wide geographic area. The reach of some stations covers several states! If you have a destination business, where your target audience is willing to travel a substantial distance to reach you, this might offer some appeal. The majority of retailers and service providers are not in this situation.

Insight

Advertising research tells us that customers are only willing to travel between five to seven miles to reach a business.

Every local TV station sells commercial time in its own unique way. However, it is a safe bet that the very best spots, during the most popular shows, are already taken—sold on the network level to national accounts.

What's left? More important, what's left that would be of interest to the target marketer?

Investigate the possibility of advertising during local news shows. These are often the most heavily watched programming on any local broadcast station, followed closely by any shows focusing on local business or sporting events.

Cable television is often much more appealing to the small business owner interested in target marketing. The wide range of stations makes it easier to position your ad in front of an audience already predisposed to be interested in your products and services. If you sell fine kitchenware, for example, you can advertise on Food Network, Fine Living, or even the Green Network. Take the target marketing even further by having your ads run during the shows most favored by your target audience. You will be pleasantly surprised to find that the rate for these slots is often much lower than you would find on broadcast television.

Buying Television Time

You cannot just call up your local network and order six 30-second commercial spots—at least not if you don't want to pay top dollar for the privilege on being on TV.

The first thing you want to do is to acquaint yourself with the station's sales rep. If you are completely unsure of what you are doing, you may want to work with a *media buyer*.

Have a media-buying strategy. Often when you commit to multiple showings of your commercial, the cost of commercial time is lower per airing.

Commercials work best when they are repeated regularly. Savvy small business owners advocate buying multiple commercial slots to run during a short period, for example, for one to three days, and then repeating the cycle each month.

def•i•ni•tion

A **media buyer** connects clients with television time, advocating for the best price and advising clients how to make the best use of it.

Insight

Media buyers tend to be independent contractors who are often loosely affiliated with a television station. Google "media buyer" plus your location or the largest city near you. For example, "media buyer + Plattsburgh " returns eight results.

Creating Targeted TV Ads

The technical side of creating television advertising is well beyond the scope of this book. Instead, focus on finding a skilled professional production team to work with. You want affordable professionals with a proven track record of producing top-notch, effective commercials.

Ways to locate this team includes asking at your local television station or ad agency. Additionally, call the businesses whose commercials you admire and ask them who produced their ads. Many times, they will be happy to point you in the right direction and share their contacts.

Let the professionals handle the technical side of things. It is up to you to come up with the concept—the idea that makes a great targeted TV ad. If you hire an advertising agency to work with you on this project, this is where you would tap into their genius and creativity.

How to Create a Great Targeted TV Commercial

For a television ad to be effective, people have to watch and remember it. In order for people to watch your ad, it has to be interesting. Think about your favorite TV commercials. Chances are they are …

- ◆ Funny.

- ◆ Hit a nerve.

- ◆ Tell you how to solve a problem.

Ideally, your commercial will do one or more of these three things. Humor is essential, because it attracts attention and gets customers talking. However, your target audience will be far more likely to buy from you when you present a solution to a common problem they experience.

On Target
H&R Block helped potential customers solve a problem with their "Ask the Box" campaign. In these commercials, a man faces his tax return with evident frustration on his face. His wife holds up the tax preparation software they are using and tells him to ask the box about the problems he is having with the return. This commercial works because it addresses a common concern customers have about tax preparation—What are they going to do if they have a problem?

Keeping It Simple

An average television ad runs for 10 to 15 seconds. TV viewers' shrinking attention span often makes a 30-second spot wasteful and unnecessary. In addition, the high cost of advertising makes it prohibitive for the small businesses.

Short ads force you to focus on a single concept. One ad, one idea is a good rule of thumb. When you try to cram too much into your messaging, you will have an ad that is jumbled and confusing. Remember, less is more!

Repetition Is Required

If you cannot afford to run your broadcast television ad often, then don't run it at all. This is one area where quantity counts. The average adult needs to hear or see your message six or more times before he remembers it.

Targeted Advertising on the Radio

Targeted radio advertising is very similar to targeted television advertising, with a few notable differences.

First and foremost, radio is markedly more affordable. Most major markets have multiple conventional radio stations, which leads to competitive pricing. Additionally, the cost of producing radio advertising is much lower than the cost of creating television advertising.

Conventional radio allows some limited targeting: you can opt to run your ads on country music stations, hip-hop stations, classical music stations, talk radio stations, and more. Each option draws a different core group of listeners. Referencing the demographic characteristics of a station's listeners enables you to pinpoint your target market.

Satellite and streaming radio offer a greater ability to target market. These stations are far more niche-oriented. However, they do have a broader geographic range, which limits their usefulness as a target marketing tool if you are focused on a local market. There is not much point telling customers halfway around the world about your services when you want to attract customers to your Main Street location.

Three Keys to Great Targeted Radio Advertising

Radio is a very intimate medium. You are talking directly to your target audience: your voice (or the voice of the actor you hire to read your copy!) is sliding directly into the listener's ear. There are three key factors you need to concentrate on when crafting your targeted advertising.

Personality

Today's customers value the relationship they have with the organizations they do business with. When customers hear your voice every morning on the radio while they drive to work, they begin to feel that they know you.

Use the intimate platform of radio to share elements of your company's personality. If you are upbeat and goofy, let that show. If you are elegant and upscale, let that show. Careful language choices, tone of voice, and background music and effects can all help the listener get to know who you are and build a desired relationship.

Frequency

People who listen to the radio listen to the radio habitually. Tuning in to their favorite shows is part of the daily routine. Capitalize on the familiar routine listeners enjoy by becoming part of the programming on a regular basis.

Successful radio campaigns hinge on how often the ads run. A great ad that only runs once is useless. Save your money!

However, a good ad that runs regularly and becomes part of the customer's consciousness motivates her to buy.

Consistency

Your radio advertising needs to be consistent with your business's branding efforts. The best radio ads use the magic of language to create a mental image, an image your customers believe in and become invested in. When they seek you out, complete with this sense of expectation, you had better deliver the experience they are looking for!

Targeted Advertising Online

There are good online ads and there are horrible online ads. Some online advertising tactics—such as pop-up ads, animated ads, ads that have no obvious way to close, ads that block content, and ads that spontaneously start playing music—have become almost universally hated.

There are other effective, strategic forms of online advertising for target marketers to use. These options include banner advertising, pay-per-click campaigns, and *unicast ads*.

def•i•ni•tion

Unicast ads are short video clips played in a browser window that offer viewers the chance to click through for more information.

From a target marketing perspective, one of the best online advertising options is contextual ads. Contextual ads display advertising on content-heavy sites based upon the copy shown in the page. Because these ads are relevant and concretely related to the text on the website the viewer chose to seek out, they have a greater click-through and conversion rate than any other type of online advertising. This means that more people actually read, click on, and buy based on these types of ads.

Targeted Yellow Pages Advertising

The Yellow Pages present a unique challenge for the target marketer. These directories, listing the telephone number, address, and increasingly, websites of businesses, are wholly unlike any other advertising medium.

Not every business needs to advertise in the Yellow Pages. How do you determine if you should? It comes down to one question: do you sell products and services that people want, or do you sell products and services that people need?

Yellow Pages use has steadily been declining, with the exception of one key consideration. It is often the first resource customers turn to when they need a business to fill a specific need that does not occur regularly.

That is why the top five Yellow Pages categories are attorneys, physicians, insurance companies, dentists, and plumbers. These are all service providers who provide services that most people do not seek out just for the fun of it. They need them at a very specific point in time—when there is a problem that needs solving.

If you are a service provider of this type, you absolutely, positively need to be in the

Yellow Pages. That is where your customers look for you. Otherwise, Yellow Pages advertising may not be the wisest use of your money.

The only other exception to this rule: restaurants!

Creating a Yellow Pages Ad

Creating targeted Yellow Pages advertising is a multistep process. Through this entire process, make sure you are keeping your target market in mind. You want your ad to do more than catch their eye. You want it to convince them that your business, among all the service providers listed in that category, is the right one to call. Here is a three-step process to follow.

Step 1: Choose the Right Directory

Depending on where your business is located, you may have more than one Yellow Pages option to select from. Small and rural communities generally have one guide, while the larger cities have several. There are also niched Yellow Pages, geared to the specific segments of the community. Some cities have Yellow Pages specifically for women, for business owners, and for ethnic and cultural groups.

When selecting a Yellow Pages directory, you will want to pick the one that attracts the largest number of people in your target audience. With that said, pay careful attention to circulation numbers and reputation. It is a good idea to be in the directory people in your community are actually using.

Pay special attention to the geographic regions covered in a directory. If all of your customers live in one neighborhood but would visit your business in another location, such as the community they work in, it behooves you to appear in both guides.

Step 2: Determine Categories

All of the listings in a Yellow Pages guide are arranged in categories. Each category will have a heading, such as Insurance. It may also have subheadings, such as Insurance-Automobile, Insurance-Health, Insurance-Life, and so on.

Most small businesses will only need to appear under one heading. Choose your heading based on the answer to this question: where will your customers be most likely to look for you?

Step 3: Create Your Ad

There are three types of Yellow Pages ads. Listings are just that, listings of your business name and phone number. Space ads are slightly larger, offering additional information including your address, website, and perhaps a motto or tagline. Display ads are very similar to display ads in the newspaper. They allow you more space for more information and graphics. Remember when advertising, the powerful maxim "A picture paints a thousand words."

Danger Zone

Before placing your ad, ask your customers and prospects in which sections they would look to find your type of services. Because these guides appear annually, you must wait 12 months before you can change a wrong position.

When creating your Yellow Pages ad, focus on two elements: provide all essential contact information, and answer the most common questions your target audience would likely have.

For example, a home heating oil company might list the following information in their ad:

Home, Farm, Business

This answers the question, "Where do you deliver to?"

Fuel Oil, Gasoline, Kerosene, Diesel Fuel

This answers the question, "What types of fuel do you have available?"

Cash Discounts, Budget Plans, Automatic Delivery

This helps answer the question, "How am I going to pay for this?"

Insight

Use display ads in directories that appeal to the majority of your target audience. Space ads and listings are good options only if you are advertising in a directory in a secondary market.

24-hour burner service, 24-hour emergency service

This answers the question, "What do I do about the fact that my furnace isn't working?"

Targeted Advertising: Signage

Signs are an often-overlooked advertising tool, yet good signage can be a very effective target marketing tool. Signs not only identify your business; they also communicate what you do and a fair amount about how you do it, in just a matter of seconds.

A great sign can convey your company's personality to the public. If you are one of many businesses of a similar type in a crowded location—one more restaurant along a popular avenue, for example, or one more T-shirt shop on the boardwalk—you need a sign out there to let the public know why you are different, and why you are the right choice for them.

Off-site signs, displayed away from your business premises, can be extraordinarily effective at driving traffic to out-of-the-way, difficult locations.

Putting It All Together

No matter what advertising format you select, it needs to be consistent with and reinforce your target marketing strategy. Nothing can kill a company quicker than dissonance: if the experience the customer has does not meet the expectations the advertising creates, you are doomed. Here is how to avoid that.

As the Expert

Use advertising that highlights your organization as the source for the best knowledge, the best insight, and the best guidance. Copy-heavy ads work well with this strategy, as well as checklist and "what you need to know" approaches.

Making It Fun

Humor, quirky graphics, and insider humor can do a lot to help you capitalize on targeted advertising. Be careful not to be too self-referential to avoid making anyone feel dumb for "not getting it."

Exclusivity

Make a point of using the language, symbols, and graphics that will resonate strongly with your target audience and create an "insider" feel. Phrases like "Only the best" and "It's not for everyone" appeal strongly to target markets that value exclusivity.

The Least You Need to Know

◆ Find the right advertising medium to connect with your target market.

◆ Make sure that you develop a clear, concise message.

◆ The key to advertising success is simplicity and repetition.

◆ When in doubt, ask your customers for their help and advice.

Tooting Your Own Horn

In This Chapter

♦ The scope and nature of public relations

♦ PR as a lifestyle choice

♦ Do-It-Yourself PR strategies every small business owner can use

♦ Public relation's role as damage control

Your biggest competitor, Joe Jones, is smiling out from the newspaper's front page this morning. Another colleague is on the news, pontificating on the five best ways your customers could save money and enjoy greater personal joy. A third is a guest blogging on the most popular blog on the web. And here you are, wondering how they all did it.

It boils down to two simple words: public relations. The media doesn't wake up one morning and say, "Hey, today I'm going to go interview Joe Jones because I picked his name at random out of the phone book."

They interview Joe Jones because Joe Jones made a deliberate strategic decision that he wanted to be interviewed. He set about letting the press know he was there and what he was good at talking about, and, most important of all, he made himself available.

It's called public relations, and you can do exactly what Joe's doing. In this chapter, we're going to tell you how.

Understanding Public Relations

Let's start off with some definitions. What is public relations? It's a simple question that can have a really complex answer, depending on who you talk to. For our purposes, public relations is the art of attracting the attention of people at large (hence the "public" part of the equation) and focusing it on your business.

In short, you want your business thrust into the spotlight, the center of attention, the star of the show. The spotlight can be harsh; a big part of public relations is making sure your company presents itself in the most favorable light possible! You want to look good for your public!

There are a number of ways to attract attention, but the most efficient way to put your business in front of numerous eyes all at once is to work with the media. Getting coverage in newspapers, magazines, and other publications increases your visibility and enhances your credibility. Appearing on television, radio, or web shows drives the same effect. If you want help with this, seek out *booking* or *media agents*. Their extensive media experience will help make this minefield easier for you to navigate. However, if you go this route, expect to pay big bucks!

There are countless public relations professionals out there who are ready and able to help you position your company in the public eye. They often do a great job—at a great price! Good PR is expensive.

def•i•ni•tion

> **Booking agents** or **media agents** are public relations professionals who specialize in getting their clients placed in the media. Generally, they focus on TV and radio appearances.

At the same time, it is difficult to exactly measure the results of a public relations campaign. Long-time target marketers say, "With advertising you pay, and with PR you pray!"—a sentiment that speaks directly to the uncertainty inherent in the nature of public relations.

After all, you can have the best story ideas in the world. You could be the ideal talk show guest. You might even have the perfect combination of style, sass, and stuff that makes Oprah's staff perk up their ears … but if the timing's not right, no one's going to pay any attention.

That's why many small business owners opt to do their own PR. This is a great idea—if you're willing to accept that public relations does require a substantial amount of time. It's not a cash-intense option, but the nuts-and-bolts work of public relations— cultivating relationships, drafting press releases, making media appearances—takes time.

Insight

Public relations is an ongoing process. Plan on committing to a continual effort of promoting your business at every opportunity for maximum results.

Integrating Public Relations and Target Marketing

Public relations shines as a target marketing tool. All the work you've done identifying your customers is essential to your public relations efforts.

Among the information you've gathered is media consumption patterns. You know what publications your customers like to read, what websites they visit, what shows they watch, and more.

Consider this list your PR to-do list. The more often you appear in the media that's important to your target audience, the more important, prominent, and successful you're going to appear. The majority of customers like to do business with companies that appear to be successful and established, so chances are great that you will increase sales of your products and services with a high-profile media presence.

Creating a Media List

A media list is a comprehensive, personalized directory of media professionals who interact with your target audience. On this list, you'll find the names of reporters who write the stories your customers talk about, the anchors who host the news segments your customers watch, the bloggers who your customers read every single day, and the publishers who put out the magazines your customers subscribe to.

It sounds great, doesn't it? There's only one drawback to a media list, and that's the fact that *you* have to create it.

Public relations is a relationship-driven practice: the more people you know, and the stronger the relationship you have with them, the better you'll do.

Here's how to create your media list.

Step One: Compile a list of target venues. On this list, you want to include every publication your target audience reads, every show they watch, every radio station they listen to, every website they follow.

Step Two: Identify what you want from each venue. Would you like to be interviewed? Appear as a guest blogger? Introduce handy tips during the local news? Designate a goal for each venue on your list—it's okay if you have the same goal (e.g., to be quoted in an interview) for several venues.

Step Three: Pinpoint the contact person. Each venue will have its own contact person. Newspapers have reporters and editors, television and radio shows have producers, and websites have bloggers or hosts.

Step Four: Locate contact information for this person. This isn't as hard as it sounds. Many newspapers and publications have a "Have a Story Idea" section, with information on how to contact the appropriate department. Failing that, look for an editorial or submissions blurb, often found on the publication's website.

To identify the contact person for a radio or TV show, the easiest route is to go to the show's website. There is often a "Want to Appear on the Show" tab, with contact information. If you can't find that, look for the "Contact Us" button and send an e-mail detailing why you'd like to be a guest on the show. Remember to focus on what the show's audience would gain from seeing you—not what being on the show would do for you!

To contact a blogger or website host, look for a contact tab, and get in touch via e-mail.

Danger Zone

A media list is a dynamic document. Media professionals change jobs often, so you should update your information at least once a quarter. You don't want to waste time and energy contacting people who aren't there!

Step Five: Contact people as you have stories to tell. Your media list is like any other tool: it only helps you when you use it! Use your media list as a starting point for cultivating relationships. Contact people when you have a story idea, when you're holding an event or have won an award, or when you have relevant commentary to offer on the news of the day.

You also want to use your contact list to send thank-you notes after you've appeared in the media. A little bit of graciousness and appreciation goes a long way to establishing strong working relationships.

What Is the Media Looking For?

It's a lot easier to establish a good relationship with the media when you know what they want from you. It goes without saying that not every media pro is the same: what's critically important to one might not matter at all to another. With that in mind, there are a few things that strike a cord with every media professional out there. Here's what they are.

A Good Story. The media is in the story-telling business. If you want to be covered, you need to have a story to tell. Before you contact the media, ask yourself: "What's my story?"

The main characteristics of a good story are that it's unusual, engaging, and has a human angle. For example, the fact that your security company offers protection for barns is not a story. The fact that your security company, in the course of performing normal barn-protecting duties, stopped a valuable racehorse from being stolen hours before the big race? Now, that's a *newsworthy* story!

The essential elements of a story can be broken down into six questions:

- ◆ What happened?
- ◆ When did it happen?
- ◆ Where did it happen?
- ◆ Why did it happen?
- ◆ Who did it happen to?
- ◆ How did it happen?

Make sure you have answers to all of these questions!

A "local" angle. A "local" angle is a nice way to say, "Who cares?" A story has to be likely to interest the venue's customers—readers, viewers, or listeners—in order to get some coverage. You must be able to articulate why your contact's customers are going to care about this story.

def•i•ni•tion

Newsworthy is the term the media uses when "something's important enough to report." This standard changes publication by publication, medium by medium. For example, creating a contest might land you on the front page of the local paper but is unlikely to merit a line in *The Wall Street Journal*.

Ease of access. Make it easy for the media to contact you! Always, always, always provide your contact information. Include your phone number and e-mail address. Never assume that your contact has this information—they don't. Answer your phone. Return e-mails promptly. The easier you are to contact, the more often you'll be contacted!

Dependability. Provide verifiable information. Be honest. If you use stats and numbers, tell the reporter where they come from. A good media professional will fact-check everything you say, but frankly, most don't take the time. That being said, if you're supplying erroneous, off-the-wall information, no one's going to call you for a second interview.

Graphics. A 1,000-word story is great. A 1,000-word story with pictures is even better!

Get in the practice of collecting high-resolution digital images of your business. The best images are full of action: crowds in your store, an agent working with a customer on the details of the person's policy. Focus on the real, everyday aspect of your business, rather than formal, posed, head-and-shoulders shots—boring!

If you take a picture of your customer and you want to use it for promotional purposes, get her permission. This is especially important if your customers are children—you need parental consent to use those images.

The Perfect Press Kit

Press kits are packets of information designed to help reporters learn about your organization in the most efficient way possible.

A press kit can be a tangible paper product, filled with photos, fact sheets, and a company history. Post this same information online on your website—increasingly the presentation of choice for busy reporters.

def•i•ni•tion

A **news release, media release, press release,** or **press statement** is a written or recorded communication directed at members of the news media to broadcast something claimed as having news value.

Each organization's press kit differs slightly, but most contain at least some of the following elements:

- Company background sheet
- Copy of the most recent *press/news release*
- Fact sheets/statistical information/sales data
- Images, including one of your business logo
- Contact information

Public Relations as a Lifestyle

As you read through the rest of this chapter, there's one thing to keep in mind. Small business owners who benefit the most from public relations commit to using it as the major tool in their marketing and advertising arsenal. They make public relations part of their lifestyle. You've met these people. They're the ones who, in the course of a two-minute chance conversation at the grocery store, can suss out who you are, tell you what they do, and suggest a way that the two of you should consider working together in the future. It seems to come effortlessly to them. They manage to let everyone in town know about their business without talking about it to the extent that everyone starts running in the opposite direction when they approach.

As much as I'd like to say there's a quick and easy way to master this type of lifestyle public relations, there's only one route to success—and that route requires patience. Practice talking about your business in everyday conversation until it comes naturally to you. You must learn to toot your own horn, and not rely on others to do it for you.

Danger Zone

Balance is everything! Talk about your business too much and you'll turn off more people than you turn on. Recruit an objective friend to help you differentiate between positive PR and negative boasting.

What You Can Do Yourself

Every small business owner can cultivate and maintain relationships with media professionals. Like anything you do, it gets easier with practice. Chances are you're not going to wind up in *Time* magazine after your first attempt at PR, but that doesn't mean you shouldn't keep trying!

Make it easy for yourself by understanding the best way to approach each media venue. The following are proven strategies for approaching print, online, and other media venues.

PR in Print

Print media, as the oldest and most established media venue, has the most hide-bound and tradition-laced methodology to securing coverage.

Insight _____

When you present a reporter or editor with a press release or story idea, you're pitching the story. A pitch is a de facto short advertisement for your story idea—a 10- to 15-word explanation of why the paper should tell your story.

The best way to reach the print media is via a press release. The press release is a short document that presents your story idea in an abbreviated format.

You have three to five paragraphs to convince the reporter or editor to cover your story—99 percent of that decision comes from your first paragraph. Make sure you have a story to tell before you send a press release!

The Press Release

When creating your press release you don't have to reinvent the wheel. Simply follow the sample template, adapting as needed to fit your business.

FOR IMMEDIATE RELEASE

FOR FURTHER INFORMATION:

<Contact details here for your company>

HEADLINE

CITY, STATE, DATE—Introduce your story, preferably with a strong "hook" that captures reader attention and interest.

<Next paragraph>—In this paragraph, introduce the relevant facts you want the reader to focus on.

<Next paragraph> Tie together the human-interest story introduced in the first paragraph with the factual and benefits information in the second paragraph. Add information about the benefits readers could expect for themselves.

<Next paragraph> As needed, to complete your story. The best press releases are only three to five paragraphs.

<Final Paragraph> Use this space to share critical information about your company: who you are, where you do, your tag line, and contact information.

======

© Year <Your company name>. All rights reserved. <Your company name> logo are registered trademarks of <your company>. Other brands and product names are trademarks of their respective owners.

For More Information <Contact Info> Also use this space to let editors know if graphics are available.

Danger Zone

Don't let a publication's appearance fool you! Even the most outrageous consumer magazine targeted to a fringe target market appreciates professionalism behind the scenes.

Press releases work best when you send them to a targeted group of media venues that serve your target audience. You have a common set of people to please. People who are interested in your products and services are the same readers the editors and writers strive to serve.

What About Press Conferences?

Press conferences are handy in two instances. The first is when you want to respond to a lot of media attention all at once—which is why you see politicians, celebrities, and big businesses holding press conferences. It saves them time, energy, and money.

Insight

A press conference may be the most efficient way to spread the word when using public relations as a damage-control strategy.

Danger Zone

Holding a press conference to broadcast a pseudo-event, that is, an event staged specifically to capture media attention with little to no news-worthy substance, will sit badly with the media and will damage any credibility you've developed!

The second reason to have a press conference is to introduce the media to something they're currently unfamiliar with and are likely to be interested in. As you might have guessed, such situations are rare.

Approach press conferences lightly: you should have a superior story to make a press conference valid. The vast majority of business owners can have wildly successful careers without ever holding a press conference.

The Electronic Press Release

Print-only publications are a dwindling minority. Rarer still are those publications that don't have any type of web presence, or that shun e-mail in the everyday course of business.

E-mailing your press release is perfectly acceptable, provided you follow some common courtesies: send releases only when you have something newsworthy to report; put the press release as the body of the e-mail, not as an attachment; and include a link to your website. Clearly identify yourself as the sender and be honest in your subject line.

There are numerous web-based press release services, which distribute your press releases to organizations all around the globe. Approach such services with caution: many do not have a stellar reputation for delivering quality content, which means they're ignored by most media outlets.

Additionally, you have to consider the value of those worldwide placements: if your target market lives within 7 miles of your business, what good does it do for you to appear in the daily paper halfway around the world? The best strategy for the small business owner is to spend more time focusing on getting into a small pool of appropriate publications than to devote less time approaching a wide range of periodicals, which may have zero interest in your products and services.

PR Online

Online media is evolving at a tremendous rate. Online media includes web-based versions of traditional print media, online streaming video, streaming radio, and a growing number of blogs that have transcended the personal website model and now serve as alternative news outlets. This variety means there's no one set way to best promote yourself to online media venues. Your best bet is to spend some time on the site where you want exposure and make sure you fully understand the site and how it works before pitching yourself as a potential guest or your story idea.

Traditional print-based model websites often have an editor or publisher who controls the content. That's the person you need to make contact with.

To appear on an online television or radio show, you'll need to do a little detective work. The most consistently successful method is to search for the show's host, and contact them directly through the show's website.

Compared to tracking down online hosts, contacting most bloggers is a snap. If they don't offer a contact e-mail address, leave a comment on their blog. If they're interested, they'll respond—guaranteed!

> **Insight** _____
> When considering an appearance on online television, think visual and short: most shows are only a few minutes long.

PR in Other Media

When approaching television and radio, you have two options. The first, and easiest, is to appeal to their local news department. More challenging is to secure a guest spot on a locally produced television or radio show. Still more challenging, but great if you can land it, is to appear on a national show.

Let's approach each of these separately, as the process for each differs slightly.

Local News

The process for approaching television and radio news broadcasts closely resembles contacting print news outlets. Send a press release to the appropriate contact.

Bear in mind that television is a visual medium, which means that you must let the producer know what he can expect to see. If there's a specific time and location to best showcase your story, let him know.

For example, a press release centering on a celebrity's scheduled appearance at your Grand Opening might include the following line:

> The Grand Opening event is scheduled to begin at 7 A.M. and end at 5 P.M. Miss VaVoom will be appearing from 4 to 4:15 P.M., and will be signing autographs for 30 minutes.

Arming the media with the appropriate information means that cameras won't show up until just before Miss VaVoom's scheduled appearance.

Locally Produced Television and Radio Shows

The following is a three-step process to appearing on a locally produced television and/or radio show.

Step 1: Sit down, watch, and familiarize yourself with the show you want to appear on. Determine why you would make a good guest.

Step 2: Approach the producer of the show. Explain what you'd like to do and why you think you'd be a good fit. If the producer's amenable, do everything possible to make the most of your appearance. Make sure to ask the producer for any clothing tips—you don't want to wear a blue shirt against a blue background!

Step 3: Make sure you get a recording of your appearance. You'll need that when you're ready to hit the big time.

National Television and Radio

Appearing on some national shows requires a booking agent or publicist to make the introductions. However, opportunities still exist without one.

Be open to both cable and broadcast television shows, as well as conventional and Internet radio. Identify those shows most enjoyed by your target market.

From there, it's a matter of identifying and contacting the producers. Make sure your pitch is on target and highly polished. Most television producers won't take a chance on an untested guest: include copies of your local recording so the producer can see how well you do live.

Using Public Relations as Damage Control

Public relations also encompasses how you, as a business owner, respond to problems and challenges as they arise. In an ideal world, you'd only have great news to report and everything would be sunshine and roses all of the time.

However, that's not always the case. From product recalls to local politics to disgruntled customers, scenarios of all types occur over the course of your business life, some of which require a public response.

The goal of public relations when you're facing a difficult situation is to put as good a face as possible on the situation. This is often called damage control (or crisis PR)—using public relations tools to prevent your brand from further damage.

On Target

A coyote wandered into a Chicago Quiznos shop in 2007—unusual news at best! Quiznos, with masterful quick thinking and strategic use of viral marketing techniques, presented the news in an upbeat, positive way, creating a media sensation—and surely driving more than a few sandwich sales!

Putting a good face on the situation is not as easy at it may sound. Here's the essential need-to-know information public relations experts recommend when you're facing reporters who want the real dirt.

Be Proactive

It's tempting to hope that ignoring the problem will make it go away—but that's seldom the case. You can't have your head in the sand. Addressing situations head on is the best strategy.

Be Prompt

Time is of the essence. Any time there's a negative situation affecting your organization, you want to address it as soon as possible. Delay creates doubt and mistrust.

Insight

It's hard to be prompt when you don't know what to say. Remember, something is always better than nothing. A statement that says, "We're aware of the situation and we're looking into it" can buy you much-needed time.

Be Prepared

Know what you're going to say before you start answering questions. Think through your position and have talking points prepared.

Be Honest

Damage control (crisis) public relations requires absolute honesty. Take it for granted that in this situation the media will check facts. Only present verifiable information. For major issues, check with your attorney before issuing any statements.

Putting It All Together

Public relations works best when it is integrated into your overall targeted marketing strategy. You want to make sure that all of your communications reflect your business's brand, effectively conveying elements of your business's personality to the public.

Here's how to integrate public relations.

As the Expert

Focus on identifying story opportunities that allow you to present the depth of your knowledge. Emerging trends serve as a great starting point. Offer to explain what the trend is, what it means, and what your potential customers need to know.

Making It Fun

Use public relations to highlight the fun, the exciting, and the unusual. Contests and events—the more eye-catching, unusual, and visual the better—attracts media coverage, particularly during the slow news periods.

Exclusivity

Be strategic with your public relations plan. Greater than any other target marketing strategy, exclusivity is dependent upon the appropriate medium. Focus on identifying and appearing in the best of the right publications. Appearing in too many places dilutes your brand.

The Least You Need to Know

♦ Getting media coverage in publications and appearing on television, radio, or web shows increases your visibility and enhances your credibility as the expert.

♦ To reach the right media, do your research and know exactly which publications your customers like to read, what websites they visit, what shows they watch, and more.

♦ Approach the media with an appropriate story angle that appeals to their readers, viewers or listeners—your target audience.

♦ Public relations is an ongoing discipline of continuously looking for new and exciting angles of your business to expose to your target market.

Part 4

Actions Speak Louder Than Words

You can attract new customers all day long, but if you can't effectively hold onto them, your business will never grow. In this part, you'll discover the power of client retention.

The most powerful and most overlooked resource any small business owner has lies within his or her customer files. Therein lies a tremendous amount of profit potential, both from future sales and in the phenomenal gold mine that referral business can bring.

Tapping into this gold mine does require work and resources—but the reward is exponentially greater than the investment. Read on to learn how to recruit an unpaid army of salespeople and lock in customer loyalty!

Chapter **18**

Now You've Got Them— Keep Them!

In This Chapter

- ◆ Understanding what customer retention is—and isn't
- ◆ Learning the value of holding onto existing customers
- ◆ Finding out how customer retention can save you money
- ◆ Recognizing the value of customer referrals

At this point, you have done it: you have successfully used target marketing strategies to attract new customers to your business. They encountered you online, in person, or in the media, and decided to take the plunge and check you out.

Is your work done? Far from it. It is not time to say, "I'm all done with this marketing thing now." That might be tempting—but if you abandon target marketing now, you'll be shooting the cash cow.

Customer retention is target marketing distilled to its purest, most powerful form. Every concept, every thought, every idea that we have covered up to this point now has to catapult to the next level. You want to take that focused spotlight of target marketing and intensify it to a white-hot laser beam, all with one sole purpose: to keep the customers you already have coming back for more!

The largest, most familiar example of customer retention in action is just a quick key stroke away on your nearest computer. Go to Amazon.com and observe the master of the game. Amazon.com built their business—in fact, some would say this is the core of their brand—by catering to their existing customer base.

When you shop at Amazon.com, the online bookseller does everything possible to make you come back. They keep track of what you buy, and offer suggestions of books and products you might like based upon previous purchases. They solicit your opinion, and make your reviews part of their selling platform. They will even e-mail you when your favorite author has a new book available!

Dispelling the Myths of Customer Retention

Customer retention is one of those topics everyone talks about and rarely altogether understands. There is so much emphasis on the 80/20 rule—80 percent of your business comes from 20 percent of your customers—yet few business owners place any emphasis on discovering who these best customers are or what it takes to keep them satisfied.

There are a few pervasive myths out there about client retention, and we might as well face them right now and get them out of the way. Let's take a peek at three of the most common.

"It's Too Expensive!"

Discovering who your existing best customers are and marketing directly to those individuals is actually less expensive than most mass-marketing efforts. Because you are reaching customers with a demonstrated, proven interest in your products and services, you will realize a higher response rate.

For example, a general direct mail campaign averages a 2 to 3 percent response rate. Send a targeted direct mail piece to the right people in your existing customer base, and you will realize a response rate of over 40 percent.

The greater response and conversion rates on targeted campaigns to your existing customer base makes client retention a far more cost-effective tool than any other marketing strategy out there.

"All of my customers already know this stuff!"

"Why do I have to tell my customers when the new spring line comes in? Spring comes every year!"

This type of comment is really common. That's sad, because it's born completely and totally out of the business owner's pride. It takes a certain amount of arrogance to assume that your customers are thinking about you at all, much less that they know what you're doing at any given time.

That is why smart accountants send their customers notices well ahead of tax time to ensure they'll have the best, most convenient appointment times. They understand that the onus of keeping track of what's important falls on them—not on their customers.

"It Takes a Lot of Time!"

We will meet you halfway on this one. If you've never, ever marketed to your existing customer base, and you have no customer data whatsoever, it'll take you a little bit of time to get started. This means developing a "getting started" strategy.

That being said, once you've collected your customer data, marketing to your customer base is no more time-consuming than traditional marketing and advertising.

In fact, in some cases, reaching out to your existing customer base can take less time than designing a brand-new general interest campaign.

For example, sending out an e-mail blast letting your entire list of golfing fanatics know that you have just added the world's best sports-injury specialist to your massage therapy practice will take 10 minutes, tops. Give them a tempting, time-sensitive incentive, and chances are you will see some instant results. Place the same content in a print advertisement in your local newspaper, and it will be at least a day before you hear anything, not to mention the time it will take to design and lay out the ad.

Why Is Customer Retention So Important?

Customer retention is the secret weapon in the target marketing arsenal. It is the single-most powerful, cost-effective way to boost your bottom line. Selling to your existing customer base will enable you to generate more traffic, sell more merchandise or services, and actually save money on marketing costs.

It is a win-win-win scenario all the way around. Customer retention is full of benefits, with very little downside. The benefits can be split into two primary categories: customer retention can save you money, particularly when it comes to advertising and marketing costs; and customer retention can enhance your brand and make you look good both in front of your community and around the world!

How Customer Retention Can Save You Money

At a certain point, you always have to assess how much of a bang you're getting for your marketing buck. That is just good business, and we talked about this way back in Chapter 2.

Customer retention takes the cost savings you realize by adopting target marketing methodology and grows them exponentially. Because you are reaching out to existing customers, who are already predisposed to purchasing your products and services, with offers that are highly likely to be of interest to them, you'll have a far greater response rate than both marketing to the public at large and even carefully targeted advertising campaigns to new customers.

Cost of New Customer vs. Existing Customer

Attracting new customers is one of the most expensive aspects of running a business. This is particularly true for new and start-up businesses that don't have an established brand or community connection to capitalize upon.

Why is attracting customer attention so difficult? There are a million other things vying for customers' attention: their families, their jobs, their hobbies and pastimes, community obligations, the gym, you name it. Everyone has a packed schedule—when was the last time you heard anyone say, "Oh, I wish I knew what to do with all my time?"

Drawing attention to yourself in the midst of all of this competition is difficult and potentially expensive. We've just spent several dozen pages illustrating ways to accomplish this, preferably without spending all your cash, but make no mistake: attracting new customers means committing a substantial investment.

The lion's share of this time and effort goes into what marketing experts call "establishing a baseline presence." Establishing a baseline presence means simply presenting yourself as a player in your community: people know you're there, and they have some vague idea of what you do, even if they've never stepped foot inside your door.

The need to establish a baseline presence and make that initial contact with a customer requires a greater investment than attracting the attention of someone who already knows you are there. Because they have already done business with you before, they have a very clear understanding of what you do and what kind of experience they'll have, which means that your investment in time, money, and energy is far less.

Insight _____

Advertising experts tell us that the cost of attracting a new customer is six to seven times more expensive than communicating with your existing customer base and persuading them to come back.

The Lifetime Value of a Customer

When a customer walks into your business for the very first time, how much is she worth to you?

It depends. If a customer buys one piece of merchandise, or uses your services one time—you prepare one tax return for her, or cut her hair one time, for example—she might have just cleared the investment it took to attract her business in the first place.

As we just talked about, new customers are expensive: you have to invest in advertising and marketing. You've got the cost of your signage. You might even attribute part of your location costs directly to the need to attract customers.

You recoup some or all of these costs when a customer comes in and does business with you. However, if a customer comes in once, never to return, it is really a zero-sum game: you've recouped your investment in that customer—but now you have to attract another customer to replace the one who never returns. You are spending money, but you are not getting any further ahead.

Profit happens when you have repeat customers. Customers who are already sold on your business will return without you having to do any other advertising—theoretically. Your merchandise is so great and your service is so spectacular that the customer won't be able to go anyplace else.

That's an ideal theory. It doesn't, however, work in the real world. The average consumer has a very short attention span; if you don't keep your company's marketing message directly in front of him, he's going to forget about you.

Not only will they forget about you, but they'll go to your competitor, who is offering merchandise that's just as great or services that are just as spectacular. That's just the way the world is.

Danger Zone _____

In a down economy, many companies make the really big mistake of cutting their marketing budget completely. Nothing could be worse, because once you're out of your customers' sight, they will forget about you. If money is tight, reduce your budget until things start looking up, but keep your name out there even if on a much more limited basis. That way, when the economy turns around, you won't have to start all over again from scratch.

So don't fall into the trap of thinking your customers will automatically return once you've brought them into the store. They won't. These customers aren't automatic.

What they are is presold.

A customer who has already found you and had a good experience with you is more likely to return to you if you give them a reason to come in. They've had fun, they've found value, they've finally discovered someone who knows how to handle their hair—and you've made it clear to them, via your customer retention efforts, that you want them to come back.

Being sought after this way is flattering, and appealing, and effective. Customers like the attention.

Repeat customers build what is known as a lifetime value. This lifetime value is the cumulative amount that a customer spends with you over the course of your relationship. It's a number that can grow pretty quickly, especially if you become someone's regular store or business.

For example, let's say the average transaction at Betty's Spa Space is $100—a massage, plus some scented candles on sale.

If a customer comes in one time, Betty's made $100.

If that customer comes in three times in a year, now Betty's made $300.

Let's say Betty has an aggressive client-retention program. She e-mails her customer about some new spa packages. She makes a special note of what this particular customer likes to buy—let's say deep tissue massage—and when there's a special on this type of service ("Bring a friend for a 50 percent discount") she phones that customer up to let her know.

Her attention pays off. This customer becomes a "regular," once-a-month client. Add to that a special holiday gift card she buys—massages for the whole family—plus other accessories, and suddenly, in one year, Betty's made $1,500.

Now let's look at this over the lifetime of Betty's Spa Space. We'll assume that this business is open for 10 years, and buying patterns remain the same for that entire period. That means …

- In the first scenario, the one-time customer: Betty makes $100.

- In the second scenario, the "stop in now and then" customer: Betty makes $1,500.

- In the third scenario, the regular customer: Betty makes $1,500×10 = $15,000.

These numbers might not be exciting in and of themselves. But that's just one customer. Consider what would happen if you could transform every customer into a regular customer? What would happen if you could transform your one-time customer into a regular?

You would make a ton more money, that's what would happen. Realizing the full lifetime value of your customers is one of the most efficient, effective ways to enhance your profitability and build a better business.

> **Insight**
>
> Wal-Mart, a company that knows a little bit about doing business, estimates the lifetime value of a customer to be $200,000. When you consider that the average transaction at Wal-Mart is approximately $80, it becomes clear that bringing customers back regularly is an essential part of doing business.

Referral Value of a Customer

The final reason that customer retention is a great bottom-line idea requires that you understand some basics of human nature. Almost everyone likes to brag. Everyone likes to be in possession of knowledge no one else has. Everyone likes to have the secret to tell.

Which is great news, if you're the secret.

Customer retention hinges on building a strong relationship with your customer. Once you have that relationship established, you've put them in a position of power.

You see, now your customers have a secret. You've given them something to brag about.

When your customer is complimented on her great new outfit, she can smile and say, "Let me tell you about this awesome little boutique … they have the best things, and they always know exactly what I want." When your customer's colleague complains of an aching back, your customer will say, "You have to see my chiropractor. He takes such good care of me."

What we're illustrating here is the referral value of your customer.

We've all heard how someone who has a bad experience in a business will tell at least six people (or if he gets online, six million people!). But what often gets missed in these discussions is the fact that someone who has a good experience with a business will tell two or three people about it—and potentially more, if prompted for information.

If one of those two people decide to check out your business based on the referral of your existing customer, you've acquired new business without incurring any additional advertising or marketing costs!

Looking Good While Doing It!

While money is nice—very nice—there's another benefit of customer retention that is just as critical and compelling. This is the role that customer retention has in your brand-building efforts and the impact it has upon your community standing.

The world may be getting smaller every day, thanks to technology and globalization. Surprisingly enough, this global shrinkage has placed a new premium on relationship building. Today's consumer wants to do business with an organization that they know and feel connected to.

The only way to build a relationship with people is to communicate with them! Reaching out to connect with your customers is now more affordable than ever, especially with web-based tools. Neiman Marcus always said, "Give the lady what she wants!"—and what the lady (and gentleman!) wants is a relationship with you.

Brand Building

Customer retention is a great way to differentiate your business from your competitors. Using regular communication, targeted mailings, and promotional campaigns, you're demonstrating that you care about your customers—as individuals!

Rest assured that this alone will set you apart from the vast majority of your competition. Megaretailers and huge institutions treat their customers as little more than numbers. They're training their customers to get used to being ignored and marginalized.

While there will always be customers who are willing to accept this treatment (generally in exchange for lower prices), there will also always be customers who are not. Individualized attention, even in the form of sales solicitations and marketing messages, are appealing to that growing segment of the customer base who want to be recognized as individuals, as special, as worthy of attention. This is a golden strategy for the target marketer.

Branding your organization as the one that truly understands and cares about its customers is a good place to be. Capitalize on the fact you're there, listening to your customers, and continually reaching out to them. You can be the company that is there for its customers, more than any logo on a screen or megainstitution who can't be bothered to answer their own phones.

You might never be able to match the big companies in size, scope, price, or marketing budgets, but where you can meet and beat them is with individualized attention and consistent demonstration of concern for your customers. That's a critical differentiation, one that you can use to build a great brand.

Emphasizing Business Relationships

Customer retention is a real-world demonstration that you understand we're all connected. The Internet has changed the definition of a friend, and by extension, the premium we now place on relationships.

Not long ago, most people would have a dozen friends. These were friends they knew from their hometowns, their jobs, their community organizations.

Now a person can have 500 friends on Facebook who they've never met. These friendships are very influential—and the impact of these virtual relationships has directly spilled over into the business world.

There is a huge hunger to know. Customers don't want to shop at nameless shops, owned by someone halfway around the world. They don't want any old person in a white coat to be their doctor. There's a real value on knowing the person behind the product, the soul behind the service.

Continually reaching out to your customers through customer-retention efforts gives customers the opportunity to know you. Yes, this may only be surface-level knowledge.

But the more you communicate with your customers, the better chance you have of forging a relationship with them. You can't form a relationship all by yourself. You need to engage with customers where they are.

Insight

How much do you know about Ben & Jerry's Ice Cream, beyond its vaguely hippie-esque philosophy and tie-dyed cartons? Probably not much, but it was that bit of personality and branding that allowed legions of ice cream fans to bond with the company, forging a long-lasting, profitable relationship.

Your Community Standing

Customer retention can enhance your standing in the community. It doesn't take long to develop a reputation, especially in a small town.

Yes, bad news travels faster than good: insult the mayor's wife in the morning, and the whole town will know before lunchtime.

However, good news travels, too. It is your job to generate good news. Customer-retention efforts can do that. For example, if you're one of Dave's Soda & Pet City's customers in Agawam, Massachusetts, you'll be able to talk about the springtime car wash coupons you receive just as the snow turns to mud and your car needs a good cleaning.

Simple gestures can generate tremendous word of mouth and positive goodwill. Everyone likes to do business with the "nice guys"—and everyone wants to get in on the good deals.

When people discover that they need to be a good Dave's customer to get the free car wash, more than a few start picking up their dog food at Dave's.

Additionally, unique and creative customer-retention ideas can occasionally generate media interest in your organization. Having the local paper talk about what you're doing for your customers (such as the pizza owner who guaranteed every one of his regular customers in town a free pie if the hometown team won) will certainly create some buzz!

The Least You Need to Know

- ◆ Understand the lifetime value of your customers.

- ◆ Shower your customers with individualized attention and they will keep coming back.

- ◆ Simple gestures can generate tremendous word of mouth and positive goodwill.

- ◆ Differentiate yourself from your competition with specific customer-retention strategies.

19

Link Into Your Customers with Database Marketing

In This Chapter

- ◆ Learning database marketing essentials
- ◆ Recognizing the value of selling to your existing customers
- ◆ Understanding customer data and how to use it

We've talked about the value of the ultimate in target marketing: reaching out to your existing customer base with offers that you know are going to appeal to them as well as be effective.

Understanding the what and why is important. Now it's time to focus on the how. That's the role of database marketing.

How Database Marketing Works

Effective *database marketing* analyzes customer-buying patterns and enables you to create targeted campaigns based on buying behavior.

def•i•ni•tion
_____

Database marketing is the practice of marketing directly to your
existing customer base.

For example, if you're a restaurant owner and you
know that you have a core of customers who order
lobster each and every time they come in, and you
want to have a lobster-themed event or promotion,
you can pull the list of regular lobster customers and
send them personalized invitations.

If you own a home décor store and you have customers who are loyal Christopher
Lowell (interior designer and TV personality) fans, you can generate a list and make
sure they're the first ones to know when he makes a special appearance at your shop.

Database marketing also allows your relationship with your customers to evolve over
time. For example, if you own a spa collect your customers' birthday month and send
them a special card with a 20 percent off coupon to encourage them to come in for a
massage.

By tracking their purchases over the years, you can develop a sense of who your customers are and what they each like.

This level of individual service and attention is impossible if you don't know who your
customers are and what they value.

That's why data collection is so critical to database marketing. It is the raw material
that makes the magic possible!

Understanding the Technology

Database management gets easier day by day. What was difficult and cumbersome
years ago now gets handled by low-cost software programs and online applications.

A database is simply a record of all of your customers' information, including how to
contact them and what they like to buy. The neat thing about having all of this information computerized is that you can search it, in an almost infinite number of per-
mutations, until you end up with a list composed only of people who are interested in
what you've got to say.

For example, if you're a jeweler, you can access your database to discover which of
your customers collect sapphire jewelry, who has a wife or daughter or sweetheart
with a September birthday, who has a September birthday himself, and who just likes
the color blue.

Add to that a list of people who favor jewelry by a certain designer, such as Jennifer
Meyer.

That way, when Jennifer Meyer releases a fantastic sapphire pendant, you know exactly which customers to contact. You can send out a brief e-mail message, replete with a picture of the piece and some copy highlighting its features, and the pendant practically sells itself.

The benefit of database marketing is that pinpoint precision, the ultimate in target marketing. Because you're dealing with people you already have a relationship with, some of the sales resistance is already gone.

Marketing in this fashion is not necessarily viewed as advertising by your customers. Instead, it is often seen as service: something you do to take care of your customers and make sure they're informed of the things that would be of the most interest to them.

Building Relationships Through Database Marketing

Database marketing enables you to begin to reinforce your relationship with your customers. One of the main benefits of online target marketing is the prominence customers put on having a relationship with the organizations they do business with; they're acclimated to having that relationship take place in the virtual world.

Database marketing takes that same relationship and has it play out in the real world, with tangible forms of communication, such as direct mail and telephone calls. It's a way for customers to feel a real, genuine, authentic human connection with your organization. That's becoming increasingly rare, and hence, is becoming increasingly valued.

Additionally, database marketing takes some accepted online target marketing tools and refines them. Rather than sending a general e-mail blast to everyone on your list, using database marketing you would send a specific message of extreme interest to a few customers who would be highly motivated to act on it.

An important aspect of database marketing is that it plays out over time. An organization can communicate with its customers for years, even decades. This communication forms a large part of the company's personality; customers bond with the company they've come to know through regular communications.

> **On Target**
>
> J. Peterman, the exclusive, upscale clothing company, carved out a successful niche in the competitive mail-order clothing market by conveying a strong sense of unique identity to a carefully maintained customer list for years and years.

What You Need to Know

There are two levels of customer knowledge: the macro level of knowledge, and the micro level. The macro level—the "big picture" level—is about viewing your customers as a group. Taken together, many of your customers live in this neighborhood, and they make this amount of money, and they prefer to wear clothes from this designer. Your customers watch this type of movie and listen to this particular kind of music. They shop at your store or patronize your business, and businesses that resemble yours, because they share a certain number of unifying traits that make them predisposed to enjoy the experience you're providing.

That's great. That type of customer knowledge is crucial to target marketing.

Now, however, we've got to concentrate on the micro level of information: the specific data you need to get in touch with an individual customer.

The critical must-have information you need on that personal, micro level includes the following.

Things You Ask Directly

◆ **Name** The customer's name. If you plan on using titles in your correspondence (Mr., Mrs., Ms., Miss) make sure to learn which one the customer prefers.

◆ **Address** The customer's mailing address.

◆ **Phone number** A home or work number where you can reach the customer.

◆ **Cell phone number** A cell phone number where you can reach the customer.

◆ **E-mail** The customer's e-mail address.

◆ **Preferred contact method** What's the best way to reach the customer? Does he prefer phone calls, text messages, or e-mail contact?

Danger Zone

Customers hate spam—and more than a few have been burned by business owners who send junk e-mails. Don't be surprised when some of your customers give you phony e-mail addresses!

Things You Learn About Your Customers

Over the course of your relationship with your customers, you're going to learn different things about them. Some of these can be tracked automatically for you, depending on your technology. Others will require a little insight and judgment on your part, but it's knowledge well worth having so that you can market more effectively to your customers:

- **When they like to do business with you** Do you see this customer weekly? Monthly? Seasonally? Once a year? Different businesses have different frequency expectations: a good customer for a local coffee shop might stop in daily, while a good customer for an accountant might visit the office three times a year. Either way, you want to know how often you see this customer, and when. Using technology, it's even possible to track what time of day you see your best customers.

- **What they buy** What is this customer's favorite brand? What type of merchandise does she purchase? What sizes does she buy?

- **Customer type** Is this person a regular customer, someone you see like clockwork? Or does she only come in for sales events, cherry-picking low prices?

  There are countless numbers of customer types: you can identify categories that are relevant to your market. The names aren't as important as the behavior. You want to know how you can expect this customer to act on a typical day.

Why Do You Need This Information?

There are two reasons you need these particular sets of data. The first and obvious reason is that if you want to market to your existing customer base, you have to have a concrete, tangible way of reaching them.

You can't call someone without his phone number. You can't e-mail someone without a working e-mail address. You can't send direct mail without knowing a physical address!

The second set of data enables you to hit the target marketing bull's-eye.

Everything you learn in the second set of information enables you to craft messages and offers that are almost guaranteed to appeal to your target audience. Response rates will be higher, as will subsequent sales.

> **On Target**
>
> When Dave Ratner, owner of Dave's Soda & Pet City, a four-store chain in Massachusetts, wants to promote new wild food, he sends an offer to the wild bird enthusiasts on his list. Sending this information to his entire list would be wasteful and ineffective.

How to Collect Data from Your Customer

Collecting customer data is a continual, ongoing process. As you meet new customers, you want to capture their information and begin a relationship with them. As the customer continues to do business with you, you want to pay attention to what you've learned, enhancing your understanding of your customers each and every time they visit.

There are two ways you can capture customer data. One is using computer-based technology, and the other requires a little more elbow grease.

Using Technology Effectively

Most businesses already have some sort of technology that enables them to track customer data. In a retail situation, that is known as the Point of Sale (or POS) system. In a service provider's setting, client files and billing software generally track at least a rudimentary level of customer activity.

Understanding Loyalty Cards

Loyalty cards—also known as preferred customer cards, frequent buyer cards, club cards, and more—are, if used correctly, a sophisticated database marketing tool.

Every time a customer uses a loyalty card, his transaction should be recorded, either by a POS system or in whatever other system you've developed.

Information recorded then should include the following:

- What the customer bought.
- How much the customer paid.
- When the customer came in.

Insight

You may very well have the technology you need, and not know it. Take a good look at your computer system. Does it have a database or client-tracking function—or can you simply buy a module to upgrade what you've got?

Individually, none of this information is all that critical—although it's nice to have for billing disputes and bookkeeping purposes. But in aggregate, when you've collected all of a customer's purchases, over the course of time you'll be able to discern purchasing patterns and tailor specific marketing campaigns that will appeal to that customer—and to your other customers who share that same purchasing pattern.

To get people to sign up for loyalty cards, point out the benefit of having a card. Customers are deluged with loyalty cards: you need to differentiate yours by making it valuable to your customers.

Hotels have been particularly effective with loyalty cards, as travelers value the savings on rooms, room upgrades, and other perks that come with the card. The perks are enough to encourage some regular travelers to consciously opt for the hotel they have the card for, rather than "whoever's closest to the airport."

Loyalty cards and frequent buyer programs have proven to be very appealing to high-income customers, which is something to keep in mind if that's the target market you're after.

Offering the Right Incentive

Your customers' information has value, and they know it. Few customers are going to share their information with you just because it's a nice thing to do. There's a fear factor associated with giving out information.

Spell out the incentive the customers will get from sharing their information with you. Make sure all your employees know and understand the incentive program. That way, when someone asks why she should share her phone number or e-mail address, they'll have a response at the ready.

Great incentives for customer information are honest and straightforward. You don't need a fabulous sales pitch here. Just tell the customers why you will be contacting them:

- To ensure they're kept up-to-date with all the latest information—a new program, book, etc.

- To make sure they never miss an appointment.

- To secure the best appointment times (great for accountants, massage therapists, and hairdressers!).

- To let them know about a great sale.

- To inform them when their favorite merchandise comes in.

The incentive should appeal to what the customer values saving. Most customers value saving time and saving money, so when you appeal to either or both, you'll be in great shape.

Back To Basics: Going Without Technology

If your business doesn't have a Point of Sale system or a computerized bookkeeping system, you're going to have to collect this same information manually. This is a lot more work than relying upon computerized systems, but the rewards are well worth the labor.

Five Ways to Manually Collect Data

Manually collecting data requires having either your customer or your staff write down all of the contact information needed to reach them. Then, after you've collected the contact information, you need to organize it into a usable format. A business card serves the same purpose.

This can often be done by entering all of the information into a program such as Microsoft Excel or even an online address book application such as Zexer.

Five common ways to include customer data manually include the following:

- **Simply asking for it** Simply asking customers for their contact information can be surprisingly effective, especially in more informal settings. A simple "guestbook" can effectively capture contact information with minimal pressure.

- **Offering to send a newsletter or special coupons** Be straightforward with your customers. Saying, "If you give us your name and address, we'll send you special coupons on the stuff you like to buy" garners an amazingly high response rate.

- **Giving an incentive** Have customers fill out a contact card in exchange for a percentage off the day's purchase or a coupon for their next visit.

- **Contests and drawings** Everyone likes to be a winner. Set out a box to collect names and addresses that customers fill out to win a prize. It costs you nothing except the prize! The prize can also be a percentage discount off a certain service you offer.

◆ **In the course of business**   Special orders, refunds, and the normal course of some types of business require the customer's contact information. Make one extra copy of the contact information for marketing purposes. This strategy is sometimes called "mining your client list," and it's a great way to begin database marketing.

How to Organize This Information

The better organized your information is, the more use you'll get out of it. That means more effective marketing campaigns.

Ideally, you want your client information to be searchable by the following:

◆ Zip code

◆ Customer type

◆ Buying patterns

◆ Merchandise preferences

◆ Amount spent with you

Categorizing information in this manner will enable you to quickly generate a list of the customers who would be the ideal recipient of your promotional and marketing efforts.

The Dark Side of Customer Data

Because customers have been burnt by some of those unethical marketing pests, they are obviously concerned about sharing certain information with you. This is especially true if they are a brand-new customer where there is a minimal relationship.

If you are going to collect customer data, you have to make a promise to your customers. This promise has two parts. The first part is that you'll never use the information to annoy, aggravate, or spam the customer. Everybody's flooded with marketing offers all the time, and they don't want to sign up for more junk mail.

The second part of the promise is that you'll never sell, rent, or share your contact list. It's a matter of trust and respect: you're asking your customers to trust you with their information, and they're trusting you not to open them up to tons of unwanted attention from every company in the world who has something to sell.

Danger Zone _____

Selling and renting customer information can be really lucrative, especially if you've got a great list. At the same time, your vendors and suppliers might offer you a discount if you share your customer's contact information with them. It's a great idea—as long as you don't mind your customers hating you forever! The money's not worth it!

How to Protect Customer Data

Protecting customer data is a critical concern. Huge companies such as TJ Maxx and Hannafords Supermarkets both had public relations nightmares when their customers' credit card information was accessed.

Incidents like that have a spill-over effect, which makes customers leery of sharing their personal information. Help make them feel secure by doing the following three things.

Limiting Access to Customer Data

The customer database in your store should only be accessible on a need-to-know basis. This means that your employees are only getting into customer contact information when they need it—to process a return, for example, or for billing purposes.

The less access your employees have to customer contact information, the less opportunity there is for information to be stolen or abused.

Working Only with Reputable Third-Party Vendors

Many database-marketing techniques involve working with third-party vendors. These third-party vendors handle the logistics of telemarketing or e-mail marketing.

It is essential that you work only with reputable, well-established third-party vendors in these cases. These companies need to be committed to ethical treatment of customer data; you don't want to find out after the fact that your third-party vendor sold your list.

Observing Internet Security Protocols

Make sure your computer's security settings are kept up to date, and that customer data lists are not available online. Websites can and do get hacked, and there are people out there who aren't above breaking into other business computers to gain a competitive advantage. Always observe standard Internet security, and be smart about how you protect your company's intellectual assets.

The Least You Need to Know

♦ Database marketing analyzes customer-buying patterns and enables you to create targeted campaigns based on buying behavior.

♦ Whether you use technology or not, make collecting customer data an ongoing "must-do" activity.

♦ Create an incentive program that is valuable and meaningful to your customers.

♦ Dispel customer concerns that you will do anything untoward with their information.

20

Making a Direct Connection

In This Chapter

♦ Understanding the power of direct mail

♦ Taming the fear of telemarketing

♦ Embracing e-mail marketing

♦ Learning the art of gift-giving

♦ Boosting your business with the client-retention cycle

We've said it before and we'll say it again: 80 percent of most small business's profits come from 20 percent of their customers. It's essential to keep that 20 percent happy, and to give them a reason to keep coming back to you.

It is impossible to overstate the importance of relationships in business today. More than ever, customers want to do business with organizations they feel a personal connection with.

If you are going to have a personal connection with someone, you need to communicate with that person. You can't bond with silence. And, because you, as the business owner, are the one who wants the bond, you need to be the one to take the initiative. It is incumbent on you to reach out and make the first step—or the first dozen steps—in establishing and maintaining this profitable relationship.

Knowing Your Options

There are an almost infinite number of ways to make a direct connection with your customer. You're limited only by your time and your creativity. The point of the exercise is to let your customers know you're thinking about them, that you value their business, and that you want them to come back regularly.

It's entirely possible to spend hundreds and hundreds of pages detailing the many, many ways you can contact your customers, but to keep it simple, we're going to focus on the top three most common:

- ◆ Direct mail
- ◆ E-mail marketing
- ◆ Telemarketing

These are proven effective tools that any small business owner can use.

Another powerful strategy is gift-giving, which is a little bit different, but amazingly effective in strengthening your relationship with your customer.

Somebody Sent Me a Letter

Direct mail can loosely be defined as any commercial message printed on paper delivered through the mail to existing or potential customers. This includes letters, postcards, magazines, books—you name it!

Creativity and innovation is the order of the day in direct mail.

Insight

Jon Goldman, a direct-marketing specialist, designed the concept of "lumpy mail" to create attention over the traditional "flat" mail. He has many different campaigns he offers clients, and one highly effective one is the "Worry Doll" mailer, which he offers clients when sales are in a slump.

It consists of an interoffice envelope with punched out holes to enable you to peek inside to see what makes the thing so lumpy. Recipients want to open it immediately to know what's causing the lumpiness inside the envelope. A hand-woven sack of tiny worry dolls. Once the readers pull out the little worry dolls, they start reading your letter, wondering, "Why did they send me these little worry dolls? What's this all about?" In the end, you will make a huge impression and generate a ton of phone calls or hits on your website with this.

Direct mail does have its detractors. Decades of junk mail and clumsy campaigns have turned people off by mail as a marketing outlet. However, smart strategic use of direct mail has built many businesses.

The Benefits of Direct Mail

Direct mail has a few distinct benefits.

First and foremost, it is relatively easy to pin-point and reach a highly targeted market with direct mail. Your first port of call is to access your existing database of customers and send appropriate offers to people you already do business with.

Next, direct mail enables you to easily and efficiently reach out to new customers.

List brokers maintain categorized lists of consumers, delineated by any number of characteristics. You can purchase these lists when trying to expand your market share and reach new customers who are likely to be interested in your products and services. If you have any concerns about information privacy, make a point of only purchasing opt-in lists. The best brokers offer only opt-in lists.

> **On Target**
>
> L.L. Bean, the privately held retail company based in Freeport, Maine, specializing in clothing and outdoor recreation equipment, has built their billion-dollar empire through their mail-order catalogs.

> **def•i•ni•tion**
>
> A **list broker** specializes in direct mail campaigns. They maintain and sell lists of consumer addresses.

Direct mail is highly customizable. For instance, you can address customers by name and speak to them as individuals. In a culture that values personal attention, this is a big plus.

Finally, direct mail is tangible. It actually exists. It's something customers can see, touch, hold on to, stick up on their refrigerator, or put in their purse. Postcards and letters are familiar, and are often retained for reference purposes. Novelty direct mail pieces are often kept just because they're "cool"—an ad that keeps on giving.

What About the Cost?

It is a common misconception that direct mail is expensive. After all, you've got the cost of designing a piece, producing it, and then mailing it. That all adds up.

When you add in the truism that a great direct mail response rate is 1 to 2 percent, it looks like a losing game—unless you have very deep pockets and can afford to mail your offer to 2 million people.

Let's be honest, direct mail as a mass-marketing tool is expensive. Target marketing with direct mail, on the other hand, is very cost-effective.

The trick to direct mail as a target marketing tool is to make your offer relevant and irresistible. You have to understand your target audience and what appeals to them. This means designing unique direct mail pieces.

> ### On Target
>
> Rick Segel, a retail expert who owned a women's specialty store, once sent 100 of his very best customers an invitation to a special sales event at his store. Included in the invitation was one high-quality, attractive woman's glove.
>
> To get the other glove, the recipient had to attend the sales event. There was no obligation to buy anything.
>
> However, a considerable number of the respondents did buy. And even more important, over 80 percent of the people who received a glove came in to claim the other one.
>
> On a per-piece basis, the glove mailing was expensive. However, when you consider the very high response rate, as well as the number of sales that the event generated, the cost of the campaign became much more realistic.
>
> The moral of the story: money spent on direct mail that doesn't work is money wasted. Money spent on targeted direct mail that produces results is the best investment you could make!

The Logistics of Direct Mail

For a small business owner to profit from direct mail, the campaign has to be extremely targeted, very creative, and well implemented. Follow the following three-step formula to make the process easier.

1. Include an offer.

The first thing to consider is your offer. Every direct mail piece you send must include an offer or call to action. While larger companies can send direct mail pieces to build brand awareness, doing so is not financially possible for the majority of companies.

So begin by deciding what you're going to offer your customers. This is the purpose of your direct mail piece: you need to have a clear vision of what you're going to use to entice your customers to come in.

2. Decide on a format.

Postcards are great. They're easy to design and produce and are very affordable. On the downside, they don't stand out from the crowd as unique and individual. Check out www.1800postcards.com or www.modernpostcards.com for cost-saving postcards.

Sales letters have long been the gold standard. There's tons of research and science out there on crafting the perfect sales letter—you'll want to check Appendix B for resources. For many purposes, a sales letter is the route to go, particularly if you're catering to an upscale, literate, or traditional target market.

Lumpy mail is a recent trend in direct mail, which couples traditional direct mail with a "goodie"—a premium or giveaway item enclosed to get recipients to open the mail and pay attention to what you have to say.

3. Select your recipients.

Select the appropriate names from your mailing list (or access the list you've secured from a list broker) and send your direct mail pieces out.

This may sound like a tremendous amount of work. It may be. Unless you're sending out a very limited number of pieces (less than 100) direct mail marketing can become a job in and of itself.

That is why many small organizations turn to third-party vendors, often known as mailing houses, direct mail fulfillment services, or literature distribution centers, to handle the task.

Insight

Track the effectiveness on your direct mailing piece by attaching a code or keyword to your offer. That way you'll be able to track how many customers come to you as a result of your direct mail efforts.

These services also help ensure that your mailings are in compliance with the Do Not Mail registry. Just as individual consumers can opt out of e-mail marketing and telemarketing, they can choose to not receive direct mail solicitations.

Pick Up the Phone

To avoid the negative connotations telemarketing has, you want to be very selective and strategic when calling your customers. You want to convey an impression of "providing customer service," not "calling to sell me something."

For example, when your physician calls to remind you that you've got an appointment coming up, is that a sales call? Chances are you don't think of it that way. It's simply your doctor making sure you don't miss a visit, right?

Yet medical practices that make reminder calls to their patients have a significantly lower last-minute cancellation or missed appointment rate than those practices that don't call. When you consider a last-minute cancellation or missed appointment is money the practice isn't making, ensuring patients do show up for their scheduled appointments is, in effect, a sales call.

Adopting that model for your customers is simple. You want to take a customer-service-oriented view of calling. Ask yourself: What would my customers want to know?

If they're loyal buyers of a particular brand, they may want to know that brand is on sale.

If they're regular customers who have very tight schedules, they may want to know you're extending the evening and weekend hours of your practice.

Each industry will have its own examples of information your customers will want to know.

The Logistics of Telemarketing

When you have information that a select group of your customers will want to know, create a list of those customer's phone numbers.

Then, call them when they are not likely to be home. Generally, this is during the workday. You want to talk to the customer's answering machine, not to the customer!

When you get the machine, leave a short message that's clear, direct, and to the point. For example,

> "Hi Joanne! This is Arnie, from Terry's Tack. We've just gotten in a new line of Corriente saddles that would be perfect for you, especially with the show season just about to start. They're on sale 20 percent off through Thursday, if you'd like to check them out."

That's it. Leave the message, and hang up.

Write out the message you want to deliver and then read it verbatim in a chatty and upbeat tone.

What Happens If You Get the Customer?

You will occasionally get a real, live person at the other end of the line. Don't panic! Simply deliver your message quickly and clearly. There will be people who hang up on you. Don't take it personally. We're conditioned, as a people, to hang up on telemarketers.

Calling all of your customers who would be interested in a particular bit of information can take time. If you have 100 customers who would be interested, and a message takes a minute to deliver, you're looking at nearly two hours out of your day!

Sometimes that's okay, particularly if the middle of the day is a down time for your business. Other times, that might not be tenable.

There are third-party vendors who handle the logistics of telemarketing. Generally, you provide them with a list of the numbers you want to call, and record your message. They automate the process, delivering your message to all of the numbers on your list. They also ensure none of your numbers are on the Do Not Call registry.

Just Hit Send

We're all connected. We're all online, all the time—in our office, on our cell phones, during our commutes. And what are we doing online?

We're checking e-mail. The average user checks his e-mail at least six times during the workday. He's online on the weekends as well, just to see what's shown up in the inbox.

Any time a large percentage of your target market demonstrates a shared, common behavior, a marketing opportunity exists. In this instance, it's a fairly safe assumption that your target market reads e-mail.

> **Insight**
>
> According to The American Management Association, on average we spend 1 hour and 47 minutes a day checking e-mail. (Eight percent of people spend four or more hours a day dealing with e-mail, which is terrifying, and neatly addressed in *The Idiot's Guide to Information Overload*.)

How E-Mail Marketing Works

E-mail marketing is simply delivering your marketing message via e-mail. This is a low-cost, highly effective way to connect with your customers. However, you've got to do it right. Mess up, and you'll alienate your customers—or worse, wind up in jail!

Effective e-mail marketing embraces The Three Rs: you reach out to your customers Rarely, you keep your message Relevant, and you always, always Repeat what makes you appealing to your target audience.

Rare: Just because you can e-mail your customers every single day doesn't mean that you should. Keep yourself in check. One e-mail per week is plenty—and if you have an elegant, upscale image, that might even be too much!

Relevant: The point of database marketing is to cater to your customers' desires on an individual level. Apply this to your e-mail marketing; send messages only to those customers who will be interested in what you have to say.

Repeat: Every e-mail needs to reinforce your brand. From the colors and font used to the language choices you make and the offers in the e-mail, make sure it fits. Your customers should be able to tell an e-mail comes from your organization without searching for a signature!

The Logistics of E-Mail Marketing

E-mail marketing can be as simple or as complicated as you'd like it to be. For the ultimate in target marketing, you, as the business owner, write an e-mail directly to your customer:

> "Hey, Bob! I know you were looking for a new drill press, and we've just gotten the new Makita drill press on the truck this morning. It's going for $599, but if you want to check it out before we put it on the floor this weekend, we'll give it to you for $579. Yours, Joe from Joe's Tools."

This type of e-mail is great, but it's difficult to provide this level of customized service and attention all the time.

That's why you need a database of your customers' e-mail addresses, preferably sortable into categories that make sense for your business.

If you're an accountant, you should be able to sort your e-mail addresses by individual accounts, small business accounts, corporations, and nonprofits, for example.

A women's apparel retailer may want to sort by size, favorite designer, or clothing type—cruise wear, formal apparel, sports clothing.

Having a sortable list means you can send e-mail messages only to those customers likely to be interested in the offer.

Once you have a sortable list, here is the four-step process you follow to send e-mail marketing messages:

1. Decide what your message is going to be. Are you informing your customers of a new product? Is there a special event or sale you want them to attend? Has something in the news affected them—and you want them to know it? This will appear as your subject heading.

2. Craft your message. Make sure your message is formatted in such a way that it clearly comes from you. Make sure your graphics and logos are consistent with the ones you use in your business and advertising.

   The most important part of your message needs to be in the top-right corner. This is the section that appears first in most preview panes—if you don't catch the customers' attention here, they're not going to open the e-mail. Bear in mind that this is a snap decision. How quickly do you go through *your* e-mails? Your customers move just as quickly!

   > **Insight**
   >
   > The offer isn't always the most engaging part of the e-mail. Potentially entertaining, funny, or informative e-mails get opened at a much higher rate than plain sales pieces.

3. Decide who is getting the message. All offers don't appeal to all customers. Choose carefully, and select the appropriate names from your e-mail list.

4. Send.

What About SPAM?

No sooner does a technology emerge than someone finds a way to abuse it. Because it is both easy and affordable to send e-mail, it has become the marketing platform of choice for some less-than-ethical businesspeople, who peddle everything from bogus vacation homes in Borneo to once-in-a-lifetime Nigerian investment opportunities.

Fraudulent and junk e-mails, collectively known as SPAM, have become a huge problem. As a result, congress enacted the CAN-SPAM act of 2003, which dictates, among other things, that all commercial e-mail must contain an opt-out provision, comply with content rules, and be sent only in a certain fashion.

Keeping track of all the CAN-SPAM regulations can be problematic—but failing to do so can cost a business owner plenty in the way of fines and sanctions. Additionally, a company that gains a reputation as a spammer has not done itself any favors.

That is why many organizations that choose to conduct e-mail marketing campaigns do so by using the services of a third-party vendor. A number of companies handle the logistics of e-mail marketing. For a nominal price, they format the content you supply and send it to the appropriate names on your list. They handle compliance issues and unsubscribe requirements. Check out www.constantcontact.com for this type of service.

Everybody Likes Presents

Gift-giving is a great way to make your customers feel appreciated and valued. More than any other strategy in this section, this one's about client retention rather than directly driving sales.

Gift-giving is a well-established way to express gratitude. The very phrase "a token of our esteem" sums it up: you give your customers a gift because you appreciate their support of your business.

There are two ways to go about gift-giving. You can have a traditional gift that you deliver to your customers every year at a certain time. For example, one massage therapist gives chocolate roses to her clients every Valentine's Day. A hairdresser gives her clients compact mirrors just before her town's biggest gala event.

Another route involves spontaneity. Give small but meaningful gifts to customers who stop by your business location or visit your website on a random day. Don't announce these gifts: delivering them is part of the surprise. You can also deliver the gifts via the mail, with a note explaining that this is your company's way of saying thanks for their business. If you're particularly upscale, consider using a courier service for a gift to truly stand out—chocolates and flowers are the most common.

What Makes a Great Gift?

Be unique. Be creative. Gifts given by companies range all over the map. Merchandise can work really well.

Make sure whatever you send is of interest to your target audience.

Other business owners have reinforced their relationship with their customers by giving away logo clothing or caps.

> **On Target**
>
> Fire Mountain Gems often tucks a little something extra into their packages as a thank-you—some new beads or charms.

The Logistics of Gift-Giving

Determine what you're going to give, and who you're going to give it to. If you're only giving gifts to a certain segment of your customers, make sure the selection criteria are well defined.

For example, you may give gifts only to those customers who spend $1,500 a year with you. Or who you see every week.

Some business owners choose to give gifts to all of their customers.

Depending on the size of your gift campaign, you may want to have a third-party vendor handle the logistics. This is easy as pie: you provide them with a list of customer addresses, and they provide the gift and package and mail it to your customers. Keep in mind that this tends to be an expensive option.

> **On Target**
>
> The Naked Turtle Restaurant started with a few quirky t-shirts for their best customers. The apparel became so popular that they wound up selling a line of clothing and creating a profitable secondary revenue stream.

Spontaneous gifts are usually smaller, spur-of-the-moment deals, although they still require planning. Make sure you have adequate supplies on hand, and let your staff know how you want the presentation of the gifts handled.

You can even consider a donation to a charity that's meaningful to your target market as a gift.

> **Danger Zone**
>
> Make sure that your gift matches your image. A cheap gift that breaks the first time a customer uses it will reflect negatively on your image.

Do-It-Yourself or Outsource

Keeping in touch with your existing customer base is a lot of work. It becomes even more work when you adapt the tools described in this chapter to reach out to new customers. No matter what strategy you adopt, you wind up having to ask yourself a critical question: is this something we can do in-house, or is it better to hire someone else to do it?

The answer to this question will depend on a number of factors:

- Do you have the time and ability to do the job yourself?
- Is doing the job yourself the best use of your time?
- Is doing the job yourself going to save you money?
- Do you have the resources needed to do the task yourself? Direct mail, for example, often requires a bulk-mailing permit.
- Do you want to do the job yourself?

Pay particular attention to the regulations surrounding any method you select. Telemarketing is subject to the Do Not Call registry. Direct mail has Do Not Mail requirements, and e-mail marketing is covered by the labyrinthine regulation of the CAN-SPAM act. If you cannot comply with all these regulations, bringing in a third-party vendor may serve as a prudent move.

Working with a Third-Party Vendor

There are four considerations when working with a third-party vendor.

Ability. A third-party vendor should be able to perform the task desired while complying with all applicable regulations. In addition, you want a vendor who can provide guidance and insight to enable you to realize maximum value from your marketing efforts.

Reputation for performance. Work with an established company. You don't want to be somebody else's learning curve. This is too important, with your company's reputation hanging on the line. Look online: there your choices are not limited by geography.

Cost. As with any promotional campaign, you need to have a budget for direct mail, e-mail marketing, and telemarketing campaigns. The same is true for gift-giving.

Factor in the cost of a third-party provider, and secure the best service you can for your money.

Many third-party vendors are willing to negotiate on price if you plan numerous campaigns with them. This is something to keep in mind when planning campaigns. Remember the discussion in Chapter 16 on advertising—repetition and consistency work.

Ethics. You need to work with a third-party vendor who will protect your customer's contact information. Security is paramount. A third-party vendor should not under any circumstances sell your contact list information nor mine it for their own purposes. Make sure that you have a written contract in place before beginning your work together.

Understanding the Client-Retention Cycle

Keeping your customers your customers poses many challenges. Loyalty is rare in today's marketplace. There's always a better deal, shinier and newer merchandise, or more attractive services.

It's a fact that you will never retain all of your customers. However, it's important to keep a handle on who your customers are, how many of them you're holding on to, and what offers they're responding to.

Loyalty cards, customer tracking, and other daily operations covered in Chapter 18 can demonstrate who your customers are, and how often you're seeing them. Regularly examine this data. It should provide a clue, as should your sales numbers. Remember that 80 percent of most businesses' profits come from 20 percent of their customers.

To understand what offers appeal to your base, you need to embrace the SMART cycle.

Being SMART

Every campaign you mount in order to hold onto your existing client base must be strategic. It must deliver results that more than pay for the campaign. It must, in short, be SMART.

Set goals. Before you begin a campaign, you must have a clear goal or objective in mind. Make this goal specific and quantifiable. For example:

By engaging in this telemarketing campaign, I will call 200 people, and 50 will respond, resulting in $8,500 worth of sales.

Measure Results. After you have conducted the campaign, look at your results and compare them to the goal you set. For example:

By conducting this campaign, I called 200 people. 30 responded. I made $6,000 worth of sales.

Adjust. Few campaigns are perfect the first time out. Changing the language, the offer, the timing of the call, or any number of factors can impact the results. For best results, pick one item to change before trying again. For example:

In the next phone campaign, I will offer a 15 percent discount instead of 10 percent.

Repeat. Conduct another campaign to see if you have better results. With the new offer, for example:

I called 200 people. 65 responded. I made $10,000 in sales.

Test. Even the best campaigns must be examined regularly. Offers tend to become less effective over time, and you want to change methodologies when you get less response, fewer buyers, or when your competition begins to copy what you're doing.

The Least You Need to Know

- Make your direct mail fun, exciting, and, most of all, relevant and irresistible.

- Give people an incentive to do business with you—a discount, or an extra something.

- Consider working with a third-party vendor for consistency and frequency of your marketing campaigns.

- Include a gift-giving strategy into your target marketing plan.

Chapter 21

Don't Go It Alone

In This Chapter

- ◆ Understanding partner relationships
- ◆ Exploring target marketing with partners
- ◆ Outlining partnership options
- ◆ Assessing opportunities

Many hands make light work. That's good news for small business owners who want to embrace target marketing but who don't necessarily have the time or resources to try everything outlined in this book, especially all on their own.

Working with a partner can make life much easier. When you develop marketing concepts, identify prime target marketing opportunities, create and implement campaigns and more, you're ahead of the game. It all becomes easier when there are two (or more!) sets of eyes looking at the project.

In this section, we'll investigate how you can form effective target marketing partnerships or, to borrow the old Beatles' sentiment, "How to get by with a little help from your friends!"

Understanding Partner Relationships

A journey's only half as long when you share it with a friend! So the saying goes, and the sentiment holds true here, when applied to target marketing endeavors.

While every organization needs their own unique, well-constructed target marketing plan, there will be occasions over the course of your business life where you have the opportunity to partner with other organizations. Working together to achieve common marketing objectives can be a great idea, provided you're smart about it.

Why Is It Smart to Work with a Partner?

There are many clear benefits to working with a partner for target marketing purposes. Five common benefits are as follows:

- Save money by sharing marketing expenses.

- Extend visibility by participating in a larger marketing campaign than you'd be able to manage alone.

- Access marketing resource relationships your partner may already have established. For example, if your partner already knows a reporter, or a great sign printer, or a fabulous podcast host, she can introduce you!

- Benefit by being affiliated in the customer's mind with another strong, established brand.

- Get exposure to fresh, new ideas and a different perspective. This is essential, because small business owners tend to develop tunnel vision, from focusing long and hard on their own ideas.

Types of Partner Relationships

In an equal partnership, everything is shared on an equal footing: costs, benefits, risks, and rewards. For example, if you buy advertising space with a partner, in an equal relationship, you can expect to occupy half the ad space. You also should expect to pay half the bill!

Unequal partnerships are exactly what they sound like: there is an uneven distribution of cost and benefits in any marketing campaign. This seems unattractive on the surface, yet there are many reasons why small business owners enter unequal partnerships.

Three common reasons include the following:

◆ The business is too small or lacks resources to compete on an equal footing with larger partners.

◆ The perceived benefit of participating in a campaign is too small to merit more involvement from a partner.

◆ Test-marketing, in an attempt to explore new markets without incurring substantial expense.

If you're interested in partnership opportunities, you need to be proactive. Yes, there are times when opportunities just fall into your lap, but sitting around waiting for those times could cause lots of frustration and disappointment.

Your professional associations and local community groups are often the first place to start exploring partnership opportunities. Creating a partnership can be as simple as having a discussion with a few like-minded business owners. Alternatively, it could be as complex as entering into a formal arrangement, devoted to ongoing larger marketing endeavors.

Insight

Tradeshow exhibiting and magazine advertising are two areas where group participation has proven to be extraordinarily effective: both may be too pricey to approach alone, yet can be a more manageable expense when shared.

Defining Your Options

Partnership opportunities exist any place you have an existing working relationship with another organization. Additionally, the potential for partnership opportunities exists in an infinite number of places. The fact is that you have to take the initiative and see how responsive other business owners would be to the idea of teaming up.

Partnership arrangements differ from a one-time deal, where you ally yourself with another organization for one campaign or event, to arrangements that continue for longer periods, providing ongoing benefits to both partners.

Insight

Be willing to make the first move! Ask the organizations you already have a relationship with if they're open to partnerships. You never know if they already have a program in place!

Partnering with Your Vendors

Vendors are the companies that sell to you. If you're a retailer, you buy your merchandise from a number of vendors. If you're a manufacturer, a vendor supplies the raw materials you use to make your products. If you're a service provider, your vendors are the companies that provide the supplies and resources you need to do what you do. For example, a massage therapist's vendors might include lotion suppliers and massage table manufacturers.

Vendors are often open to marketing partnerships, because the more that you sell, the more money they make. The benefit is clear and direct, which is why many vendors aggressively promote marketing partnership opportunities.

Danger Zone

A vendor can kill you with kindness. Because they want their name in as many places as possible, they might provide signage, advertising, logos, e-newsletter templates, and the like. It's possible for their brand to overwhelm yours. Keep an eye on the balance!

How Does It Work?

How can your vendors help you? Many vendors already have programs in place. They might provide signage or fixtures for the retail environment. Cooperative advertising, where the vendor shares in advertising or promotional expenses, is a common model for many types of businesses.

Vendors are also a good resource if you're looking to sponsor a community event. They'll cough up the cash if you can ensure that their name is featured prominently. All you need to do is ask!

What Do They Get Out of It?

Vendors want their names out there as often as possible. Brand awareness is just as critical to a vendor as it is to you!

At the same time, don't lose sight of the fact that you provide vendors with advertising access they wouldn't ordinarily get. For example, a clothing manufacturer can advertise all they want, but without a venue for people to buy the clothes, that money isn't necessarily being well spent. When they "buy into" target marketing opportunities you've identified, they realize the power of positioning in front of their target audience.

Joint Ventures

A joint venture is simply two or more businesses agreeing to work together for a specific purpose. By cooperating in a very real, tangible way, both organizations benefit.

Ideally, you'll want to explore joint venture target marketing with an organization whose products and services complement your own. For example, a small art gallery joined forces with an interior decorator. Because they shared a customer base, the gallery owner was thrilled at increased sales, and the interior decorator became renowned for adding that unique, original art touch to her work.

Remember, you're looking for a target marketing joint venture. This method works best when you're working with businesses that share your target market! If you're spending time and money trying to reach out to customers well outside your ideal demographic, you're just wasting your resources!

> **Danger Zone**
>
> Beware of a joint venture with a company that commands power and prestige in the marketplace. It's only a good fit if you're targeting their same market. To join forces just for the prestige could be wasteful.

How Does It Work?

A joint venture is the most flexible and free form of all the target marketing partnership opportunities. Your arrangement will be what you and your partners agree upon.

To make your partnership work, communication is essential. Start the joint venture process by sitting down with your proposed partners. Discuss what you want to accomplish by working together. Spell out goals and objectives and the method you're planning to use to attain those goals and objectives.

Make sure everyone understands his or her responsibilities and obligations. Then put this all in writing and run it by a lawyer, so that should a dispute arise, you have the original agreement to refer to.

> **Danger Zone**
>
> "Internet joint-venture marketing" is the latest set of buzzwords favored by get-rich-quick scam operators. Some online opportunities are legitimate, but they're the minority. Do your research!

What Do They Get Out of It?

Because joint venture target marketing partners share a target audience, the primary benefit is one of efficiency. Your partners get their message out to their customers for a fraction of the price of going it alone.

> **Insight** _____
>
> Customers judge us by the company we keep. The partnerships and alliances we enter are branding decisions. Before making any final decisions, it's critical to ask a very important question: "How will entering this partnership affect how my customers think about my business?"
>
> Don't feel bad about asking that question. You better believe the other business owner is asking it. If your reputation isn't going to enhance theirs, they're not going to want to partner with you!

Affiliate Programs

Affiliate programs are a web-based form of joint target marketing. You need to look no further than Amazon.com to see this concept in action—but you don't have to be an Amazon-size organization to make affiliate marketing work for you!

How Does It Work?

Affiliate marketing, in its purest form, is the art of paying for customer referrals. Let's go back to Amazon.com to demonstrate how this works.

> **Insight** _____
>
> If you get a lot of traffic to your website or blog, affiliate marketing for a larger organization offers a nice, passive revenue stream: you make money without doing any work! However, you need to do your homework first.

Amazon.com, of course, is a well-known online book, media, and everything-else retailer. They stock just about everything you can think of, but that doesn't mean they can promote everything they sell.

However, if you, on your business website or blog, mention a product sold by Amazon, and link to their site, and someone reading your site clicks on the link and purchases the product, you make a commission. (As of this writing, it's 4 percent.)

If you operate some or all of your business online, it's well worth exploring affiliate marketing. Affiliate marketing can be highly targeted. If you're very selective about whom you allow into your affiliate program, you can control to some degree who sees your ads.

Designing an affiliate marketing program for your business takes some work. However, the investment of time and resources can be well worth it. When you start driving more traffic to your website, and people buy from you, you generate more income! An easy concept to understand.

The nice thing about affiliate marketing, from the business owner's perspective, is you only pay your affiliates when the customers they refer buy!

What Do They Get Out of It?

Affiliates are generally pretty crystal clear about their motivation: sending customers to your site makes them money. It's as simple as that.

In fact, legions of professional bloggers have carved out successful careers for themselves creating high-traffic, high-visibility blogs, loaded with affiliate marketing links.

Danger Zone

Lie down with dogs, wake up with fleas! The Internet is full of less-than-ethical individuals, and many of them purport to be willing affiliates. Before you enter any agreements, take the time to check out the site they'll be linking from. Remember your reputation!

Channel Partners

The channel partner model has its roots in the IT world. Basically, a channel partner resells services or products on behalf of a larger vendor.

Some channel partners enhance the offerings they get from the original vendor, making the product or service more valuable to the end customer. This type of arrangement is known as a Value Add Reseller, or more commonly, a VAR Channel Partner.

How Does It Work?

There are two ways to look at the channel partner model from a target marketing perspective. The first is as the channel partner. Having access to products and services that would ordinarily be beyond the scope of what you can provide makes your business more appealing.

For example, you might be a great web designer, but if you also provide site hosting because you're a channel partner with BlueHost, then you've become that much more valuable to your customers.

The second option is to create your own network of channels to distribute your products and services. By creating a network of channel partners, you're cutting out the middleman and eliminating the costs of dealing with a third-party distributor. However, this is not a minor undertaking. If you consider this option, be prepared to commit substantial amounts of time and resources to establishing the program.

What Do They Get Out of It?

If you enter a channel partner arrangement as a reseller, you're enhancing your organization's appeal and generating sales for the manufacturer. They enjoy increased profitability and wider distribution.

If you create your own channel network, your partners are likely to be in the relationship to offer a wider range of products and services than they could do on their own. In addition, they make money on each sale—a lucrative incentive.

Evaluating Potential Partners

Any time you ally your business with another organization, it's a critical branding decision. Really think through the choices you're making, to ensure that you protect your business's reputation.

Being approached for a joint venture or other target marketing partnership opportunity is exciting. It can be taken as a sign that you've arrived. There's nothing more flattering than other business owners saying they want to work with you.

However, proceed with caution. Don't let your ego overtake the business side of this proposition. When you enter into a target marketing partnership, you're in a situation where elements of what happens, when it happens, and how it happens will be beyond your control. You need to be sure you're comfortable giving up that control.

Assessing the Relationship

When considering target marketing partnerships, keep your focus on the quality of the relationship. This type of alliance can only work if both parties to the agreement feel like they're benefiting from the deal.

To help stay focused, ask yourself the following questions:

How will entering this partnership positively impact my business? Identify the goals and objectives you hope to achieve by entering this partnership. Be realistic: this isn't the time to get your head caught in the clouds!

How will entering this partnership negatively impact my business? Everything has a cost. Identify the cost of participating in this target marketing partnership opportunity. Weigh if this cost is acceptable. Don't forget to move beyond dollar and cents accounting: consider intangibles, like your reputation in the community.

What will I be expected to do for my partners? Get a clear list of what you're expected to do. Is there a financial contribution? Are you supposed to spend time placing articles and doing interviews? Are you committed to flying to the industry conference in Toledo or Thailand? Get a clear list ahead of time. Avoid being blind-sided by stealth expectations!

Is this partnership the best possible company to ally myself with? You don't have to dance with the first person who asks! Once you start considering target marketing partnership opportunities, critically assess all of your options. You want to ally yourself with the company your target audience will find the most appealing!

What is this company's reputation? Who else are they partnered with? Do your research before saying yes. Get online and Google potential partners. If you find hate sites aimed at the organization or lots of negative commentary, joining forces with them may not be your wisest move.

At the same time, consider who they're already keeping company with. Do you want your company's name forever linked in the public mind with those organizations?

What marketing campaigns can be created centered on the new alliance? If you're going to join forces with an organization, there should be a reason. What target marketing campaigns do you see happening that benefit both companies? Brainstorm, alone and with your potential partner. You want to see how much creativity and insight they're bringing to the table. It's important to know and understand their strengths and weaknesses.

How much input will I have in partnership decisions? Basically, how much say do you get? This can be a critical consideration: if you're convinced a certain campaign is going to be a disaster, do you still have to fund it? Can you opt out of marketing projects if they don't work for you?

How will problems be handled? As tempting as it may be to assume that nothing ever will go wrong with your partnership, prudent business owners address problem resolution ahead of time. Personality conflicts, different decision-making styles, and divergent viewpoints make for great TV but can really wreck your target marketing plan. Discuss how you'll handle conflict and who has the final decision-making power.

Pitfalls and Perils of Partnership

There may be safety in numbers—but misery loves company! How can you determine if the partnership you're entering into will enhance your business or detract from it?

There's no sure way, short of a magic crystal ball, to read the future. However, you can be aware of certain common scenarios that signal trouble on the horizon. If you see any of these "red flag" scenarios creeping into your target marketing partnership, take action and address them immediately. Consider the following scenarios:

Your partner doesn't trust you—and you don't trust him! Once trust has been removed from a relationship, that relationship, for all intensive purposes, is over. You can't do good business with someone you don't trust. If you find yourself questioning the other party and doubting his word, get out, and get out fast!

You know what you're doing, but your new partner is completely clueless. Different levels of competency make for a rocky relationship. This is particularly true in the marketing world, where there are so many interpretations of what works and what's foolish. Serious conversations are in order!

You're sure your partner is great. You just never see her. Or talk to her. Or e-mail her. For a partnership to work, there has to be communication. If you can't reach your partner, or she can't reach you, there's a real issue in the relationship. Bridge that gap and change the dynamic, before it is too late!

You were sure this partnership was going to increase your sales 1,000 percent—and so did your partner. Now nobody's happy. Entering a partnership with unrealistic expectations is a surefire route to failure. Take time to spell out quantifiable, objective goals at the beginning, and create benchmark goals to track your progress. It's fine to aim high—but not out of the galaxy!

You want to reach young, career-oriented, tech-savvy women, and your partner's after the gray granny set. For a target marketing partnership to work, you must share a target audience with your partner. Spend time spelling out exactly who falls into your target market. Be specific, and never assume you share target markets!

As soon as your customers heard about the new partnership, they had one thing to say: "Why?" Ideally, a target marketing partnership will make total and complete sense to your customers. They'll look at the relationship and say, "Of course!"

If Smuckers Jam and Jif Peanut Butter did a campaign together, customers would likely react well—the two items complement each other, and there's a natural relationship between them. Take that same Smuckers Jam and partner it with windshield washer fluid, and you'll have some cognitive dissonance on your hands! Don't create confusion for your customers.

The Least You Need to Know

- Working together to achieve common marketing objectives is a great idea, but be smart about who you choose to partner with.

- For a joint venture to be successful, your products and services should complement each other.

- When you ally your business with another organization, realize that your brand reputation is vulnerable.

- When you consider target marketing partnerships, keep your focus on the quality of the relationship.

Glossary

advertising rate card   Document containing prices and descriptions for the various ad-placement options available from a media outlet.

advertorial   Where an advertisement masquerades as editorial coverage.

advocate   A person who publicly supports or recommends a particular cause or policy.

affiliate programs   Web-based form of joint target marketing.

affinity   Likeness based on relationship or causal connection.

animated ads   Advertising that uses movement (animation) to create attention.

annual conference   Meeting organized by a specific group held every year in the same or a different location.

anthology   Collection of literary pieces, such as poems, short stories, or plays.

association publication   Newsletter, magazine, or journal published by a specific association to keep its members informed and up to date with information in the specific industry or community.

authenticity   Something that is real, genuine, and trusted.

avatar A computer user's self-representation or alter ego in a three-dimensional model used in computer games, or in a two-dimensional picture used on Internet forums and other communities.

B2B community Business-to-business; a term commonly used to describe commerce transactions between businesses, as opposed to those between businesses and other groups, such as business-to-consumers (B2C) or business-to-government (B2G).

baby boomers Term used to describe a person born during the post-World War II baby boom (1946–1964).

banner ad A graphic that appears on a web page that is usually hyperlinked to an advertisers website; it's typically a large headline or title extending across the full page width.

beliefs Something believed or accepted as true, especially a particular opinion or doctrine accepted by a group.

belly-up Business dealings that go badly wrong.

benchmark A point of reference for a measurement such as goals.

blog Short form for weblog; an online chronological log of information kept by an individual, group, or business.

blog commenter A person who comments on someone else's blog.

blogger A person who blogs.

blogging The act of posting on blogs.

blogosphere The Internet blogging community on the world-wide web.

booking agent Also known as a media agent, this is a public relations professional who specializes in getting his or her clients placed primarily on television or radio.

brand Concrete symbols such as a name, logo, slogan, and design scheme that convey the essence of a company, product, or service. The key objective is to create a relationship of trust.

brand analysis Measures the relative strength of one brand against another set of competing brands.

brand loyalty When customers have a high relative attitude toward the brand, which is exhibited through repurchase behavior.

brand recognition Reaction created by the accumulation of experiences with the specific product or service, both directly relating to its use and through the influence of advertising, design, and media commentary.

brick-and-mortar   Refers to a company that possesses a building for operations, which offers face-to-face consumer experiences.

buying motivator   Something that stimulates (someone's) interest in or enthusiasm for buying something.

buzz   A highly intense and interactive form of word-of-mouth communication.

call to action   A request for the customer to do something, generally to place an order.

CAN-SPAM Act   Establishes requirements for those who send commercial e-mail, spells out penalties for spammers, and gives consumers the right to ask e-mailers to stop spamming them.

cause marketing   Refers to any type of marketing effort for social and other charitable causes.

cell phone advertising   The use of text messages to notify customers of special deals and banner ads to sponsor items, such as ringtone downloads.

channel partner   Resells services or products on behalf of a larger vendor.

chat room   Online place to meet and communicate with friends who share your interests—from entertainment to sports, to politics and pop culture.

column   A regular recurring piece or article in a newspaper, magazine, or other publication written by columnists.

comment card   An easy way for customers to express their satisfaction directly to you.

communications platform   Planned marketing that comprises objectives, target audience, major selling idea, benefits, and a creative strategy.

community-building tools   There are three basic kinds of community-building tools: web-based, e-mail–based, and chat-based. Each has specific strengths and weaknesses.

community conversation   Brings together diverse groups of people who share what they think and feel, and to listen to what others think and feel.

community shopper paper   A community newspaper that links businesses and myriad special products with thousands of readers and advertisers.

competitive edge   Enables a company to create superior value for its customers.

conclusive market research   Draws some conclusion about the issue being researched.

conference call   A telephone call where two or more people participate. It may be set up so that the called party merely listens into the call and cannot speak.

content distribution sites   A system of computers networked together across the Internet that cooperate transparently to deliver content, most often for the purpose of improving performance, scalability, and cost-efficiency, to end users.

cooperative advertising   Where the vendor shares in advertising or promotional expenses.

customer base   A group of current clients and consumers a business serves. In the most ideal situation, a large part of this group is made up of repeat customers.

customer retention   Keeping customers and not losing them to competitors.

customer satisfaction   A measure of how products and services supplied by a company meet or surpass customer expectation.

cutting-edge   The state-of-the-art developments in a field.

cyberspace   A global computer network, linking all people, machines, and sources of information through virtual space.

damage control public relations   Also known as crisis public relations. It provides options to consider in the midst of a crisis brought on by adverse or negative media attention.

data collection   A term used to describe a process of preparing and collecting information.

database marketing   The practice of marketing directly to your existing customer base.

demographic analysis   Includes the sets of methods that show measurement and dynamics of populations.

demographics   Information about people's lifestyles, habits, population movements, spending, age, social grade, employment, etc.

differentiation   Involves identifying, leveraging, and promoting characteristics of a business that are distinctly different from a competitor's.

discussion forum   An area within a website where you can discuss any aspect of a particular topic with other online users around the world.

e-commerce   Electronic commerce, consists of the buying and selling of products or services over electronic systems such as the Internet and other computer networks. Also known as Internet commerce.

early adopter   Customers who are the first to try a new product or service. They don't mind paying higher prices for the privilege to be first.

echo research   Research you conduct in the everyday course of business with your customers.

editorial   An article in a newspaper or magazine that expresses the opinion of the editor, editorial board, or publisher.

editorial calendar   Shows the major editorial features planned for forthcoming issues of a newspaper, magazine, and similar publications.

entrepreneur   Person who organizes and operates a business or businesses, taking on greater-than-normal financial risks in order to do so.

event collateral materials   Includes a wide range of documents that companies use to promote themselves at an event such as a tradeshow.

exploratory market research   Preliminary research to clarify the exact nature of the problem to be solved.

ezine   A periodic publication distributed by e-mail or posted on a website. They are typically tightly focused on a subject area.

fad   A custom, style, etc. that many people are interested in for a short time; passing fashion; craze.

family structure   Sometimes referred to as family dynamics, it considers size and roles individuals play.

fandom   A passionate community group; fervent admirers of a specific product.

feasibility study   Evaluation of a contemplated project or course of action, according to preestablished criteria, to determine if the proposal meets requirements. An analysis is also made of alternative means of accomplishing the task.

flash animation   An animated film created using animation software. The term also refers to a certain kind of movement and simplistic or unpolished visual style.

franchise   License granted by a company (the franchisor) to an individual or firm (the franchisee) to operate a business where the franchisee agrees to use the franchisor's name; products; services; promotions; selling, distribution, and display methods; and other company support.

fulfillment service   An independent service contractor that fills large and small customer orders on behalf of a company.

generation   A term used to describe an age grouping that consists of 10 or more years.

Generation X   A term used to describe the generation of people born between the approximate years of 1965 to 1981.

Generation Y   Sometimes referred to as "Millennials" or "Net Generation," people born between 1982 and 2000.

generational strategies   Marketing programs aimed at the different generations.

ghostwriter   A professional writer paid to write books, articles, stories, reports, or other content that are officially credited to another person.

globalization   The process of transformation of local or regional phenomena into global ones.

Google Analytics   Free online facility for obtaining traffic analysis by adding code to all website pages.

GPS system   Global positioning system used to tell you where you are geographically.

guarantee   A promise or assurance, especially in writing, that something is of specified quality, content, benefit, etc., or that it will perform satisfactorily for a given length of time.

hook   A clever phrase or melody used to capture the consumer's attention and help make the advertising message more memorable.

hype   Extreme promotion of a person, idea, or product.

image analysis   Objective and quantifiable report based on how an organization is viewed by a specified group.

inbound links   Links from another website pointing to your website (like a friend calling your house from his house).

independent contractor   A person or company retained to perform work for another, often under a written contract, whereby control is subjected to the end result and not as to how the work is performed; the independent contractor is not an employee.

Internet retailing   Selling products on your website.

information superhighway   Term used to describe the Internet and virtually all associated computer networks.

IT   Information technology.

jargon   The language, especially the vocabulary, peculiar to a particular trade, profession, or group.

joint venture   Two or more businesses agreeing to work together for a specific purpose.

keyword   A word or phrase entered into a search engine in an effort to get the search engine to return matching and relevant results.

layout   The whole design of a single page in a magazine, brochure, etc.

layperson   A person who is not a member of a given profession.

life coach   An advisor who helps people with problems, decisions, and goal attainment in daily life.

lifetime value   A marketing metric that tends to place greater emphasis on customer service and long-term customer satisfaction than on maximizing short-term sales.

link swapping   Reciprocal link exchange with another website—they link to your site and you link to theirs.

list broker   A business that maintains and sells lists of consumer addresses for use in direct mail campaigns.

loyalty cards   Used in loyalty programs—structured marketing efforts that reward, and therefore encourage, loyal buying behavior. Often a loyalty card, rewards card, points card, advantage card, frequent buyer card, or club card is a plastic or paper card that identifies the holder as a member in a loyalty program.

market growth   When the overall demand for a product being sold has increased.

market saturation   When the overall demand for a product being sold has reached its maximum capacity.

market-share analysis   Indicates how well a company is doing in the marketplace compared to its competitors.

marketing materials   Any piece of material that helps promote a company.

marketing message   Feelings, usually expressed through words, that convince potential customers your products or services provide a solution.

Maslow's Hierarchy of Needs   Maslow set up a hierarchy of five levels of basic needs. Beyond these needs, higher levels of needs exist.

mass marketing   A market coverage strategy in which a company decides to ignore market segment differences and go after the whole market with one offer.

media   A means of communication, especially of mass communication, such as books, newspapers, magazines, radio, television, motion pictures, and recordings.

media buyer   Connects clients with television time, advocating for the best price and advising clients how to make the best use of it.

media consumption   Refers to an individual's usage or consumption of specified media or a media vehicle.

megachains/retailers   Refers to supersize stores, eateries, or hotels, such as McDonald's, The Gap, or Hilton.

merchandise   The manufactured goods bought and sold in any business; the stock of goods in a store.

meta tags   Electronic word tags or coding statements that are used to describe various aspects about a web page.

microblogging   The practice of sending brief posts to a personal blog on a microblogging website, such as Twitter.

mindset   An attitude, disposition, or mood.

mobile phone marketing   Emerging as a powerful component of any interactive marketing mix, as it provides an opportunity for interaction with users who may otherwise not be willing to interact.

national campaign   A promotion that is conducted throughout the country.

natural attrition   The gradual reduction in employees by natural means, for example, retirement, resignation, or death.

networking event   A meeting organized to cultivate business friendships and acquaintances.

news release   Also known as media release, press release, or press statement; a written or recorded communication directed at members of the news media to broadcast something claimed to have news value.

news site   Website dedicated to helping people stay up to date on current events.

niche marketing   A strategy that addresses the need for a product or service for a narrowly defined group of potential customers.

Nielsen Ratings   Measures television, radio, and newspaper audiences in their respective media markets. Also offered as an online service.

online brochure   Promotional material created to be used on a website.

online education   Learning material of all levels offered through a website.

online publication   Publications such as periodicals, magazines, newspapers, and more, offered on a website.

pitch   A short advertisement of a story idea.

podcast   A method of distributing multimedia files (audio/videos) online using feeds for playback on mobile devices and personal computers. Podcasts are created by podcasters.

poll   Used to get the opinions (of people) by asking specific questions.

pop-up ad   An ad that appears in a separate window on top of content already onscreen.

populace   A group of people forming the total population of a certain place.

PowerPoint   A presentation software program included as part of the Microsoft Office package.

premium item   A prize, bonus, or award given as an incentive to purchase products, enter competitions initiated by business interests, etc.

press conference   The calling together of the press to announce significant news and/or events.

primary market research   The process of planning, collecting, and analyzing data relevant to marketing decision-making.

print advertising   Advertising in newspapers, magazines, catalogs, or mailers, usually using some combination of photographs, illustrations, and copy.

print on-demand   Books printed as they are sold rather than printed in large quantities.

product positioning analysis   A marketing technique that maps out consumer perceptions of product attributes.

professional advocacy   Paying a professional to encourage or support an activity that helps a consumer, company, or organization to secure its product.

professional connection site   Web-based services that enable professionals to construct a public or semipublic profile within a bounded system.

promotional strategy   Choosing a target market and formulating the most appropriate promotion mix to influence it.

psychographics   Data describing the psychology of specific target audiences.

public data   Data open without restrictions to the public.

public opinion studies   The aggregate of individual attitudes or beliefs held by the adult population.

questionnaire   A formal, written, set of closed-ended and open-ended questions that are asked of every respondent in the study.

ranking   Relative placement in a list.

readership   Refers to the number of people reading a particular publication.

relationship marketing strategies   Developed from direct-response marketing campaigns, these marketing strategies emphasize the long-term value of keeping customers.

return policy   A document that explains a merchant's policy regarding the return of products by customers.

satellite radio   A digital radio signal that is broadcast by a communications satellite, which covers a much wider geographical range than terrestrial radio signals.

search engine optimization (SEO)   The process of improving the volume and quality of traffic to a website from search engines via "natural" ("organic" or "algorithmic") search results for targeted keywords.

searchable catalogs   Online catalogs you can flip through to find what interests you, or simply type in what you're looking for.

secondary market research   Also known as desk research, is information that already exists in one form or another.

shelter magazine   A publishing term used to indicate a segment of the U.S. magazine market—specifically referring to aspirational lifestyle magazines about the home, décor, furnishings, and gardens.

signage   Any publicly displayed information that is presented in the form of words, symbols, and/or pictures. When displayed at a tradeshow, it's referred to as "show signage."

Silent Generation, The   A term used to describe the generation of people born from 1923 to 1943.

site analysis   Identification and evaluation of a site or sites to satisfy a given use or objective.

social network   A web of interconnected people who directly or indirectly interact with or influence each other.

sound bite   A brief, content-rich phrase.

sponsorship   The practice of a company funding a program in order to advertise or sell a product.

streaming radio   Radio programming that is downloaded, on-demand, iteratively to the viewer's computer.

submission   The exchange of information for purposes of publication.

syndication service   Service that buys articles, stories, columns, photographs, comic strips, or other features and distributes them for simultaneous publication in a number of newspapers or periodicals in different localities.

Technorati   A real-time search engine dedicated to the blogosphere. It only searches through blogs to find exactly what you're looking for.

test-marketing   Small test runs of new products or marketing techniques to determine effectiveness before making a full commitment.

third-party vendor   A supplier that provides goods and services that will in turn be supplied to the customer.

tip sheet   A "how-to" publication containing information or tips for a particular business or service.

tradeshow   An exhibition organized so that companies in a specific industry can showcase and demonstrate their latest products and services, study activities of rivals, and examine recent trends and opportunities.

trend   The direction in which the market is heading. Three categories of trends are major, intermediate, and short-term. Trends move in one of three directions: up, down, sideways.

trend spotter   Someone who spots trends.

unicast ads   Short video clips played in a browser window that offer viewers the chance to click through for more information.

U.S. Census Bureau   Largest depository of public information, with data updated regularly.

Valpak campaign   A full-service direct-marketing organization that features coupon savings from over 50,000 advertisers each year from local to national brands. The blue envelope, their flagship product, is delivered to over 45 million homes each month in the North America.

video blog (vlog)   Blogging using video.

video clip   A piece of video film footage.

video hosting platform   An Internet website that enables individuals to upload video clips.

viral marketing   A marketing phenomenon that facilitates and encourages people to spread a marketing message, "like a virus," primarily through "word of mouth."

virtual business card   Business cards bearing business information about a company or individual, shared electronically.

webinar   A seminar conducted remotely over the web.

wiki   Piece of server software that allows users to freely create and edit web page content. The collaborative encyclopedia Wikipedia is one of the best-known wikis.

word-of-mouth marketing   The person-to-person passing of information, especially recommendations, but also general information, in an informal manner.

YouTube   A video-sharing website where users can upload, view, and share video clips.

zoned edition   A publication that is distributed to a specific state or region.

Resources

Knowledge is power! The more you know, the better target marketer you will be. In this appendix, you'll find a number of resources you can use to enhance and augment the information you've gained from reading this book.

Each topic section includes web-based and print resources.

Market Research Basics

Market Research Surveys:

www.freeonlinesurveys.com

www.surveymonkey.com

www.zoomerang.com

The Marketing Teacher
www.marketingteacher.com/Lessons/lesson_marketing_research.htm

Marketing Research Association
www.mra-net.org/

Inc.com Resource Center
www.inc.com/guides/marketing/24018.html

The Complete Idiot's Guide to Marketing, Second Edition by Sarah White, published by Alpha (2003)

Market Research Made Easy by Don Doman, published by Self-Counsel Press (2006)

Trends

Marketing Trends:

www.marketingtrends.org

www.trendsspotting.com

www.trendwatch.com

Trends lend themselves to blogging, and here are some entertaining and informative blogs that focus on trends:

http://interactivemarketingtrends.blogspot.com

http://trendtracker.blogspot.com

Small Business Trends
www.smallbiztrends.com

Hottest Small Business Trends
http://sbinformation.about.com/cs/bestpractices/a/aa122202a.htm

The National Federation of Independent Business Small Business Economic Trends
www.nfib.com/page/sbet

Meatball Sundae: Is Your Marketing Out of Sync? by Seth Godin, published by Portfolio (2007)

Demographic/Psychographic Information

U.S. Census Bureau
www.census.gov

SBDCNet National Information Clearinghouse
www.sbdcnet.org/SBIC/demographics.php

Small Business Labs
http://genylabs.typepad.com/small_biz_labs/demographics/

The Official Business Link to the U.S. Government Business.Gov
www.business.gov/guides/advertising/market-research/index.html

The Ultimate Small Business Marketing Toolkit: All the Tips, Forms, and Strategies You'll Ever Need! by Beth Goldstein, published by McGraw-Hill (2007)

Successful Business Research: Straight to the Numbers You Need—Fast! by Rhonda Abrams, published by The Planning Shop (2006)

Web Design for Business

WebSite Tips
http://websitetips.com

The Internet Digest
www.theinternetdigest.net

Always Be Testing: The Complete Guide to Google Website Optimizer by Bryan Eisenberg and John Quarto vonTivadar, published by Sybex (2008)

Web Design and Marketing Solutions for Business Websites, by Kevin Potts, published by Friends of ED (2007)

Search Engine Optimization

Search Marketing Trends
www.searchmarketingtrends.com

The Small Business Guide to Search Marketing
www.searchengineguide.com/

Keyword Research Tools:

www.keyworddiscover.com

www.wordtracker.com

www.spyfu.com

The Complete Idiot's Guide to Growing Your Business with Google by Dave Taylor, published by Alpha (2005)

Search Engine Marketing, Inc.: Driving Search Traffic to Your Company's Web Site (2nd Edition), by Mike Moran and Bill Hunt, published by IBM Press (2008)

Search Engine Marketing, by Andreas Ramos and Stephanie Cota, published by McGraw-Hill (2008)

Blogging

Blogging Sites:

www.wordpress.com

www.blogger.com

www.typepad.com

Blogging Resources:

www.technorati.com

www.wordpress.org

www.newsvine.com

www.mybloglog.com

Blogging Tips for Beginners
www.problogger.net/archives/2006/02/14/blogging-for-beginners-2

Learning About Blogging and How to Blog
http://lorelle.wordpress.com/2005/08/29/learning-about-blogging-and-how-to-blog

Ezine Articles: "Blogging"
http://ezinearticles.com/?cat=Internet-and-Businesses-Online:Blogging

Blogwild!: A Guide for Small Business Blogging, by Andy Wibbels, published by Portfolio (2006)

The Secret Power of Blogging: How to Promote and Market Your Business, Organization, or Cause With Free Blogs, by Bruce C. Brown, published by Atlantic Publishing Company (2008)

Blog Schmog: The Truth About What Blogs Can (and Can't) Do for Your Business, by Robert W. Bly, published by Thomas Nelson (2007)

Podcasting

SmallBizPod: "How to Podcast for Small Business"
www.smallbizpod.co.uk/blog/2008/10/25/how-to-podcast-for-small-businesses-2

Easy Free Ways to Podcast
http://howtopodcast.blogspot.com

WebProNews: "Why and How to Podcast"
www.webpronews.com/topnews/2006/10/03/why-and-how-to-podcast

Podcast Alley
www.podcastalley.com

Podcasting Tools
www.podcasting-tools.com

Podcast Academy: The Business Podcasting Book: Launching, Marketing, and Measuring Your Podcast, by Michael Geoghegan et. al., published by Focal Press (2007)

Promoting Your Podcast: The Ultimate Guide to Building an Audience of Raving Fans, by Jason Van Orden, published by Larstan Publishing (2006)

Webinars

Web Conferencing Services:

www.gotowebinar.com

www.webex.com

www.webconference.com

www.infiniteconferencing.com

The Webinar Blog
http://wsuccess.typepad.com

BNet Business Network: "How to Conduct a Successful Webinar"
http://jobfunctions.bnet.com/abstract.aspx?docid=341204

eHow "How to Record Webinars"
www.ehow.com/how_2257947_record-webinars.html

BusinessKnowledgeSource.com: "How to Create a Webinar"
www.businessknowledgesource.com/technology/how_to_create_a_webinar_025959.html

Better Than Bullet Points: Creating Engaging e-Learning with PowerPoint, by Jane Bozarth, published by Pfeiffer (2008)

Social Networking

Top Social Networking Sites:

www.facebook.com

www.ning.com

www.myspace.com

www.youtube.com

www.linkedin.com

www.flickr.com

www.twitter.com

Social Bookmarking Sites:

www.digg.com

www.reddit.com

www.delicious.com

Social Calendar
www.meetup.com

What Is Social Networking
www.whatissocialnetworking.com

Small Business Search Marketing: "Social Media Local Networking"
www.smallbusinesssem.com/social-media-local-networking/1327

TheStreet.com: "Social Networking Can Be a Friend Indeed"
www.thestreet.com/story/10430499/1/social-networking-can-be-a-friend-indeed.html

Facebook Marketing: Leverage Social Media to Grow Your Business, by Steve Holzner, published by Que (2008)

Social Media Is a Cocktail Party: Why You Already Know the Rules of Social Media Marketing, by Jim Tobin and Lisa Braziel, published by CreateSpace (2008)

Twitter Revolution: How Social Media and Mobile Marketing is Changing the Way We Do Business & Market Online, by Warren Whitlock and Deborah Micek, published by Xeno Press (2008)

Advertising 2.0: Social Media Marketing in a Web 2.0 World, by Tracy L. Tuten, published Praeger Paperback (2008)

YouTube and Video Blogging

YouTube
www.youtube.com

Things You Should Know About Video Blogging
http://net.educause.edu/ir/library/pdf/ELI7005.pdf

How to Do Things.com: How to Video Blog
www.howtodothings.com/computers/a3803-how-to-video-blog.html

Ladies Who Launch: "How Video Blogs Will Help Grow Your Business"
www.ladieswholaunch.com/magazine/how-to-video-blog/1714

Freevlog—Get Started Video Blogging
www.freevlog.org

YouTube for Business: Online Video Marketing for Any Business, by Michael Miller, published by Que (2008)

Plug Your Business! Marketing on MySpace, YouTube, blogs, and podcasts and other Web 2.0 social networks, by Steve Weber, published by Weber Books (2007)

Cell Phone Marketing

Cell Phone and Mobile Marketing: Five Things to Consider Before Starting a Mobile Marketing Campaign
http://search.techrepublic.com.com/search/cell+phone+and+mobile+marketing.html

Mobile Marketing Association
www.mmaglobal.com

Mobile Marketing Watch
www.mobilemarketingwatch.com

Word-of-Mouth Marketing

Word-of-Mouth Marketing Association
www.womma.org

George Silverman's Word-of-Mouth Marketing Blog
http://wordofmouth.typepad.com/george_silvermans_word_of

Five Word-of-Mouth Marketing Strategies for Your Business or Website
www.doshdosh.com/word-of-mouth-marketing-strategies

How to Change the World: A Practical Blog for Impractical People
http://blog.guykawasaki.com/2008/06/the-inside-word.html

The Complete Idiot's Guide to Guerrilla Marketing, by Susan Drake and Colleen Wells, published by Alpha (2008)

Word-of-Mouth Marketing (Revised Edition) by Andy Sernovitz, Seth Godin, and Guy Kawasaki, published by Kaplan Publishing (2009)

Building Buzz to Beat the Big Boys: Word-of-Mouth Marketing for Small Businesses, by Steve O'Leary and Kim Sheehan, published by Praeger Publishers (2008)

Networking

No More Cold Calling: The Breakthrough System That Will Leave Your Competition in the Dust by Joanne Black, published by Business Plus (2007)

The Secrets of Savvy Networking by Susan RoAne, published by Grand Central Publishing (1993)

Business by Referral: A Sure-Fire Way to Generate New Business by Ivan Misner Ph.D. & Robert Davis published by Bard Press (1998)

Riches in Niches: How to Make It BIG in a Small Market by Susan Friedmann, CSP, published by Career Press (2007)

Mastering Niche Marketing: A Definitive Guide to Profiting from Ideas in a Competitive Market, by Eric V. Van Der Hope, published by Globalnet Publishing (2008)

Guerrilla Networking: A Proven Battle Plan to Attract the Very People You Want to Meet, by Jay Conrad Levinson and Monroe Mann, published by Morgan James Publishing (2007)

Talk Up Your Business: How to Make the Most of Opportunities to Promote and Grow Your Small Business, by Mary Morel, published by Allen & Unwin (2006)

Tradeshow Marketing

Tradeshow Tips
www.thetradeshowcoach.com

Trade Show Marketing.com
www.tradeshowmarketing.com

Finding Tradeshows:

www.tsnn.com

www.thetradeshowcalendar.com/index.php?BNR=susan

Exhibitor Magazine
www.exhibitoronline.com

Tradeshow Exhibitors Association
www.tsea.org

Center for Exhibition Industry Research
www.ceir.org

International Association of Exhibitions & Events
www.iaee.com

The Complete Idiot's Guide to Trade Shows by Linda Musgrove, Alpha Books (2009)

Trade Show & Event Marketing: Plan, Promote & Profit, by Ruth Stevens, published by South Western Educational Publishers (2005)

Writing Web Copy

Word Strategist
www.caseacecopy.com

Copywriting Blog
www.copyblogger.com

"Writing Web Copy That Works"
www.marketingprofs.com/4/dwyer1.asp

"How to Write Effective Web Copy"
www.isitebuild.com/web-copy.htm

"How to Write Killer Copy for the Web"
www.bellaonline.com/articles/art1684.asp

"10 Tips for Writing Effective Web Copy"
www.webpronews.com/topnews/2004/04/22/tips-for-writing-effective-web-copy

Promote Your Business: How to Write Effective Marketing Material for Your Small Business, by Mary Morel, published by Allen & Unwin (2004)

Web Copy That Sells: The Revolutionary Formula for Creating Killer Copy Every Time, by Maria Veloso, published by AMACOM (2004)

Words That Sell by Richard Bayan, published by McGraw-Hill (2006)

Being a Good TV Guest

"Do's and Don'ts for TV Appearances"
www.businessknowhow.com/marketing/tvinterview.htm

"5 Easy Tips to Becoming a Great TV Guest"
www.bigbadbookblog.com/2008/03/19/5-easy-tips-to-becoming-a-great-tv-guest

"Tips on Becoming a Good TV Guest"
www.bigbadbookblog.com/2008/05/02/tips-to-becoming-a-great-tv-guest-part-ii/

"How to Promote Yourself as a TV Guest"
www.frugalmarketing.com/dtb/getontheair.shtml

All About Public Relations
www.aboutpublicrelations.net/uccamerona.htm

Making News: A Straight-Shooting Guide to Media Relations, by David Henderson, published by iUniverse Star (2006)

Inside Stuff: Mass Media Pros Reveal The Secrets of Using Radio, TV & Newspapers for Public Relations, Free Advertising, Internet Marketing, Website Promotion, and Small Business Publicity [AUDIOBOOK], by George McKenzie, published by 101PublicRelations.com (2003)

How to Make the Most out of Every Media Appearance, by George Merlis, published by McGraw-Hill (2003)

Being a Good Radio Guest

"Be An Excellent Talk Radio Guest: 10 Tips for Success"
www.midwestbookreview.com/bookbiz/advice/talkradio.htm

"The Radio Interview"
www.community-media.com/interview.html

"Preparing for a Media Interview"
www.fullcirc.com/rlc/mediainterviewprep.htm

"How to Be a Great Radio Guest"
www.fullcirc.com/rlc/mediainterviewprep.htm

The Media Interview
http://themediainterview.com

Riches in Niches Radio
www.wsradio.com/internet-talk-radio.cfm/shows/Riches-in-Niches-Radio.html

Ready, Set, Talk!: A Guide to Getting Your Message Heard by Millions on Talk Radio, Television, and Talk Internet, by Ellen Ratner and Kathie Scarrah, published by Chelsea Green Publications (2006)

Advertising

Advertising Articles:

http://advertising.about.com/cs/a.htm

http://ezinearticles.com/?cat=Business:Advertising

"Small Business Advertising"
http://smallhomebusiness.suite101.com/article.cfm/small_business_advertising

"How to Advertise Your Small Business on the Radio"
www.essortment.com/career/advertisesmall_ttcl.htm

International Advertising Association
www.iaaglobal.org

American Advertising Federation
www.aaf.org

The Complete Guide to Writing Web-Based Advertising Copy to Get the Sale: What You Need to Know Explained Simply, by Vickie Taylor, published by Atlantic Publishing Company (2008)

The Unfair Advantage Small Business Advertising Manual: How to Use Newspaper, Direct Mail, Radio, Cable TV, Yellow Pages, and Other Advertising by Claude Whitacre, published by Unfair Advantage Retail (2007)

Advertising: Principles and Practice by William D. Wells, Sandra Moriarty, John Burnett, published by Prentice Hall (2005)

Public Relations

"Tips, Guidelines, and Templates for Writing an Effective Press Release"
www.prwebdirect.com/pressreleasetips.php

"How to Write a Social Media Press Release"
www.copyblogger.com/social-media-press-release

Public Relations Society of America
www.prsa.org

PR Leads
www.prleads.com

PR News & Tips
www.ereleases.com/pr/prfuel.html

I See Your Name Everywhere: Leverage the Power of the Media to Grow Your Fame, Wealth, and Success by Pam Lontos, Andrea Brunais, published by Morgan James Publishing (2008)

Unleashing the Power of PR: A Contrarian's Guide to Marketing and Communication, by Mark Weiner, published by Jossey-Bass (2006)

6 Steps to Free Publicity: For Corporate Publicists or Solo Professionals, by Marcia Yudkin, published by Career Press (2003)

Press Releases Are Not a PR Strategy, by Linda B. VandeVrede, published by VandeVrede Public Relations, LLC (2007)

Database Marketing/POS Systems/Protecting Customer Privacy

"Database Marketing"
www.businesstown.com/Marketing/lowcost-database.asp

"Direct marketing, mobile phones, and consumer privacy"
www.entrepreneur.com/tradejournals/article/178895275.html

"Using Point-of-Sale Software for Your Small Business"
www.fastupfront.com/business-articles/business-technology/
using-point-of-sale-software-for-your-small-business

"Point Of Sale Systems"
www.abcarticledirectory.com/Article/Point-Of-Sale-Systems/96896

POS Systems Buyer's Guides
www.buyerzone.com/computers/pos/buyers_guide1.html

"Protecting Customer Privacy Information"
www.ittoday.info/Articles/Protecting_Customer_Privacy_Information.htm

Database Marketing: The Ultimate Marketing Tool by Edward Nash, published by McGraw-Hill (1993)

Big Business Marketing For Small Business Budgets, by Jeanette Maw McMurtry, published by McGraw-Hill (2003)

Direct Mail

"Direct Mail"
www.smallbusinessnotes.com/operating/marketing/directmail.html

Small Business Marketing
www.postcardsmart.com/directmailblog

"8 Reasons Why Direct Mail Is So Powerful"
www.score.org/m_pr_17.html

"Direct Mail Services: Outsourcing for Profit"
www.manta.com/coms2/page_VS_direct_mail

"Benefits of Direct Mail"
www.usps.com/directmail/benefits.htm?from=directmailhome&page=whyusedirectmail

Direct Marketing Association
www.the-dma.org/index.php

The Complete Idiot's Guide to Direct Marketing by Robert Bly, published by Alpha Books (2001)

The Complete Guide to Direct Marketing: Creating Breakthrough Programs That Really Work, by Chet Meisner, published by Kaplan Business (2006)

Internet Direct Mail: The Complete Guide to Successful E-Mail Marketing Campaigns by Robert W. Bly, Michelle Feit, Steve Roberts, published by McGraw Hill (2000)

Advanced Email Marketing by Jim Sterne, published by Lyris Technologies, Inc. (2003)

Effective E-Mail Marketing: The Complete Guide to Creating Successful Campaigns by Herschell Gordon Lewis, published by AMACOM (2002)

Telemarketing

Telemarketing Articles:

www.buzzle.com/articles/telemarketing

www.all-biz.com/RelId/8376/ISvars/default/Telemarketing.htm

"Telemarketing: How to Have a Quiet Evening at Home"
www.privacyrights.org/fs/fs5-tmkt.htm

Telesales Tips from the Trenches: Secrets of a Street-Smart Salesman, by Joe Catal, published by Business By Phone (2002)

Telemarketing Success for Small and Mid-Sized Firms, by Tony Wilkins, published by Xlibris Corporation (2004)

E-Mail Marketing

"E-Mail Marketing Basics for Small Business"
www.allbusiness.com/marketing/direct-marketing-e-mail/2595-1.html

"Small Business E-Mail Tutorial"
http://website101.com/email_e-mail

E-Mail Marketing Articles
www.benchmarkemail.com/res_index.aspx

E-Mail Marketing Glossary of Terms
www.benchmarkemail.com/res_glossary.aspx

E-Mail Marketing Software
www.constantcontact.com/index.jsp

Email Marketing: An Hour a Day, by Jeanniey Mullen and David Daniels, published by Sybex (2008)

The Truth About Email Marketing, by Simms Jenkins, published by FT Press (2008)

Internet Direct Mail: The Complete Guide to Successful E-Mail Marketing Campaigns by Robert Bly et. al., published by McGraw-Hill (2000)

Outsourcing

"Top 10 Tips for Outsourcing Success"
http://entrepreneurs.about.com/cs/beyondstartup/a/uc041003a.htm

"Outsourcing—Even Small Business Outsourcing—Is In!"
www.startupnation.com/articles/1276/1/small-business-outsourcing.asp

"Business Process Outsourcing"
www.smallbusinessbible.org/businessprocessoutsourcing.html

"Make Outsourcing Work for You"
www.businesslink.gov.uk/bdotg/action/
detail?type=RESOURCES&itemId=1073791040

"100 Small Business Tips and Tricks for Effectively Outsourcing to India"
www.hrworld.com/features/100-tips-outsourcing-india-021508

The Black Book of Outsourcing: How to Manage the Changes, Challenges, and Opportunities, by Douglas Brown and Scott Wilson, published 2005.

Smartsourcing: Driving Innovation and Growth Through Outsourcing, by Thomas K. Koulopoulos and Tom Roloff, published by Platinum Press (2006)

Index

W–X–Y–Z

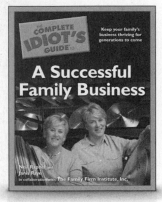

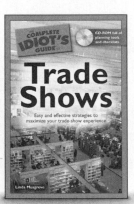